THE IVP NEW TESTAMENT COMMENTARY SERIES

James

George M. Stulac

Grant R. Osborne
series editor

D. Stuart Briscoe
Haddon Robinson
consulting editors

INTERVARSITY PRESS
DOWNERS GROVE, ILLINOIS, USA
LEICESTER, ENGLAND

InterVarsity Press
P.O. Box 1400, Downers Grove, Illinois 60515, U.S.A.
38 De Montfort Street, Leicester LE1 7GP, England

InterVarsity Press, U.S.A., is the book-publishing division of InterVarsity Christian Fellowship, a student movement active on campus at hundreds of universities, colleges and schools of nursing in the United States of America, and a member movement of the International Fellowship of Evangelical Students. For information about local and regional activities, write Public Relations Dept., InterVarsity Christian Fellowship, 6400 Schroeder Rd., P.O. Box 7895, Madison, WI 53707-7895.

Inter-Varsity Press, England, is the book-publishing division of the Universities and Colleges Christian Fellowship (formerly the Inter-Varsity Fellowship), a student movement linking Christian Unions in universities and colleges throughout the United Kingdom and the Republic of Ireland, and a member movement of the International Fellowship of Evangelical Students. For information about local and national activities write to UCCF, 38 De Montfort Street, Leicester LE1 7GP.

USA ISBN 0-8308-1816-2
UK ISBN 0-85111-673-6

Printed in the United States of America ♾

Library of Congress Cataloging-in-Publication Data

Stulac, George M., 1944-
    James/George M. Stulac.
       p.   cm. —(The IVP New Testament commentary series)
    Includes bibliographical references.
    ISBN 0-8308-1816-2
    1. Bible. N.T. James—Commentaries. I. Bible. N.T. James. English. New International. 1993. II. Title. III. Series.
BS2785.3.S88 1993
277'.9107—dc20   *93-18088*
                                                      CIP

British Library Cataloguing in Publication Data

A catalogue record for this book is available from the British Library.

17	16	15	14	13	12	11	10	9	8	7	6	5	4	3	2	1
06	05	04	03	02	01	00	99	98	97	96	95	94	93			

For those to whom I have been blessed
to be a pastor:
the InterVarsity students,
Bethany Presbyterian Church,
Memorial Presbyterian Church,
and my family—
Barbara, Bob, Sara, David and Dan

General Preface

In an age of proliferating commentary series, one might easily ask why add yet another to the seeming glut. The simplest answer is that no other series has yet achieved what we had in mind—a series to and from the church, that seeks to move from the text to its contemporary relevance and application.

No other series offers the unique combination of solid, biblical exposition and helpful explanatory notes in the same user-friendly format. No other series has tapped the unique blend of scholars and pastors who share both a passion for faithful exegesis and a deep concern for the church. Based on the New International Version of the Bible, one of the most widely used modern translations, the IVP New Testament Commentary Series builds on the NIV's reputation for clarity and accuracy. Individual commentators indicate clearly whenever they depart from the standard translation as required by their understanding of the original Greek text.

The series contributors represent a wide range of theological traditions, united by a common commitment to the authority of Scripture for

Christian faith and practice. Their efforts here are directed toward applying the unchanging message of the New Testament to the ever-changing world in which we live.

Readers will find in each volume not only traditional discussions of authorship and backgrounds, but useful summaries of principal themes and approaches to contemporary application. To bridge the gap between commentaries that stress the flow of an author's argument but skip over exegetical nettles and those that simply jump from one difficulty to another, we have developed our unique format that expounds the text in uninterrupted form on the upper portion of each page while dealing with other issues underneath in verse-keyed notes. To avoid clutter we have also adopted a social studies note system that keys references to the bibliography.

We offer the series in hope that pastors, students, Bible teachers and small group leaders of all sorts will find it a valuable aid—one that stretches the mind and moves the heart to ever-growing faithfulness and obedience to our Lord Jesus Christ.

Introduction: James's Redemptive Message

It should be our joy to read and to teach the epistle of James as a message of redemption. The problem is that James does not seem to fit readily enough our concept of redemption. We describe our redemption as "salvation by grace alone," and James writes so much about deeds!

It is not a new problem, of course. Donald Guthrie summarized the history well: "The Epistle of James has suffered much through misunderstanding, the most notable example of which was Martin Luther's oft-quoted description of it as an epistle of straw. The course of nineteenth-century criticism dealt a further blow against the epistle and has left in its wake a general inclination to regard James as a product of an inferior Christian outlook in contrast to the strong meat of Pauline theology" (1990:722). J. B. Mayor in part explained the limited popularity of James's epistle in early history by observing that "it seemed to contradict the teaching of the great apostle to the Gentiles" (1892:li). As recent a commentary as that of Sophie Laws asserts that "the epistle of James is an oddity. It lacks almost all of what might be thought to be the distinctive marks of Christian faith and practice" (1980:1).

There have been many variations of views concerning the theological intent of the letter, which are necessarily involved with views concerning the historical origin of the letter. Guthrie excellently reviews the alternative theories and the evidence to be weighed (1990:723-46). The views may be summarized as three primary alternatives.

1. *The traditional view of authorship:* that the letter was written by James the Just, brother of Jesus, from his position as leader of the church in Jerusalem. Among those who have held this viewpoint, some (e.g., Parry, Tasker) have dated the letter late in James's life, around A.D. 60-62, and have regarded the letter as an argument against a misuse of the Pauline letters to Rome and Galatia. Others (e.g., Mayor, Kittel, Moo, Davids) have dated the epistle earlier in James's life, probably prior to the Council at Jerusalem in Acts 15, before Paul's letters and before the controversy over admission of Gentiles to the church.

2. *The later Christian context for authorship:* that the epistle was written within the Christian community in the late first century or early second century, at least in part as a response to some form of Pauline teaching. Scholars (e.g., Harnack, Dibelius, Ropes, Laws) holding variations of this view propose somewhat different identities for the author— a Christian writing deliberately under the pseudonym of James, or some other Christian by the name of James, or an anonymous writer whose message was later attributed to James. The common elements in these theories about the epistle of James are a date later than the life of James the Just and a dependence upon Pauline teaching as the context for the writing.

3. *The pre-Christian Jewish context for authorship:* that most of the epistle of James was originally a Jewish work written in pre-Christian time and later adapted for the Christian community. Scholars holding some form of this view (originally Spitta and Massebieau) see James's concern for law and deeds as reflecting an earlier Jewish emphasis rather than a later Christian response to Paulinism. They identify 1:1 and 2:1 as the primary Christian additions to the Jewish text.

These issues are important for determining the proper use of the epistle today in Christians' study and in the church's teaching. Is James properly and consistently a message of redemption, fitting well with the other New Testament teaching on salvation? Or is it, to some degree, an aberration from the larger redemptive history and theology recorded in the Bible? How is James to be taught and preached today? We can seek answers to these questions historically and theologically, and then we will seek applications homiletically.

Historical Issues The theological issues in the epistle can be addressed first in the historical context for the writing of the letter. If it was written after Paul's letters were being circulated, then there was at least the theoretical possibility of an anti-Pauline intent in the writing of James. Our endeavor to understand James's theology of redemption must begin, then, with an accurate understanding of the authorship and historical setting.

The debate begins with consideration of the early church fathers' references to James's epistle. Origen cited the letter as Scripture authored by James. Eusebius also treated the book as genuine, and he recorded that James was being "read publicly in very many churches." But he noted that some in his day "disputed" James's authorship of the letter, and that "not many of the ancients have mentioned it" *(Church History* 2. 23). This perceived scarcity of citations in the church fathers has led some modern scholars to doubt the traditional authorship and early dating of the letter of James. J. B. Mayor attempted to refute this skepticism with quite a list of references to James by the early church fathers (1897:lii-lxviii), though Peter Davids's more recent commentary finds much of Mayor's list questionable (1982:8).

But even if Davids's assessment is more judicious than Mayor's on this point, the scarcity of early citations can be regarded as a piece of nonevidence which does not require a late dating for the epistle. Furthermore, a late dating leaves unanswered some other questions which are much more adequately resolved by an early dating (discussed in the following pages).

The debate continues with examination of the linguistic and literary skill exhibited in the letter. The question is whether the quality of writing would require an author more educated than James the son of Joseph and Mary, or at least a significant editing by a later redactor. Davids, for example, attributes the letter to James the brother of Jesus but sees the necessity of an editing by "an amanuensis with considerable ability in literary Greek" (1982:13). Motyer, on the other hand, finds this kind of theory too speculative and warns against unnecessary assumptions— including the assumption that such literary skill could not have been found in James. Motyer would rather "congratulate" James on his somewhat surprising but not improbable quality of Greek (1985:18-19).

Moo also finds Davids's amanuensis theory "unnecessary." As to whether the writing of the epistle would have been beyond James's ability, Moo finds the evidence lacking: "Without knowing the details of James's education, the extent of his travels or the people with whom he associated, this question is impossible to answer" (1985:25). Even Laws, while arguing that "James" is a pseudonym rather than the author's actual identity, does not do so on the grounds of unlikely linguistic proficiency. She dismisses that argument: "It is certainly no longer possible to assert with complete confidence that James of Jerusalem could not have written the good Greek of the epistle, since the wide currency of that language in Palestine is increasingly appreciated" (1980:40).

A third issue of debate in the question of authorship is the amount of familiarity with, and reference to, the person and teachings of Jesus. This is the point at which Laws cannot believe authorship by James: "It must seem extraordinary that a Christian with such an especial knowl-edge of, indeed relationship with, Jesus, should give him so small a place in his writing" (1980:40). However, Laws's assessment is surprising in light of the abundant documentation that James's epistle is saturated with the teachings of Jesus. She recognizes only seven or eight references to the Synoptic teachings of Jesus (1980:3).

Mayor, however, lists almost sixty possible references to the Synoptic Gospels in James (1897:lxxxv-lxxxvii). More recently, Simon Kistemaker has elucidated the relationship between James and the Synoptic Gospels, especially in Matthew 5—7 (1986:55-61). Davids also provides a helpful chart listing thirty-six references by James to specific verses of Jesus' teaching in the Synoptics, plus several more references which he calls "general parallels in thought" (1982:47-48).

Analyzing such material all through James's letter, J. A. Robertson sum-marizes that in James the words of Jesus "drop out freely and spontane-ously, as from a mind that had so absorbed them that they had become part and parcel of its very self" (cited in Ross 1954:17). The expositor of James should make use of the work of R. R. Williams ("much of James reads like the gospel *of* Jesus rather than the gospel *about* Jesus"), C. F. Schmid (describing James's letter as "the echo of the discourses of Jesus" and Jesus' Sermon on the Mount as "the model of the Epistle of James") and W. L. Knox (noting the similarity in structure between James and Jesus' teaching in Luke 6) (Williams, Schmid and Knox all cited in Adamson 1976:22).

The primary remaining area of debate about authorship has to do with the theology argued in the epistle, especially in relation to Pauline theology. I discuss this area in the section on theological issues below. For now, the evidence supports the traditional view of authorship: that the epistle was written by James the brother of Jesus as the recognized leader of the church in Jerusalem.

An early dating of this letter also makes clearest sense of the content of the letter. Davids, for example, endorses the view that the epistle was authored by James between A.D. 40 and 50. He convincingly argues for the early diaspora of Acts 8, rather than the later dispersion after A.D. 70, as the setting for James's letter. His well-supported conclusion is that the letter was written by James the Just, the brother of Jesus, in a Palestinian (not Hellenistic) culture, either as a unified pastoral message or as a compilation of brief messages, to the Jewish Christians scattered in the time recorded in Acts 8:1-3. Consider how this conclusion then provides explanation for some of the questions raised from the content of the letter.

1. Why is there comparatively little citing of the letter by the early church fathers? The relative obscurity of the epistle is most readily explained in the context of an early dating—the setting of persecution and scattering recorded in Acts 8. This was primarily a Jewish persecution, not a Roman one. It would have seemed to be a terrible scattering at the time (making James 1:1 an appropriate description), even though the later scattering by Roman persecution would be much more extensive. Later, in the more widespread and increasingly Gentile church, Paul's letters would understandably have received more attention than this letter by James addressed primarily to Jewish Christians in an earlier and more limited scattering. (Cf. Guthrie 1990:725-26 and Davids 1982:2-22.)

2. Why does the author not identify himself in more detail? Again, the

early dating of the letter provides the likely answer. From all records we have of the early church, we know of only two men with the name of James who would have been sufficiently known and respected to be able to send a letter like this to scattered recipients with no further introduction of himself. One was James the son of Zebedee. He was martyred in A.D. 44, and most scholars agree that the letter of James would have been written later than that. Tasker, for example, writes that "it is almost impossible to date the Epistle as early as his authorship would demand" (1983:22). This leaves James the brother of Jesus, known as James the Just, as the only other likely author of the letter (Guthrie 1990:726). Resolving this question also brings into clearer focus the value which the letter carried. James identifies himself in no greater detail not only because he does not need to do more but also because "the Epistle of James is a quasi-prophetic letter of pastoral encouragement, and, no less, of pastoral rebuke, proceeding from an unquestioned right of pastoral vocation and authority. . . . The Epistle of James comes from the center and head of the Christianity of its day, and speaks with all the pastoral authority of its source" (Adamson 1976:20-21).

3. Why does the author attempt to present an anti-Pauline argument, especially in chapter 2 regarding the issue of faith and works? If the author of this epistle is attempting to refute Paul's letters to the Romans or Galatians, or to combat an abuse of Paul's teaching, then this letter would have to be given a later date. The answer, of course, is that the supposed confrontation between James's legalism and Paul's doctrine of grace is a misunderstanding of both James and Paul. We ought to suspect this is so first from James's abundant use of Jesus' teaching in Matthew 5—7. The epistle of James is no more anti-Pauline than is the Sermon on the Mount. The proper understanding of the theology in both James and Paul will be addressed in the discussion of the theological issues; then, in the section on the homiletical issues, one of the tasks of exposition must be to expose the redemption-by-grace context for James's message. For now, as we treat simply the historical questions of date and authorship, the perceived disagreement with Paul is best explained by the early dating of this letter at the hand of James, writing earlier than A.D. 50, before Romans and Galatians had been written by Paul. James is not responding to Romans or Galatians; he is not trying to correct a

misunderstanding of Paul's letters. Rather, James is writing as a Christian in the context of Jewish tradition, attempting to refute a Jewish-Christian misunderstanding of the lordship of Christ. (See Davids's discussion of this, 1982:19-21.) This also explains why James is silent about the Jewish-Gentile controversy and the Council of Jerusalem recorded in Acts 15: the letter was written prior to those developments.

Now what is the theology with which James addresses people who are living in the trials of the Acts 8 persecution? Is it a theology of redemption by grace or a theology of legalism?

Theological Issues James's concerns for the people in this historical context are theological, especially in the strong ethical application of the theology. His writing goes far beyond merely sympathizing with his readers in their hardship: he wants to strengthen them for moral victory in their hardship. Thus Douglas J. Moo is impressed that "James' genius lies in his profound moral earnestness" (1985:9). But even the ethical issues have a more fundamental origin. His moral earnestness is theologically contextualized in redemption. The teacher or expositor of the epistle of James will need especially to display James's convictions related to the following theological themes.

Christology Sophie Laws is not alone among commentators in seeing a "distinctly limited christological interest" in James (1980:46). A. M. Fairbairn even referred to "the poverty of James's Christology" (cited in Adamson 1976:23). But a distinction must be made between deliberate explanation of a theme (which may be lacking if it is not an author's primary purpose) and views expressed on that theme (which may still be quite rich and significant). Certainly an explanation of Christology is not a major concern for James's purposes in this letter. On the other hand, he is deeply concerned for the moral application of Christology to our lives, and his references to Christ do indicate a high christological view. Thus Davids warns against unwarranted conclusions from the limited discussion of Christology by James: "Here utmost caution must be exercised, for the Christology of James is an assumed Christology. The author refers to ideas as needed; he feels no compulsion to explain Christology" (1982:39).

James calls Jesus "the Lord Jesus Christ" (1:1). We must not allow our familiarity with that phrase to cause us to overlook what magnitude of meaning it carried for those early Christians. It meant that James saw Jesus as his Master, as the divinely anointed and appointed Messiah, and as God himself. James enlarges the phrase significantly in 2:1 by connecting the term *doxa* to the name of Jesus: "our glorious Lord Jesus Christ." Tasker argues that the term may well be taken as a genitive of apposition (1983:56). Adamson agrees, interpreting it as " 'the Lord Jesus Christ, our Glory,' the 'Glory' being taken in the sense of the Shechinah, the Divine Presence" (1976:25). In 5:7-9 James looks forward to the Lord's coming again, and he refers to the Lord as "Judge." This is a significant Christology already, even if one discounts the several other references to "the Lord" as possibly referring to God rather than specifically to Jesus (in 1:8; 4:10; 5:10-11, 14-15). The significance of this view of Jesus' identity is underscored when one remembers who the author is. This is James, who knew Jesus in family intimacy as brother, now calling Jesus "our glorious Lord Jesus Christ" who is coming as "Judge."

It is also significant that Jesus' identity made James self-consciously the "servant" of his brother Jesus (1:1). The application of believing that Jesus is "our glorious Lord" is that one lives with the strong moral purity and commitment that James describes throughout the letter. This application is drawn explicitly in 2:1, revealing the thought that motivates the entire letter. Jesus is our glorious Lord and Christ; this high view of Christ presents Jesus as worthy of the devotion James prescribes for his readers even while they suffer many trials. James's intense ethical focus originates christologically rather than legalistically; it is founded on James's high view of Christ rather than his reverence for Old Testament law.

These are explicit expressions of James's Christology. One implicit expression is essential for expositors to see if we are to be faithful in presenting the redemptive message of James. It is the fact that James's message is saturated with the teachings of Jesus, as already outlined in the section on historical issues above. James's writing shows not obligatory quotations of Jesus' words but rather a thorough familiarity with and devotion to the Lord's teachings.

The christological relevance of this is to demonstrate the high authority that James evidently attributed to the teachings of Jesus. Taken with the explicit references to Jesus already cited in the epistle, this further reveals James's devotion to Jesus as Christ his glorious Lord.

The Law James uses the term "law" *(nomos)* eight times in the following (NIV) phrases.

1:25 the perfect *law* that gives freedom

2:8 the royal *law* found in Scripture, "Love your neighbor"

2:9 show favoritism, you sin and are convicted by the *law*

2:10 whoever keeps the whole *law*

2:11 commit murder, you have become a *lawbreaker*

2:12 going to be judged by the *law* that gives freedom

4:11 speaks against his brother . . . speaks against the *law*

4:11 when you judge the *law,* you are not keeping it

In addition, he refers once (4:12) to the "one Lawgiver," using the term *nomothetēs.*

Three points are valuable in discerning James's intent with these references to the law. First, in all of these references and throughout the letter, there is not a trace of controversy over circumcision or any aspect of the ceremonial law of the Old Testament. James's use of *law* is consistently concerned with the moral law. His treatment of *law* is perfectly consistent with the New Testament view that the Old Testament ceremonial law has been fulfilled in Christ's death.

Second, the thorough involvement with the teachings of Jesus, already noted in the preceding section, makes the content of James's *law* strongly Christian—that is, heavily focused on the teachings of Jesus himself. Davids concludes that for James it is primarily not the Old Testament law nor even the Gospels "but the words of Jesus himself that form the new law" (1982:50). This is not to say that James repudiated the Old Testament moral law, but that he saw it fulfilled in the teachings of Jesus.

Third, in the references listed above, even with the emphasis on keeping "the whole law," James also sees the law as something that "gives freedom." The goal of this freedom is not left obscure by James. His desire for the lives of his readers is variously described: "that you may be mature and complete, not lacking anything" (1:4), "that we might be a kind of firstfruits" (1:18) and "bring about the righteous life that God desires" (1:20). This idea of maturity and completion is James's desire for wholehearted, steadfast, undivided devotion to righteousness, carried out by unreserved obedience to Christ the Lord. James's message is this:

Since the law has been fulfilled in Christ, give yourselves completely now to becoming mature in Christ. Moo paraphrases James's concept of "mature" *(teleios)* in 1:4 as "perfection and wholeness of Christian character." This is James's desire for his Christian readers, and he encourages them intensely and forcefully to persevere in godliness.

All of this simply reflects what Moo aptly describes as James's "profound moral earnestness." There is nothing in this so far which is at odds with Pauline theology of salvation by grace. Paul, too, required obedience to the moral law, especially as taught by Jesus, to the point of commanding a church to expel from the fellowship a brother who continued in sin (1 Cor 5). What needs to be examined next is the relationship between this law and faith.

Faith and Deeds It is quite explicit in James that this obedience to Jesus' law is not an obedience apart from faith. There are sixteen references to "faith" *(pistis)* in James. (Two of these references to *pistis* are translated in the NIV as "believe" and "believers"—in 1:6 and 2:1.) Most of them are in the crucial passage in 2:14-26 about faith and deeds. In other passages faith is fundamental as the basis for prayer (1:6; 5:15), an important point to which we will return. Faith is also the starting point toward the goal of becoming "mature and complete" (in 1:3-4). That this order of relationship between faith and maturity is what James intended to express is confirmed within the 2:14-26 passage—"I will show you my faith by what I do" (2:18). This is the progression that James evidently envisions:

1. faith (as the starting point for being a Christian)
2. deeds (the life of wholehearted obedience to the law of Jesus precisely because one does have faith in Jesus, as illustrated in 2:1)
3. maturity (that goal of perfection and wholeness of Christian character)

This is a justification through faith, with good works coming forth as the natural and expected expression of faith. It does not need to be spelled out by James in the manner of Paul's writing to the Galatians, because it is not controversial in James's context as it would be later for the Galatians. "James has no need to argue about the law, but simply works from it" (Davids 1982:47). That James understands and assumes the grace of God as the source of salvation is expressed, for example, in 1:17-

18. There God is emphatically the source of every good gift and is the one who gave us birth. That James understands these gifts to be of grace is reflected by what he tells people to do in 1:21 to be saved: accept it!

But what about the crucial passage 2:14-26? The view that James's thinking stands in opposition to Paul's is in part the result of the two apostles' using identical terms with different emphases appropriate to their different contexts. One example is the term *erga* ("deeds" or "works"). Later Paul would use the term to refer specifically to works of the law intended as a basis for standing as righteous before God. But as James was writing to his people, he was referring to moral deeds flowing naturally from genuine faith—the very kinds of deeds that Paul would later command. A second term in this passage is the verb *dikaioō*, with which Abraham is described as "justified" (or "considered righteous") in 2:21. Later Paul would use this term to mean "declared to be righteous" in the judicial sense of "acquitted," a judgment that would come about on the basis of a person's faith. At this earlier time, James was using the term to mean "shown to be righteous" in the moral sense, a judgment that would have to be made on the basis of moral acts performed in the person's life.

The issue James was addressing was, Which kind of faith is genuine and saving—faith that speaks, or faith that speaks and acts? The issue Paul would be addressing was, How can sinful people ever gain acquittal and a standing of righteousness before God—by deserving it with works, or by receiving it with faith? Calvin was quite emphatic in explaining James's use of "justify": "you must understand the word 'justify' in another sense than Paul takes it. . . . As Paul contends that we are justified apart from the help of works, so James does not allow those who lack good works to be reckoned righteous" (*Institutes* 3. 17. 12). In fact, when Paul did address the question whether good works should be expected in a life of genuine, saving faith, he showed himself to be in agreement with James—as in Ephesians 2:10.

Davids correctly points out that this difference in use of terms is demonstrated by the different events from Abraham's life chosen by James and Paul to illustrate their respective points (1982:51). James's illustration is Abraham's offering of Isaac, an act of supreme obedience carried out in faith (exactly what James is encouraging his readers to practice). Later, Paul's illustration would be Abraham's belief in the promise of God in Genesis 15, an act of trust in God's grace to provide what was beyond human ability (exactly what Paul would be encouraging his readers to practice).

Spiritual Growth We have already seen James's concern that his readers grow toward complete maturity (1:3-4), so a full discussion of this theme is not needed now. But it is worth noticing that in his presentation of how a Christian develops, James shows himself to be thoroughly depending on the sovereign, redeeming grace of God. This is demonstrated in three aspects of James's discussion of trials and temptations in 1:2-18.

First, James's initial instruction for a person who desires anything he lacks of being "mature and complete" is to ask God for it. Lacking wisdom is the particular illustration James uses in the line of thought in 1:5, but his point is that growth will come from God. He emphasizes particularly that the asking is to be done in faith. This call to prayer, repeated with much emphasis at the conclusion of the letter in 5:13-20, is an important demonstration of James's reliance on God's grace. Prayer is the natural act of those who know their dependence on grace. James is most certainly teaching grace-reliance, not self-reliance.

Second, James's theology in this passage emphasizes that God is gracious. He "gives generously to all without finding fault" (Paul would have no trouble with this as an expression of justification by faith as well as sanctification by faith). "Every good and perfect gift is from above, coming down from the Father"—including the steps in the process of the Christian's growth to maturity.

Third, the work of God within the circumstances of trials reveals his grace. James characterizes trials as events that may become temptations to do evil, but that is decidedly not God's will for the Christian. God never tempts anyone to do evil, for he is holy, and he does not change like shifting shadows. He would use trials as testings by which to develop the Christian into maturity. James wants these Christians who are suffering in trials to know with assurance that God is gracious to bring good for them out of evil circumstances. We have from James a picture of God's sovereign grace at work even in trials for the full redemption of believers' lives.

The similarity between James's teaching here and Peter's teaching is another confirmation of James's oneness with the other New Testament writers. Peter uses the same term *dokimion* ("testing") in a passage similar in thrust to James 1:2-18 (1 Pet 1:3-9). Peter also urges Christians to trust in God's generous giving to supply "everything we need for life and godliness" (2 Pet 1:3). Laws concludes from such similar threads that James and Peter wrote independently but from a common viewpoint among the leaders of the early church (1980:52). Kistemaker likewise argues that James was probably written before 1 Peter, but that the close fellowship between the two apostles in Jerusalem accounts for a common teaching viewpoint in their letters (1986:55-56).

What we have found in this section on the theological issues is that the content of the epistle of James indicates it is a thoroughly Christian work (not a pre-Christian Jewish document with a slight Christian adaptation), and that in theological content it is quite consistent with the setting of the dispersion of Acts 8 (prior to, not in response to, Paul's letters). James's thought is shown to be intimately related to the teachings of Jesus and Peter, and quite consistent with the subsequent teaching of Paul. James appears to believe in both justification by grace and sanctification by grace. Indeed, his conviction about these truths would likely be the motivation for the intensity of his message. He wants Christians suffering in evil circumstances to know the grace of God redeeming their lives for moral victory.

Homiletical Issues The belief that must underlie a consistently redemptive-historical approach to Scripture is that all of Scripture reveals a redeeming God of grace who has worked unalterably for the redemption of people by delivering them from both the penalty and the power of sin. On this basis the history recorded in Scripture is searched for the continuing stream of God's redemptive work, and didactic books of the Bible are regarded as expounding the more foundational historical books. Thus Jesus rebuked his disciples for being "foolish" and "slow of heart to believe" because they had not recognized and believed the Old Testament redemptive history that revealed the necessity of his suffering, death and resurrection (Lk 24:25-27).

Certain homiletical principles flow from this. Holwerda writes that "dogmatic texts rest on historical texts and not vice versa." Hoekstra writes, "A sermon without Christ is no sermon" (see Greidanus 1970:131, 141). The homiletical goal is to display from every part of Scripture the redemptive character, the redemptive works and the redemptive goals of God.

How then would we preach the message of James redemptively? On the basis of the historical and theological issues already examined, seven points of particular application emerge for the expositor of this epistle. Preaching James redemptively will mean the following:

Preaching Christ-Centered Sermons We have seen that James is a Christ-centered message, both in its high view of Christ and in its thorough use of the teachings of Jesus from the Synoptic Gospels. Preaching from James will need to be similarly Christ-centered to be faithful in exposing James's message. If the preaching is merely moralistic without drawing the hearers to Christ as "our glorious Lord," it misses the mark. The expositor would especially do well to draw liberally from the Sermon on the Mount in preaching from the epistle of James.

Preaching Reliance on the Grace of God We have found that James wrote from an assumed context of redemption made available by the gift of God. He therefore urged people to rely on God and to practice their reliance in one most important way: turning to God in prayer, asking, believing and trusting God for anything needed. Preaching that is faithful to James will display God's redemptive grace and assure people of God's sufficient generosity. It will lead people therefore to rely on him and not on human effort for righteousness. It will call people to a life of faith.

Preaching with a Vision for Full Redemption of Lives We discovered that James's vision for his readers' lives was not small. He believed in both justification by grace and sanctification by grace, with the goal of becoming "mature and complete, not lacking anything." Good preaching from James will go far beyond mere sympathizing and moralizing for people who face trials. It will say much more than "Trust God to take care of you when you face trials." It will focus deliberately on our need for redemption, given that we are fallen people living in a fallen world. Earnestly seeking the perseverance that leads to complete maturity in Christ, redemptive preaching from James will have a high and large vision for God's work to purify people's lives.

Preaching with Application We cannot miss the practicality of James's letter. He cared to address the actual, contemporary needs of the people to whom he wrote. The faithful expositor will have to follow James's model and make careful, well-developed, clearly emphasized application to the needs of the people who will hear the sermon. They should have no trouble discerning why they should listen to a sermon from this epistle, just as James's readers must have had no trouble knowing that James cared about them in their trials and was speaking to their needs. Application must receive strong, full treatment in redemptive homiletics.

Preaching with Application to the Preacher The records we have indicate that James the Just manifested serious moral commitment in his own life. Eusebius's ancient description of James is that he was a man of extraordinary reliance on the grace of God—"frequently found upon his knees begging forgiveness for the people, so that his knees became hard like those of a camel"—and that he had extraordinary integrity—"because of his exceeding great justice he was called the Just" *(Church History* 2. 23). This brings homiletics beyond the crafting of a sermon into the shaping of the preacher's own life. James entered personally into the issues of moral integrity and full redemption about which he wrote; this is the model for the one who would preach redemptively.

Preaching the Lordship of Christ James was impressive in his "profound moral earnestness." A sermon from James that conveys a casual attitude about moral purity is simply not faithful to the text. Moral earnestness does not mean placing legalistic demands on people's lives; James did not write in such a vein. But redemptive preaching must not be tentative about the lordship of Christ. Preaching redemption by grace will be done with a passionate love for the righteousness that redemption by grace has made possible.

Preaching Church Renewal James confronted the dangers of a religion that had external Christian forms but lacked the strength of consistent moral integrity. What a critical message for the church today, if there is to be genuine church renewal! James addresses the problem in an utterly straightforward, uncompromising manner; his epistle provides a marvelous basis for preaching church renewal today.

There are those (e.g., Dibelius) who see the letter of James as a loosely connected string of moral lessons on unrelated topics. I disagree thoroughly, and in the commentary that follows I will argue for the unity of the letter. James's persistence in his central message impresses me far more than his diversity of topics. I am convinced that the shifts in topic, which some commentators see as loose editing, are the result of the one author's simple bluntness in making direct applications. James is not one to beat around the bush; he gets right to his point. But he does not give up on his central message: that genuine faith in Christ as Savior will be carried out in a life of obedience to Christ as Lord. The lordship of Christ is an essential part of being redeemed, not an optional part.

My prayer in writing and preaching is that some might more fully believe in their redemption by grace and that, as a result, they might consider it pure joy to persevere in their obedience to the Lord. I believe this was James's intention in writing his epistle.

Outline of James

COMMENTARY

☐ Called to Joy (1:1-18)

My friends Jim and Marie had devoted themselves to building what they had: a good income, a home in the country and two fine sons now grown into young men. Then came the tragedy: their older son, Jim Jr., had stopped to check the roadside mailbox near their country home, when a truck came over the hill and smashed into him. For Jim and Marie, it was the shattering of dreams. One son was dead, and the country home had become a place of sorrow rather than joy.

Soon there were additional trials. But a year later, as Jim was leaving my home one evening, he turned to me at the door and said, with a smile of puzzled but satisfied discovery, "You know, in the last year, I've lost my son, I've lost my job, and I'm making twenty thousand dollars less per year—and I've never been happier in my life."

That is an amazing statement, testifying to an amazing reality. But it was only the centuries-old testimony of Christian experience, expressed in terms of Jim's particular circumstances. I was the family's pastor, young and inexperienced. It was certainly not my skill or wisdom that had brought healing to Jim's life. He spoke of a spiritual reality that does in fact lead a sufferer to joy in the midst of trials.

For Jim, the discovery of joy did not come by denial of his loss or by some superficial sentimentality. What had happened to him in the year since his son's death was that he had committed his life to Jesus Christ. He had become what the apostle James, over nineteen hundred years before, had called "a servant of God and of the Lord Jesus Christ." James wrote about this with precisely the application my friend Jim discovered: that it is possible to "consider it pure joy . . . whenever you face trials."

James's Greeting (1:1) James introduces himself first as one such *servant of God and of the Lord Jesus Christ.* His letter will be about this servant-Lord relationship in which all Christians are to persevere. Along the way, true servants of the Lord will have to put their servanthood into practice in the midst of suffering, in choosing their relationship with material wealth, in controlling how they speak and in other life issues James will address.

At the very start of this letter, James is identifying himself as one who is self-consciously accepting this way of life for himself. His purpose in this letter does not require that he assert his apostleship (as Paul and Peter do in their letters) or his eldership (as John does in his letters). James's identity is already known to the church at large. It is only his servanthood to the Lord Jesus Christ that matters to him here, for this is the theme of his letter: How shall we live as servants of the Lord Jesus Christ?

His readers' life setting is equally pertinent to the content of the letter. He is writing to Christian Jews *(the twelve tribes)* who are *scattered among the nations.* The reference speaks of a literal *diaspora,* a scattering of these Christians mainly through persecution. Acts 8:1-3 gives the likely background. By addressing them as ones *scattered among the nations,* he is telling them at once: "I know you are persecuted; I know you face various trials; I know you are suffering." All that James will have to say to his readers is said with this knowledge of their life setting. All that he will have to say to his readers is applicable even in their life setting of suffering.

Notes: **1:1** The arguments for an early dating of the epistle of James are discussed in the introduction, pointing to a setting in the early diaspora of Acts 8 rather than the later diaspora after A.D. 70. Right away our choices concerning authorship and date affect the

Imagine the implications, drawing from the actual phrases of Acts 8:1-3. Young Christians of Jewish upbringing had become the objects of "a great persecution" by the very ones who had been their leaders in Judaism. Stephen, a loved and respected leader of this Christian movement, had been stoned to death for his faith in Christ. The church "mourned deeply for him." Meanwhile, Saul was determined to destroy the church and so was "going from house to house" forcibly taking men and women to prison. With "all except the apostles" being driven from Jerusalem, James now writes from there to believers *scattered among the nations.* Certainly among James's readers are people experiencing confusion, fear, sorrow, injustice, loneliness, poverty, sickness, loss of home and family members and livelihood—in fact, "trials of many kinds," as he acknowledges right away in 1:2.

Look squarely now at the issue those Christians were facing as they received James's letter. Would these times of suffering and uncertainty be an interruption in their servant-Lord relationship with Jesus Christ? For example, is any trial a reason not to be joyful (1:2)? Are the differences in poverty and wealth to cause favoritism (2:1-13)? Even in trials, shall we be cursing other people (3:9) or grumbling against each other (5:9)? Is loss of anything a reason to fight with each other (4:1-2)? Is sickness or other trouble a cause to cease praying or trusting in God (5:13-14)? Even in these "trials of many kinds," the servant of the Lord Jesus Christ is to continue living the life that James will describe. His burden in writing is this: "Don't put off your life of faith until times get better. Right now, in the midst of your suffering, is the very time to be putting your servanthood toward Christ into practice."

The message is clearly applicable for Christians today. When we encounter trials, what do we experience? In most of us there is probably a mixture or succession of reactions: fear ("what will become of me?"), anger ("how can they do that to me?"), self-pity ("won't somebody feel sorry for me?"), envy of others ("why aren't they suffering like I am?") and confusion ("why is this happening?"). With these reactions, we often fall into precisely the problems James addresses for his original readers:

interpretation of the text. A person teaching from this epistle can highlight James's moral earnestness even in the way James introduces himself, if indeed the author is James the Just as I have argued in the introduction.

a jealous focus on material wealth, a selfish neglect of others' needs, a judgmental spirit and hurtful speech, and a bitter fighting with one another.

The church needs a sound theology of suffering. Philip Yancey points out that Helmut Thielicke was asked once what he saw as the greatest defect among American Christians (1977:15). Thielicke's surprising reply was "They have an inadequate view of suffering." We would be helped by a more adequate study of James. His message is this: Your trial is not the time to rejoice less. Your sickness is not the time to pray less. Your loss is not the time to love others less. Rather, now is the very time to practice the joy, peace and love that we know theoretically to be the Christian life. For the Christian life is not mere theory; it is the life of the servant of God and the Lord Jesus Christ.

Therefore it must have been of more than perfunctory significance to James when he told his readers, *Greetings*. The word is *chairein:* "Joy be to you." Yes, joy! Even though you are scattered among the nations and facing trials of many kinds, do not be robbed of your joy. This joy in the midst of trial becomes the first major topic of James's letter.

Trials (1:2-12) When I was a non-Christian college student, the loving acceptance of Christian students in an InterVarsity chapter helped me to begin a serious investigation into the Christian faith. I was asking questions and discussing issues: Does God exist? How could a good and holy God allow evil? Is the Bible a reliable historical record? Are the claims of Christ true? How can I know? I was reading every book I could find on such questions. One of my non-Christian friends, whom I liked very much and whose esteem I valued, offered this commentary on my search for God: "I admire your open-mindedness." His comment made me glad.

Eventually God in his grace brought me to some answers. I accepted Christ as my Savior and gave my life to him as my Lord. Since discussions of religious issues had become a part of my relationship with my non-Christian friends, it was not long before some of my remarks exposed

---

1:2 John Stott (1978:30-56) provides excellent illumination of the progression within the Beatitudes. To review the Beatitudes here is not a digression. This is only the first of many

my new stance of belief. The friend who had admired my open-mindedness confronted me with a stare and then a question: "Are you starting to believe that Christianity?"

I testified that I had become a believer, but I was naively unprepared for his disgusted response: "I'm sorry you have become so narrow-minded."

I was perceived to have changed from "open-minded" to "narrow-minded" because I believed my investigation had yielded some answers! That was my first experience with being rejected for my faith in Christ. It was a small matter compared to the persecution many Christians have suffered. But it illustrates the promptness of the separation which comes between Christian and non-Christian, manifesting itself in diverse magnitudes of rejection.

It illustrates as well the primary focus of "trials" in James's epistle. It is not that Christians are the only ones who have ever been persecuted. Nor is the letter intended to give comfort to Christians who suffer as a consequence of their own sin. For example, people who suffer conflicts with other people because of their own malicious talk are not told to consider it pure joy; James tells them to control their tongues. When he writes about "trials," he means hardships and sufferings that Christians encounter even as they are following the Lord. This would include tragedies unrelated to their public stance as Christians, such as young Jim's death in the automobile accident. James will explicitly include poverty as one of the *trials of many kinds*. But he most particularly has in mind the trials of being persecuted, the trials that come as a consequence of one's faith in Christ.

Pure Joy (1:2) You who follow Christ have experienced this: your painful surprise at realizing you are misunderstood, criticized or held at a distance by people to whom you had hoped to draw near. You must understand this separation that divides you from non-Christians so that you can be prepared to *consider it pure joy* when you encounter the rejection.

The course of the separation was traced by Jesus in the Beatitudes. It

points that give evidence of the close relationship between James's letter and the teachings of Jesus, especially as recorded in Matthew 5—7 and Luke 6. See the discussion of this in

begins so promptly after your conversion because it is rooted in the very starting point of faith—your honest acceptance of your spiritual need as one who is "poor in spirit." That starting point sets you on a path that diverges more and more radically from the path of those who continue to rely on their own sufficiency. The difference between you and ones who do not seek after God widens when you "mourn" over your sin, for this seems mentally and emotionally unhealthy to them.

Your repentance for sin makes you "meek," but this humility is foolishness to people who are driving to get ahead by their self-sufficiency. For you, the outgrowth is that you begin to "hunger and thirst for righteousness" to replace your sin, but this hunger is not shared or welcomed by many others. This direction for your life, traced in the Beatitudes, brings you increasingly into conflict with people who are on a different course, because your course entails a thorough reversal of your values.

Jesus lovingly warned you to be prepared for it: "Blessed are you when people insult you, persecute you and falsely say all kinds of evil against you because of me. Rejoice and be glad, because great is your reward in heaven" (Mt 5:11-12). James now, with his mind saturated with these teachings of Jesus, will tell his readers about the rejoicing and about the reward.

James picks up the root idea of joy from his "greetings" (chairein) and makes it emphatic with his phrase pasan charan—"all joy" (RSV) or "pure joy" (NIV)—as if to say, "Yes, I really meant joy." "Happiness" would be a weak term to use in place of joy; moreover, it would be misleading. The translation "be happy" (LB) is only slightly improved as "supremely happy" (NEB) or as "a happy privilege" (JB). "Fortunate" (TEV) avoids the misleading impression that one should expect to feel

---

the introduction. The decision regarding whether the teachings in Matthew 5—7 and Luke 6 are from the same or from two different occasions is not critical to a grasp of James's letter. The important point here is the weaving of Jesus' teachings into the letter. In the epistle of James, the Holy Spirit has given the church a commentary on Jesus' Sermon on the Mount and Sermon on the Plain, a commentary that is rich in applications for daily life.

The student of Scripture should take note of the precise terms in this passage. As James's instruction unfolds, the use of peirasmos, dokimion and peirazō will be critical.

Moo argues for the meaning of peirasmos as "external trials of adversity" with two pieces of evidence. First, the verb face (or "meet" or "fall into") suggests that James has in mind external afflictions more than internal enticements. Second, the shift to the term testing (dokimion) in 1:3 reflects a concept of external trials. The element of a temptation will enter

happy in the midst of the trial. But James's phrase *pasan charan* is better translated "all joy" (RSV) or "pure joy" (NIV). Happiness is a subjective state, whereas James is instructing us to make a more objective judgment when he says *consider it pure joy.* "Happiness" might encourage readers to expect a carefree life or a constantly cheerful mood. Neither of these is what James has in mind. He acknowledges the presence of extremely unhappy experiences in his readers' lives. At the same time, and with no perception of any contradiction, James counsels these readers to rejoice during those very experiences of hardship.

My friend Jim, having lost son and job and income, had not had a happy year. Though he was sincere in expressing his new stance in Christ with the term "happy," it would have been more accurate to say "joyful." This joy is what we must grasp if we are going to teach the redemptive message of James accurately. James now goes on to explain why his readers may rejoice, and in his explanation we will discover the content of biblical joy.

The Spiritual Dynamics of Trials (1:2-4) To view our lives biblically (which is to view our lives accurately), we must perceive the spiritual realities. Circumstances and events are only the surface; James tells his readers to look for the deeper meaning. This is especially important in facing the *trials of many kinds.* James wants his readers to see a progression of events in the following pattern.

TRIAL ➜ TESTING ➜ PERSEVERANCE ➜ MATURITY

1. The trials. The term *peirasmos* can refer to internal temptations, but here James probably has in mind the other primary meaning for the

---

the picture in 1:13, but James's starting point is the external circumstance of hardship, especially through persecution.

There are common abuses of this theme of rejoicing in trials which the teacher of this passage must take care to avoid. One abuse is the superficial "positive attitude" that is little more than a denial of troubles. James is going to give reasons for rejoicing which squarely face the reality of the suffering but which consider other realities operating simultaneously.

1:2-4 Peter uses the same terms in 1 Pet 1:6-7 *(poikilois peirasmois . . . to dokimion hymōn tēs pisteōs).* Paul's use of James's term for perseverance has already been noted. See Davids's discussion of the parallels among these three apostolic passages: Romans 5:2-5, James 1:2-4, 1 Peter 1:6-7 (1982:65-66).

word: the external trials of adversity which his readers are experiencing. With this meaning, the term is used especially to refer to trials of persecution, as in 1 Peter 4:12.

Do not think that joy is appropriate only within a narrow range of circumstances. James calls them *trials of many kinds* to encompass the range of his readers' hardships. Shall we consider it joy when we receive unjust treatment? Is there any realistic reason for joy when I am seriously ill? In the midst of a financial crisis, or even a life of poverty without hope of improvement, does James mean for people to rejoice? If pressures in my job weigh upon me day after day, is this trial as well to be considered a time for joy? Or the huge sorrow of a family burden, perhaps a bleak marriage or a child in trouble—is even this trial included? Some of these examples will be specifically mentioned by James; all of them and more are indeed the circumstances in which to perceive the spiritual realities that give reason for pure joy.

Do not be robbed of your joy by supposing that your trial is not a suitable context for applying this passage. Instead, look for the spiritual dynamics of trials. In particular, look for the *testing* in the trial.

2. The testing. The trial is to become a testing (*dokimion*). This term in adjective form means "genuine" or "without alloy"; so the noun refers to a "test to prove genuine." The object of this testing is specifically the Christian's faith. But the biblical concept of a testing goes beyond what we have come to expect from our school experiences. Most of our school tests are designed primarily to reveal what knowledge the students already have in them. The biblical concept of a testing, as James uses it here, is one that does reveal the genuineness of the person's faith;

1:3 It is noteworthy that faith, *pistis*, is identified as the object of the testing. James should not be characterized as promoting deeds and ignoring faith, as some have done in a mistaken conclusion from 2:14-26. James knows full well the necessity of faith; he emphasizes the completion of genuine faith in the performance of deeds. The distinction between faith and deeds is merely that faith is essentially a knowledge and deeds are essentially the actions taken because of the knowledge. Calvin's search of Scripture led him finally to the conclusion that faith, reduced to its essential focus, is this: "a firm and certain knowledge of God's benevolence toward us, founded upon the truth of the freely given promise in Christ, both revealed to our minds and sealed upon our hearts through the Holy Spirit" (*Institutes* 3. 2. 7). James writes in 1:3 about the testing of this firm and certain knowledge. What one knows of God's benevolence is put to the test in trials—for the further development of faith.

but James says the test is also designed to develop something that is not yet present in full measure in the person.

This is why, for the one who wants to live by faith, the trial can be a time for rejoicing. How many people today suffer in trials of many kinds, thinking that the issue is whether they have the faith to pass the test? The spiritual reality is that God will use the trial to develop something that they admittedly do not yet possess. James says, "Rejoice in that prospect!"

3. The perseverance. What specific quality of faith will be developed through the trial that becomes a testing? James's answer is *perseverance.* This means, first, that God will give the ability to endure patiently. The Christian with this quality of faith does not give up trusting and praying even when the need continues for a long time. Second, the term carries the idea of discipline. The Christian with this quality of faith continues in a disciplined obedience to Christ as Lord even when it requires "a long obedience in the same direction" (Peterson 1980). Third, the term means steadfast faithfulness. The Christian with this quality of faith is not a part-time servant of the Lord Jesus Christ. Making the same point, in fact using the same terms, Paul wrote, "We also rejoice in our sufferings, because we know that suffering produces perseverance" (Rom 5:3).

That the testing *develops,* or "produces," perseverance is emphatic. It may be compared to 1:20, where human anger does not "bring about" the righteous life that God desires. The root verb *ergazomai* is the same in 1:3 and 1:20, but in 1:3 it carries the prefix *kata,* making it emphatic with the image of producing or creating. Human anger will not bring about righteousness, but the testing of genuine faith will certainly pro-

---

The term *hypomonē* is too weakly translated in the KJV as "patience." Better translations are "endurance" (NASB), "steadfastness" (RSV) and "perseverance" (NIV). Ropes conveys the right idea more colloquially with the phrase "staying power."

1:4 There is no need to regard James's instruction here as envisioning the attainment of a moral perfection in this life, as in the holiness tradition. What the text does give us is a vision for becoming mature in Christ. With this, the teacher of God's Word is to call God's people unashamedly to commit themselves to holiness. We are not to tolerate unholiness in ourselves with the excuse that it is inevitable; we are not to give in to sin, saying that it is inescapable. We are to persevere in dying to sin. The teacher of this passage can emphasize that we will be totally confirmed in righteousness someday, and that there is real victory to be attained along the way.

duce perseverance.

James's earnestness needs to be heard, with the very direct questions this raises. Don't you desire this quality of faith in yourself? Isn't it the desire of your heart to learn to live by faith and to be "a servant of God and of the Lord Jesus Christ" in a patient, disciplined, steadfast, faithful way? Now you have the reason to rejoice in the midst of trials! These trials provide the opportunity for the testing that will develop this quality of faith. To stop trusting and start worrying, to cease ministering and start withdrawing, to interrupt godliness and start selfishness, just because of one's anxiety over the current trials, would be precisely the wrong course to take. The spiritual realities call for joy in the opportunity to learn perseverance.

4. The maturity. Why would perseverance be so valuable? It is because there is a fourth stage in the spiritual progression: "that you may be mature and complete, not lacking anything." Perseverance turns out to be not the end in itself, but rather the lifestyle by which the servant of Jesus Christ attains maturity.

The terms James uses in this last clause of 1:4 give a picture of wholeness and completeness. Moo's good paraphrase of James's term *teleios* is "perfection and wholeness of Christian character" (1985:61). Laws describes it as being "a complete person, having integrity, unlike the divided man of vv. 6-8" (1980:54). In other words, James is holding before his readers a vision for becoming everything the Lord desires them to become.

James invites you to envision yourself in the state of spiritual maturity, rid of the jealousy or laziness or impulsiveness or impatience or bitterness or self-pity or selfishness that now mars the wholeness of your fellowship with God and the completeness of your spirituality. Do you hunger and thirst for righteousness? Do you long to be fully the person God desires you to be? If so, then you now have the full reason for considering it pure joy whenever you face trials of many kinds. The trials can be opportunities for testing to develop in you the perseverance which, when it finishes its work, will leave you mature in Christ! For

---

1:5 By repetition of the verb *leipō*, this first example flows immediately from the idea of *lacking* at the end of verse 4. Later, James's return to the theme of wisdom in 3:13-18

those who have set their hearts on becoming Christlike, this is wonderful reason for *pure joy.*

Called to Joy (1:2 Reconsidered) In the light of this spiritual goal we can now return to the beginning of 1:2 and have an idea of what James means by *consider it pure joy.* Contrast it to some unworthy substitutes:

1. Denial. It is clear from James's own recognition of the suffering that he is not prescribing a mind-game to keep oneself feeling happy by denying the reality of the trials.

2. Complaint. Praying for deliverance from a trial is appropriate, but doing so with a complaining spirit is far from what James envisions for the Christian. The goal of becoming complete is too valuable to be approached with grumbling.

3. Self-pity. Continuing in obedience to the Lord's commands would certainly be part of perseverance, but doing so in self-pity is not worthy of the goal James has in mind. Obeying while thinking "Poor me!" is different from obeying with *pure joy.*

James's vision for spiritual victory may be faced clearly and courageously. He honestly believes that in the very midst of painful trials in the Christian's life, there is definite basis for joy. If one's goal is to become mature in Christ, and if that is a goal far higher and more valuable than merely avoiding hardships, then indeed consider it joy when you meet the trials by which you attain that treasured goal. We are called to joy!

James is at this point entirely consistent with the rest of the New Testament. Jesus taught that the kingdom of heaven is like a treasure so valuable that a man would rightfully sell everything else to obtain it, and that the man would do so "in his joy" (Mt 13:44). Paul announced that we "rejoice in our sufferings" because "suffering produces perseverance" (Rom 5:3). Peter understood the Christian experience of rejoicing even in the midst of "all kinds of trials" (1 Pet 1:6).

The First Example: Lacking Wisdom (1:5-8) Two examples come to mind for James, by which to illustrate the spiritual dynamics of trials. First, what if you lack wisdom? This is an important example to

---

is an evidence of the inherent unity of the letter, in contrast to the view that the letter is a collection of unrelated teachings.

James, for he will return to the theme of wisdom in 3:13-18. It is also fitting as a first example, because it is of such urgent importance for Christians in trials. Isn't this the cry in the heart of ones who are suffering? "I don't know what to do!" 2 Chronicles 20:12 in its context illustrates well this cry for wisdom from people facing trials. James's pastoral concern takes him directly to this pressing need in his readers' lives.

It is worth taking time to identify with that need ourselves, so that we catch the significance of James's answer, for we experience the same disabling effects that James's original readers must have been experiencing.

1. Guilt. I remember an agonizing time of division in our church. I struggled with self-blame. "If only I had said this . . . or done that . . . or acted differently." I kept wondering what to do. I needed wisdom desperately.

2. Confusion. Suffering easily pushes us into the confusion of self-doubt, in which we question our actions, motives and capabilities. Such self-doubt can be devastating, for example, for parents who lose a child in a tragedy or find their child alienated in rebellion. "Why did this happen to me? Where did I go wrong? Is God punishing me? Does God love me?" We don't know what to do in the midst of that intense internal questioning, and our need for wisdom is urgent.

3. Fear. Suffering awakens the fear that things are out of control and that whatever we hold dear might be lost. As a result, people commonly withdraw to protect what they still have. This is, in part, why a wife or child may keep submitting to an abusive home situation; there is the fear that the abuse will get worse. "Maybe, if I submit, my abuser will stop." In the midst of a trial, the fear can be absolutely crippling, so that you do not know what to do. You need wisdom.

4. Anger. Trials can produce a great deal of anger, but intense anger often receives insufficient satisfaction. Yet the intensity of anger cannot be sustained. When the anger subsides without being resolved, it is

---

Translators and commentators have cited two meanings for *haplōs:* "generously" (NIV, RSV, NASB); and "without hesitation" (Mayor) or "freely" (JB). Davids is more persuaded by evidence for the second meaning, for which he uses the phrase "without mental reservation" (1982:72). Laws sees contrasts to both meanings in the context and so concludes James may have had both meanings in mind (1980:55). Moo focuses on the idea of "sin-

replaced by hopelessness. That is why counselors often regard depression as the other side of anger. The result is a loss of motivation and, again, an inability to know what to do. If you are angry or depressed because of trials, you need wisdom to get your life going again as a servant of the Lord Jesus Christ.

James is concerned to address one central need from which the other needs in these complex situations can be unraveled. In the face of such trials, what shall the "servant of God and of the Lord Jesus Christ" do? *He should ask God* for the wisdom that is lacking. This is not to dismiss the problems with a simplistic solution, but it is to face the problems with the root solution. Again the Sermon on the Mount appears as a possible basis for James's message: "Ask and it will be given to you" (Mt 7:7).

Stop and take note of what James prescribes here; it is foundational for an accurate grasp of the whole letter. For those who would portray James as simply a teacher of law, it is important to see this: by instructing his readers to ask for wisdom, James is pointing them to God's grace. This is one example of what underlies the whole epistle—James's confidence in the grace of God and his intense desire for his readers to place their own reliance there. Overlooking this, and taking 2:14-26 out of this context, some have failed to teach James redemptively.

James then leads his readers into God's grace by calling attention to four facets. As they come in the Greek word order, first God is one who "is giving." The word is *didontos,* a present active participle; it is God's constant nature to be gracious and giving. Second, God gives *to all (pasin).* The call to live by faith is extended to everyone, and no one is left without an invitation to trust in God. Third, God gives *generously (haplōs),* emphasizing that God gives freely and without reserve. Fourth, God gives *without finding fault,* or without reproaching.

You may ask God for the wisdom you need without fear, for God gives without holding your failures or lack of wisdom against you. This is the

---

gleness" in this term and captures most attractively the pastoral intent in James's use of the word (1985:63). I have drawn on Moo's language in my exposition.

1:6 James's repetition of terms carries the line of thought. *He should ask (aiteitō)* in 1:5 leads to *when he asks (aiteitō)* in 1:6. The RSV's literal rendering "let him ask in faith" *(en pistei)* makes clear the continuation of the concern about *faith* from 1:3.

assurance with which the Christian approaches God, that God is not a harsh Father who responds to our needs by reminding us of our faults. Christ has made atonement for our sin; we receive justification by responding with faith, not by trying with good deeds to become righteous enough to deserve God's favor. This salvation by grace, the very heart of the gospel of Christ, will certainly not be contradicted by God when we come to him for wisdom. God responds to his own people with grace—his undivided, unwavering intent always to give good gifts.

Believe this love from God, James continues in 1:6, and do not doubt it, for the doubt is instability. There are certain distortions of this teaching common today which should be recognized. The first distortion occurs within what is popularly known as the "name it and claim it" philosophy, when Christians are taught that they should name whatever they need in faith and so claim it as given to them. The dangers are the misplacing of faith and the raising of unbiblical expectations. Christians are sometimes led, in effect, to place their faith in the force of their own believing, and then to expect freedom from hardship or deprivation. What James is prescribing is something quite different: faith in the grace of God, which enables faith to be exercised even within hardship and deprivation.

A further distortion of the biblical teaching occurs when Christians treat James's warning against doubt (and the similar teaching by Jesus in Mt 21:21) superficially, taking it to require a willful suppression of mental doubts. This can become an unrecognized attempt to manipulate God by one's own power of positive thinking. The error has left many in bondage to fear, afraid of their own thoughts and afraid of the God who might hold their doubts against them and therefore not grant the wisdom needed. The result is a crippling of people's faith and a perversion of the very truth James is teaching: that God gives freely, without finding fault.

James certainly does place *doubt* in immediate contrast to *believe* (or, literally, in contrast to the noun *faith*) in 1:6. But James is writing about

---

1:8 The term *dipsychos* is important, as James is the only New Testament writer to use it (in 1:8 and 4:8). Its meaning should be explored in its significant Old Testament background, including Psalms 12:2 and 1 Chronicles 12:33, with the contrasting concept of a whole heart undivided in love for God (Deut 6:5; Jer 24:7; 32:39; Ps 86:11). James may also be reflecting another point in Jesus' own teaching, from Matthew 22:37. Cf. discussion by Davids (1982:74-75) and Laws (1980:58-61).

something much deeper than surface thoughts. The actual point of his warning about doubt is to expose a basic soul-condition of unbelief. That basic soul-condition is described with the term *double-minded* in 1:8. It means a double-souled person, a person whose heart's loyalties are divided, a person who has not decided to give his or her love to God. The *doubt* then is a vacillation between self-reliance and God-reliance. This person is not looking to God from a stance of faith, and for this person there is no promise that God will give wisdom. The instability of this vacillating person is captured in the vivid imagery of the unstable sea wave, and this image stands in contrast to the perseverance in 1:3 (cf. Is 57:20). The testing of faith develops perseverance, but doubt (as a root unbelief) makes a person unstable.

Now we can summarize James's use of the first illustration. If you encounter a trial and lack wisdom to know what to do, stand the test of faith by asking God for the wisdom you need. As you ask God for wisdom, do not be unbelieving toward God or frightened about your lack of wisdom. Instead, trust God to give wisdom generously. He will do so. Therefore consider it pure joy that you face the trial, for that very trial will be used by God to develop your perseverance toward maturity.

The Second Example: Lacking Money (1:9-12) James's second illustration introduces another major theme to be developed later in the epistle: one's relationship with material wealth. There are indications in the New Testament that *humble circumstances* were a common trial among Christians. In the first place, the explicit appeal to the poor in Christ's preaching likely attracted numerous poor people among the earliest converts (Lk 4:18). In addition, some Christians became poor because of deliberate persecution against them. Some may have been living in a self-imposed poverty for ethical reasons, as they refused to participate in corrupt economic enterprises. We have examples in Acts 16:19 and 19:23-29 of the gospel's economic effects, forcing a separation

---

Davids sees a progressive sharpening of the faith-doubt contrast from Mark 11:23 to Matthew 21:21 to James 1:6, with James emphasizing in the doubter a "root distrust of God: the petitioner really has no faith in God, for his whole attitude toward God is divided" (1982:73). Moo agrees that the doubting means "not so much intellectual doubt as a basic conflict in loyalties" (1985:64).

of Christians from immoral financial pursuits and resulting in a backlash of persecution. Christians suffered economically for their faith.

James evidently understood this trial to be a common circumstance among his readers. If this is a deliberate point of application by James, and not just another topic in a loose train of thought, then the spiritual dynamics of trials should be evident in this illustration. Exposition should bring out how this trial would become a testing to develop perseverance toward maturity.

To understand this, it is valuable first to consider how, even today, money is the context for some of our most common and spiritually significant trials. Because of money we are beset with fears—troubling anxieties about how financial needs will be met. Because of money we are attacked with a sense of guilt and failure. We struggle to make ends meet, and we feel internal accusations about inability to manage finances and about mistakes we must have made in financial choices. Because of money we fall into crippling self-pity, chronic complaining and envy of others who can buy and do things which we lack. These can produce a terrible bitterness of spirit that makes a desert of our personal fellowship with God. Because of money we become trapped in attitudes of greed, practices of injustice and a lifestyle of materialism. No wonder Scripture says that the love of money is a root of all kinds of evil!

Look still more deeply into the matter. Why does money evoke such destructive reactions in us? Don't we fall into these reactions especially because of the particular functions money plays in our lives? First, money functions as verification of personal worth. When we are conscious of lacking wealth (which is relative—lacking in comparison to anyone who has more, or in comparison to anything we cannot afford), the implication is that we are worth less than others and that we are less worthy for God to bless. On the other hand, if we are conscious of having wealth (again, relative to anyone else or relative to anything we want), the prideful comparisons come easily to us. The implication is that we are

---

1:9-10 James's message to *the brother in humble circumstances* in 1:9 continues to *the one who is rich* in 1:10 as one sentence, with the verb *kauchaomai* (to rejoice or exult) used in 1:9 also serving the second clause in 1:10. The parallelism between the two sides of the illustration is reinforced by the use of *tapeinos* for the apparent *humble circumstances* of the brother and *tapeinōsis* for the actual *low position* of the one who is rich.

more successful because we are worth more. Second, money functions as security. That is why a loss of job or a financial setback is so frightening. It is also why some choices can be so attractive when they are financially helpful even though they will harm our well-being. A friend admitted to me that he hates going to work because of the evil atmosphere there, but that he took the job because of the financial security it offered. Third, money functions as power or advantage over other people. It gives power for people to perform injustices against others; when we lack wealth compared to others, we feel our vulnerability.

The effect of these dynamics is to focus our lives on the pursuit of money. Financial gain becomes the increasingly decisive factor in our attention, choices and lifestyle. It becomes urgent to recognize, therefore, that these three functions of money are worldly functions—violations of the ways of Christ's kingdom. Jesus called his followers to choose between treasures on earth and treasures in heaven, for he said, "You cannot serve both God and Money" (Mt 6:19-24). He warned that material wealth is dangerous to spiritual health; in fact, "it is easier for a camel to go through the eye of a needle than for a rich man to enter the kingdom of God" (Mt 19:24). James's purpose here is to encourage Christians in material hardship not to become caught in the pursuit of wealth. What he has to say will be in radical opposition to the three worldly functions of money.

1. Against the notion that money means personal worth. First, James addresses 1:9 specifically to *the brother* as a reminder that the Christian reader is already specially accepted and loved. Second, the brother is reminded of a *high position* that has nothing to do with amount of money. (Nor does the *low position* have anything to do with the rich person's level of wealth.) Third, the brother is to *take pride* (NIV) or to "glory" (NASB) in that high position. Therefore, whatever is worth such glorying must also have nothing to do with money. Fourth, the *high position* is assumed as a fact, not proposed as a conditional possibility.

1:9-11 Jacques Ellul has explored in terms of today's economic systems how money has the function of measuring value (1984:9-33). From that standpoint, people naturally learn to pursue the goal of *having* something instead of the goal of *being* something. That is why Christians must avoid the deception of wealth as measuring value. James wants Christians to rejoice in actual value, not illusory value.

It must refer to a high position that occurs by virtue of being a *brother:* being one for whom Christ died and being claimed by God as his own. Contrary to the claim that our humble circumstances mean inferior worth, it turns out that we are declared worthy of extravagant blessing by God! We can tell ourselves now with certainty that our money does not determine our personal worth and that the first worldly function of money is a lie.

The trial of financial hardship presents the opportunity for a testing, or an exercising, of faith. Christians will engage in the testing by exulting in what they believe: the more important reality of their high position with God. This very act is a rejection of the culture's materialistic values and therefore a growth toward maturity. It will lead the Christian to renounce any anxious outlook about the future, any self-accusing attitude in financial struggles, and any complaining or jealous view toward others' comparative wealth. Instead of adopting anxiety, guilt, complaint or jealousy, the Christian will *consider it pure joy . . . because you know that the testing of your faith develops perseverance . . . so that you may be mature and complete, not lacking anything.* Further, this proper pride in their high position means that Christians' treatment of others will no longer be affected by others' wealth. Christians will repent of favoritism, an application that James will explore in 2:1-13. Thus the test of living in humble circumstances will develop perseverance to continue a life of faith, manifest in both outlook and behavior.

2. Against the notion that money means security. James reminds his readers that the rich will fade away as easily and certainly as a wild flower. *The one who is rich* is not called a "brother," for James is not addressing rich Christians. My appendix on the identity of the rich will provide a larger treatment of the conclusion that *the rich man* is a non-Christian. For now it may be noted that this exegetical decision will affect interpretation of James's other references to the rich in chapters 2 and 5. Most scholars (Adamson, Mayor, Moo and Ropes, among others) have treated *plousios* (rich) as governed by *adelphos* (brother) from 1:9 and therefore as referring to a Christian brother who is rich. At first glance, this does seem to be the most natural reading of the syntax, with the verb *kauchaomai* from 1:9 also understood in 1:10. In that case, James would be telling the rich brother to take pride in his humiliation in Christ. A major problem with this view is James's complete silence about meaning humiliation "in Christ." James was familiar with Jeremiah 9:24, and he could have elaborated on *kauchaomai* as Paul did in 1 Corinthians 1:31. Instead, his elaboration dwells entirely on the destruction of the rich person. The extent to which James emphasizes this in 1:10-11 indicates that he is speaking of rich people who will likely continue in their materialism only to find themselves brought low in the end. In general, though, he understands his Christian readers to be poor people suffering in the trial of deprivation. This fits perfectly with the line of thought already traced from 1:2, as encouragement for the poor to consider their trial *pure joy* because they know their perseverance in faith will leave them *not lacking anything*, whereas the path of materialism will lead to destruction. The syntax easily allows for this understanding, with *plousios* and *adelphos* standing as contrasting subjects of the one verb *kauchaomai*.

The later passages in James 2 and 5 confirm this view. For example, 5:1-6 will thoroughly condemn rich people, without acknowledging any saving faith in them or hope for them. Though that passage is written in the second person, it makes sense as a rhetorical addressing of persons not actually receiving the letter, written for the benefit of the ones who are reading it. The actual readers will then be addressed in 5:7, "Be patient, then, brothers . . ." Laws (1980:62-64) and Davids (1982:76-77) should be read as examples of this view that *the one who is rich* in 1:10 is a non-Christian.

Therefore James is encouraging Christians *in humble circumstances* not to be deceived by the apparent security of the rich. Three factors would especially encourage them in this regard. First, the rich person has only a *low position* to look forward to; his wealth cannot shield him from being humbled. Second, the rich person *will pass away like a wild flower.* Jesus' Sermon on the Mount would have been known to the believers; James's own familiarity with the Sermon is certainly evident in his letter. Jesus used similar imagery to illustrate the care with which the Father clothes his own children, who are of greater value than the wild flowers which are tomorrow "thrown into the fire" (Mt 6:25-34). James's imagery is a reminder of this promise of God's providence. Third, the rich person will pass away *even while he goes about his business.* This not only parallels Jesus' own emphasis in the parable of the rich fool (Lk 12:20), it also emphasizes the vulnerability of the rich at the very time they are trying to make their wealth secure. Again we can now speak with certainty: the second worldly function of money is a lie; money does not mean security.

This is a huge and liberating truth for Christians who are pressed on all sides by a materialistic society. Armed with this truth, Christians who want seriously to uproot the sin of materialism from their hearts can embark on deliberate disciplines to confront money's lie about security. Two such disciplines will be emphasized by James later in his letter. One is giving. The Christian who has repudiated money as security will be free to give to others in need, as James will require in 2:14-17. John Wesley was conscious of the value of giving for his own spiritual health when he said, "When I have any money I get rid of it as quickly as possible, lest it find a way into my heart." Though he later formulated his more comprehensive dictum "Make all you can, save all you can, give all you can," Wesley's earlier sentiment was at least founded on an honest insight that material wealth had power to put down deep roots into his heart with a false security. The other discipline is prayer, especially with thanksgiving. The Christian who has repudiated money as security will be free to refrain from grumbling and instead look patiently to God in prayer for all needs, as James will teach in 5:7-18. Together the disciplines of generous giving and thankful prayer can help today's church stand against the lie that money is security.

3. Against the notion that money means power or advantage. James now directs our attention to what is the real advantage or blessedness in life: *the crown of life.* James does not define this phrase, but some careful observations can lead us to a safe idea of its meaning. It is not something complete at the point one becomes a Christian. Rather, it is something the Christian *will receive.* It is a "crown" *stephanos,* which is a term used among the leaders of the New Testament church to refer to the Christians' ultimate goal or reward. (Cf. Paul in 1 Cor 9:25, Peter in 1 Pet 5:4 and John in Rev 2:10.) We know that one ultimate goal on James's mind is that of becoming *mature and complete, not lacking anything.* The crown must include fulfillment of that goal of true life. This crown is assured; it is *promised* to them. James wants his readers to be certain of this as they endure deprivation now. The crown is promised specifically *to those who love him.* (The NIV appropriately derives from the pronoun *him* that God is the one who has promised.) We know that this idea of loving God carried a strong emphasis on faithfully obeying him (as Jesus said in John 14:15, and as James is teaching all through his epistle). Finally, James has begun the sentence with "blessed" *makarios,* like a new beatitude recalling Matthew 5:3-10 and especially 5:11-12, where Jesus encouraged perseverance in trials "because great is your reward in heaven." Putting these observations together, the crown of life would be the ultimate reward, the fulfillment of eternal life and the exaltation with Christ which will be enjoyed by those who, because of faith in Christ, have loved God enough to live faithfully, obeying him even through trials.

James calls us to believe this: the crown of eternal life is worth more than any advantage to be gained by money in this life. Truly *blessed* is the one whose heart is set on this goal. We can now say with final conviction that the worldly functions of money are all evil lies. It remains for the church in every age to put this into practice by renouncing all worldly uses of money. We must not settle for the comparatively worthless goal of merely avoiding trials in a life of wealth and ease and comfort. We must repent of all use of wealth for unjust power over others. And we have to make deliberate economic choices according to what is morally right rather than what is financially advantageous. James will say more about this in 4:13—5:6. I have seen an example, however, in a young business executive in our congregation who was on a track to climb up the corporate and economic ladder. His job required him to be away from home so much that he was not able to see his children. He therefore made a choice of values; he changed jobs. The change hurt him financially, but it gave him the opportunity to be present with his children as they grow up.

Summary (1:12) The return to the original pair of themes (trial and test) makes 1:12 not only a conclusion to the example of lacking wealth but also a summary principle, drawing together the major elements James has been presenting since 1:2. Though I see these as unifying themes in 1:2-12, teachers should examine in their own study the issue of the unity of James's writing. Adamson is one who finds a "sustained unity" in the thought and structure of the entire letter (1976:20). Laws, representing a contrasting view, sees 1:2-12 as "a loose train of thought" (1980:62). As a result, she sees 1:9-11 as introducing a new theme rather than illustrating a continuing theme as I have presented it. She understands James to offer in 1:4 the "achieving of personal intcgrity" as "apparently an end in itself" (1980:52). She regards 1:12, then, as introducing a new motivation for enduring trials—a future reward instead of a present perfecting of character. I would agree that James envisions a future reward as well as a present perfecting. In my view, however, Laws's handling of the passage as only loosely related thoughts may lead the reader to miss one of the strongest motivations for perseverance in New Testament thinking: the continuity between present perfecting of character and future reward. The New Testament idea is that present growth in holiness culminates in a future sharing of glory with Christ. The teachings of Jesus in the Sermon on the Mount again provide the basis (Mt 5:48; 7:15-23). Peter lends parallel explanation of the early Christian leaders' teaching (1 Pet 1:7, 13, 15; 4:13-14; 5:1, 10). And John points to the same reward for Christians in persecution—the crown of life (Rev 2:10). This ultimate sharing of glory with Christ is the vision high enough with which to call people to joy in the midst of terrible trials.

Recall the complete picture now, reviewed in this one verse phrase by phrase.

1. *Blessed is the man:* This is the reason for the pure joy in 1:2. Believe that you are blessed, truly blessed in reality, in spite of any suffering or trial.

2. *who perseveres:* James repeats the theme of perseverance in 1:3-4. You are blessed if you continue trusting and obeying as "a servant of God" in spite of trials.

3. *under trial:* This includes the trials of many kinds recognized in 1:2 and illustrated in 1:5-11.

1:12 James, of course, was not writing in tidy chapters or in homiletical segments. He was writing a letter in a continuous flow of thought. I am treating 1:12 as primarily a summarizing verse for 1:2-12, but others have appropriately emphasized the ways in which 1:12 also introduces the subsequent verses. Moo, for example, groups 1:12 with 1:13-18 as the concluding segment of 1:2-12 on "Trials and Christian Maturity." Davids also sees 1:12-18 as a segment but treats it as the first part of a unit covering 1:12-25. These and other treatments should be considered. I find 1:12 most significant as a summarizing verse be-

4. because when he has stood the test: The phrase is *hoti dokimos genomenos* ("when he has become approved as by a test"). This recalls the use of the noun *dokimion* in 1:3—*the testing of your faith.* The diverse trials will make various demands on you, but do not be frightened or deceived. Trust the loving and sovereign God to use the trials as faith-growing tests for you.

5. he will receive the crown of life: Later the Lord would affirm to the church in Smyrna, "I know your afflictions and your poverty," but this would not be his entire message to them. He would also encourage that persecuted church by adding, "Yet you are rich!" In what way could they possibly be called "rich" while knowing poverty, slander, imprisonment and other persecution "even to the point of death"? The Lord's answer would be his promise, "I will give you the crown of life." That promise of the Lord in Revelation 2:9-10 is the kind of encouragement James gives the suffering Christian here, promising with the same phrase that God will give the crown of life.

6. that God has promised to those who love him: The crown of life is not a reward you are gambling for when you choose to persevere in faith. This is no wheel of fortune, in which you will have to wait until later to find out whether perseverance turns out to have been the right way of life. The crown of life is assured by God himself.

James the Just, with his deep moral earnestness, wants to help suffering Christians find the strength to make tough moral choices. He therefore calls us to face the issue of *worth*. Persevering is worth doing, because the crown of life is worth more than avoiding the trial. James calls for courageous applications of this principle. Giving up on a difficult ministry, retaliating against people who are mistreating you, withdrawing from active participation in worship and fellowship, compromising moral standards, interrupting your life of obedience, turning away from a walk of fellowship with the Lord—all these responses to adversity

---

cause (a) 1:12 gathers the major points of the preceding section and (b) 1:13 introduces a new element to the line of thought (temptation to do evil).

Cf. the crown of glory in 1 Peter 5:4 for another point of similarity between James and Peter.

Wenham's book *The Goodness of God* is a discussion of how evil can exist in a world ruled by a benevolent God and is valuable help with this larger issue in James's epistle.

assume that escaping the trial is of more value than gaining the crown of life. The Christian is called to place greater value on the goal of becoming mature and complete in Christ. With such applications, the Christian life is taken out of the realm of sentimentality and placed in the realm of significant moral choice.

When a Christian's spouse is unfaithful and abandons the marriage, is Christ still worth obeying? When a Christian's financial security is threatened or wrecked, is Christ still worth trusting? When a Christian's physical health is crippled, is Christ still worth adoring? When a Christian's family member is killed, is Christ still worth serving? When a Christian's actions are misunderstood or slandered, is Christ still worth devotion? Even if the Christian loses everything else, is Christ still worth honoring, and is the crown of life still worth the perseverance in faith? The answer is decisively yes!

"Afflictions are but as a dark entry into our Father's house," wrote Thomas Brooks. Christians through the generations of the church have borne testimony to this experience. In the midst of the suffering we are able to see little or no point to it all. So we cry to God, "Why?" Afterward, whether very soon or much later, we find such good resulting from the suffering that we reach the point of being able to say sincerely, "The good I have seen coming out of the trial, especially the benefit of my knowing God far better now, is worth the suffering it took to get me here." Because we value the Lord and his kingdom and the crown of life more than we value ease or comfort, it becomes the choice of realism and wisdom to *consider it pure joy* whenever we face trials of many kinds. "However reluctant we may be to embrace it, we know that suffering rightly received is one of the Christian's supreme means of grace" (Wenham 1974:79).

Temptations and Good Gifts (1:13-18) In the very midst of a trial, when I am feeling fear and sorrow and pain, if I am asked by a friend, "What danger or threat is there in your life now, that I may pray for you?" I would probably answer, "Pray for the deadly disease to be healed, or for my financial needs to be met, or for the people to stop doing the things that are injuring me." In other words, I would think of the chief injury being inflicted by the trial, and my foremost concern would be for the trial to be stopped. Now, in 1:13-18, comes a word of God that requires a radical change in our thinking. The Bible says that the trial itself is not the most seriously life-threatening factor. The greatest danger to me is not the wrong being done *to* me, but the wrong that may be done *by* me. The real threat is that when wrong is done to me, I may be tempted to fall into sin myself.

This central emphasis by James sometimes is obscured in the debate over the meaning of James's terms and the relationship between 1:12 and 1:13. Some accentuate a distinction between James's terms for "trial" and "temptation." Dibelius would separate them to such extreme that "the seduction by lusts in vv 13-15 has nothing whatsoever to do with the afflictions in v 12" (1976:90). Moo is more moderate in language but still puts the emphasis on a transition in subject: "Thus, despite the fact that the same Greek root *(peira-)* is used for both the outer trial and the inner temptation, it is crucial to distinguish them" (1985:72). Yet in the next sentence Moo admits that James makes so little mention of such a distinction that Moo is left guessing: "It is probably within verse 13 that James makes the transition from one to the other." Others make the opposite emphasis on the commonality of the two terms and verses. Davids, for example, proposes that "both verses refer to testing" and translates the middle of 1:13 "God ought not to be tested by evil persons" (1982:81-82). Moo is right to reject this as "a very poorly attested meaning" (1985:72), but Davids is driven to this by his failure to observe fully enough the flow of James's thought in logic and vocabulary.

The noun *trial (peirasmos)* in 1:12 and the participial verb *tempted (peirazō)* in 1:13 share a common root, and the primary contrast is not between these two terms. This does not mean that trials and temptations are identical and interchangeable concepts. But it does have two implications for our understanding of the text. First, James is continuing the line of thought about the spiritual dynamics of trials. The temptations he has in mind now are especially those that come in the context of his readers' trials—for example, the temptation to harbor hatred or to take revenge toward those who have persecuted them, or the temptation to be covetous and jealous in their economic hardship. This focuses our understanding of the passage so that we will be able to apply it honestly. Societal values might lead us to think of temptation in terms of our appetite for food or sexual pleasure. James wants us to apply the text to our temptations toward hatred and greed and envy.

Second, the really decisive point of contrast to the idea of temptation in 1:13 is the completely different term *(dokimion)* for "test" or "testing" in 1:12 and 1:3. By using 1:12 so firmly as the start of a new segment united to 1:13-15 (instead of a reference back to 1:2-4 by way of summary as I have suggested), Davids interprets James as dissociating God from the test and "denying that God actively tests anyone" (1982:79-81). There is no debate over the fact that James is warning Christians not to blame God for temptation and sin. However, James does want us to see the testing as a divinely used and positive alternative that stands in direct contrast to the temptation.

James has told us already that God desires the trial to become a test for the development of perseverance leading to maturity. The alternative possibility is now considered: that the trial may become a temptation for sin leading to death. That alternative is emphatically not God's will for the Christian, *for God cannot be tempted by evil, nor does he tempt anyone.* James is describing another dimension to the spiritual dynamic, one that stands in contrast to the one already presented in 1:2-4. We can compare the two parallel patterns now in the following way.

TESTING   ➡   PERSEVERANCE   ➡   MATURITY

TRIAL:

TEMPTATION   ➡   SIN   ➡   DEATH

James will now warn against this second pattern (in 1:13-15) and then encourage a following of the first pattern (in 1:16-18). That these two paragraphs should be so compared will be evident in the parallelism in

---

1:13 The rarity of the term *apeirastos* (characterizing God as "not tempted") has brought various translations, including "inexperienced in evil" (Hort), "un-tempted by evil" (Laws) and "ought not to be tested by evil persons" (Davids).

Moo cites Ecclesiasticus 15:11-12 from the Apocrypha as an evidence that the tendency to blame God existed long before James: "Do not say, 'Because of the Lord I left the right way'; for he will not do what he hates."

1:13-18 A further instance of common apostolic teaching with Peter is evident by comthe outline of their content.

Temptations (1:13-15) James would remember the Lord's teaching that it is not God's desire to tempt a person to live in any way displeasing to him, and that temptation should be resisted (Mt 6:13; 26:41). The flow of James's thought now is to assert facts of God's nature and God's will and then to answer questions these facts raise about the dynamics of temptation.

1. God's nature and will. God's nature is that he *cannot be tempted by evil.* This is a reminder of the holiness of God, whose moral purity is absolute, unassailable, undefiled. He is high and exalted, the Holy One of Israel, whose holiness is so pure that it is described in terms of its wondrous beauty, splendor and utter awesomeness (Ps 27:4; 29:2; 99:3). There is not the smallest trace of evil in God's nature (1 Jn 1:5), and evil cannot have any closeness to God. That is why God's holiness put despair into Isaiah's heart: "Holy, holy, holy is the LORD Almighty. . . . 'Woe to me!' I cried. 'I am ruined! For I am a man of unclean lips . . . and my eyes have seen the King, the LORD Almighty' " (Is 6:3-5). This sense of God's awesome purity is so strong in both Old and New Testaments that it would have to be the background for James when he assures us that God will not be tempted by evil.

This particular character of God leads to a particular will of God—*nor does he tempt anyone.* Not only is he holy; he requires holiness of us. His will for us is always toward holiness, never toward evil. If this is so, it raises the question about human experience that James wants to address. We all experience the temptation to do evil. What then is the origin of temptations, and how do they operate?

2. The dynamics of temptation. First, *the origin of the temptation* is emphatically the person's *own evil desire.* James's term is *epithymia,* a "desire" or "longing" especially with evil meaning. This is a call for us to take responsibility for our own lives and to deal with our sinful

---

parison of 2 Peter 1:3-4 with James 1:13-18. Common elements include emphasis on God's moral perfection; God's giving of good gifts; the complete, encompassing scope of those gifts; the urging to escape evil desires and to participate in the divine nature.

1:14 "Desire *(epithymia)* does not always have a negative meaning (cf. Lk. 22:15; Phil. 1:23), but here, as most often in the New Testament, it refers to fleshly, selfish, illicit desire. While the word often describes specifically sexual passions, the use of the singular here suggests a broader conception" (Moo 1985:73).

motives. Have you ever blamed your parents or other people for what you have become? Have you ever blamed circumstances for what you have done? Of course people and circumstances do affect us. However, one of the most significant ways we resist the work of God for our growth toward becoming "mature and complete" is that we blame factors outside of ourselves for our sin.

I recall a young man I was counseling who was beginning to deal very productively with certain relational problems and an addiction. He said, "I've been angry at my parents for years for my problems, but I see that has been a way for me to be irresponsible about my own behavior." I rejoiced when he said that, for it was a very large and courageous step of faith toward healing. James is doing us a great good by forthrightly confronting this issue—that we are tempted to sin by our own evil desires.

Second, *the action of the temptation* is to drag away and to entice. This is a hunting and fishing metaphor (dragged away as by a predator; enticed as by a lure). With both terms James is warning his readers concerning who is really in danger in the temptation. When they are tempted, they are thinking about taking some pleasure—such as the pleasure of revenge on their persecutors. But who is really being captured? Who is really in danger? The Christians themselves are the prey!

Third, *the effect of the temptation* is sin leading to death. Here James adopts a childbearing image. The person's desire does the conceiving *(syllambanō)* and the giving birth *(tiktō)* to sin; then sin's full growth culminates naturally in its own act of producing *(apokyeō);* what it ultimately produces is death. It is vivid imagery, emphasizing how natural the progression is. This attention-getting imagery is designed to stop sinners in their tracks, seeing that death is the natural and terrible end of a life of sin, not just an occasional result for some sinners. Paul stated the same truth with an image of compensation: "the wages of sin is death" (Rom 6:23). God gave Adam the same assurance about the forbidden fruit: "when you eat of it you will surely die" (Gen 2:17). James is warning Christians to see the danger, and so to abhor sin, and therefore to deny the *evil desire* from which sin comes.

Seeing this impact, we can conclude that we would be applying the verse in a way not intended by James if we derived a doctrinal statement that Christians can lose their salvation. James's concern is not for such a point of doctrine but for a life of genuine faith. He is not telling genuine Christians that they may lose their salvation; he is warning that genuine salvation comes by repentance and faith. The extremity of the warning simply shows how seriously James takes the lordship of Christ. He expects that true believers will not go on giving themselves to sin. To accept Christ as Savior is to accept him as Savior *from sin* and so to turn from sin and follow him as Lord. James's intention is that we should take the holiness of God seriously, realize the extremity of danger in a life of sin and turn from sin to follow Christ.

This is why the greatest danger to James's persecuted readers is not the wrong being done to them but the wrong they may do. Now James is ready to explain the basis for the alternative pattern: a trial becomes the good gift of a testing to develop perseverance leading to maturity and completeness.

Good Gifts (1:16-18) The admonition not to be deceived should be seen as a transition, a "hinge verse" (Davids 1982:86), directed both to the preceding ideas and to the next verses. Don't be deceived about the origin of temptation, and don't be deceived about the origin of every good gift either. It should also be seen as a verse of deep concern addressed to *my dear* [or "beloved"] *brothers.* James earnestly wants to help his readers in their suffering and to save them from the greatest danger to their lives: sin. Notice in this paragraph an outline parallel to the one in 1:13-15.

1. God's nature and will. He is *the Father of the heavenly lights, who does not change like shifting shadows.* The association of God with *heavenly lights* is an image of his exalted glory and power. The dissociation of God from *shifting shadows* is a declaration of his immutability. Both images are designed to give us assurance that we may rely upon him confidently. James wants his readers to cling to the certainty of God's unchanging love in their suffering. Furthermore, this guaranteed nature of God has led to this will of God: *He chose to give . . .* What James emphasizes is that God gives by his own will (participle *boulētheis*), not someone else's; he gives good and perfect gifts, not evil ones; in fact, every good gift is from him, not just some of them.

James intends the force of these truths to accumulate with impact on our actual beliefs about God. Especially in times of trial, is your image of God one of exalted authority, trustworthy constancy and unfailing generosity? Do you believe that God gives you good gifts? The same young man who faced his error of blaming his parents also said to me, "I've been a Christian five years, but it's been only in the last few months that I have taken God seriously. I have talked a good God-game, but I have not taken seriously his power and authority to change my life." Again I rejoiced over his humility and honesty; I have every confidence that God will deliver him from his addiction and make him someday "mature and complete, not lacking anything."

2. *The dynamics of good gifts.* First, *the origin of the good gifts* is emphatically God himself. Whether one acknowledges God as the provider of blessings is an issue of major consequence. Failure in this was, for example, a step in Israel's spiritual adultery, according to Hosea 2:5, 8, 12. James is passionate about this because he wants his suffering readers to be able to apply it in their trials. They need to believe this fundamental truth: in the midst of the trials, God has good gifts for them.

Second, *the action of the good gifts* is one of *coming down.* The implied application of this fact is that we are to look up! With the allusion to far-off heavenly bodies James evokes an image of looking up to receive something wondrous, in order that we may anticipate God's good gifts instead of looking only at the hardship of our circumstances. John Bunyan said, "Temptation provokes me to look upward to God."

Third, *the effect of the good gifts* comes in two stages. The initial effect is *to give us birth.* It refers not merely to physical birth but to regeneration, since it comes *through the word* of truth which becomes the theme of 1:19-27, where it is not God's creative word but his saving and freeing word. The contrast is to sin in 1:15, which gives birth to death (the same verb *apokyeō*). The further effect of God's good gifts is to make us "a kind of firstfruits of all he created"—that we become not only alive but also

---

1:17 These points of emphasis, that good gifts come to us from God and that God's goodness is immutable, are clear in this verse. Some of the details are unclear and subject to debate among commentators. Some of the debate concerns the meaning of James's unique description of God as *the Father of the heavenly lights* and what sort of astronomical phenomenon James has in mind. It is probably best not to read much allegorical or technical meaning into James's imagery here; "we may suspect that he intends no more than a general reference to the constant changes observed in creation" (Moo 1985:76). There are also

changed. The image of firstfruits connotes an expectation of the ultimate fruit-bearing goal of God's work in us. It is the image with which James concludes this section; its meaning will be apparent as we review the passage.

The implication of what James teaches is to encourage the application of God's own nature and will in Christians' practice. We call certain attributes of God "incommunicable" because finite beings do not possess them. God's immutability is one such attribute. But James is persistent in wanting Christians to practice God's ways and to live identifiably as the firstfruits of God's redemptive work through Christ. James is encouraging Christians to imitate God's ways, which are in contrast to their own evil desire.

The first aspect of God's character emphasized in the text was his holiness, which is so absolute that he *cannot be tempted by evil*. Our high calling as firstfruits of his creation is to have that character of holiness more and more clearly reflected in us. We imitate God in his holiness when we resist temptation because we abhor sin.

The second fact of God's character was his grace. He gives good gifts. We imitate God in this trait by graciously giving good gifts to others—even to those who are causing the trials in our lives, for we will give "generously to all without finding fault" (1:5). When we are treated unjustly and hurtfully, we will take our stand here: to rely on God to provide good gifts for us while we persevere in loving our enemies, doing good to those who hate us, blessing those who curse us and praying for those who mistreat us (Lk 6:27-28).

The third fact emphasized about God was his immutability. Even this can be reproduced in a finite form. The trait by which we participate in this attribute of God is none other than *perseverance*—the very trait which God will develop in us through the testing of trials.

This is where the topic of perseverance in trials, begun in 1:2-3, has

---

grammatical questions having to do with (a) whether James means "all God's gifts are good" or "all good gifts come from God" (Adamson 1976:74); (b) whether *good* may be a predicate adjective supplying a reading "all giving is good, but every perfect gift comes from above" (Tasker 1983:47-48); (c) whether to prefer a translation such as "with whom there is no variation or shadow due to change" (RSV) or "who does not change like shifting shadows" (NIV). Davids and Moo especially provide helpful analyses of these issues.

led us. It is James's earnest desire that Christians facing trials of many kinds should see the special privilege set before them in the circumstance of a trial. We have a goal higher than merely escaping the trial or avoiding the pain. God is at work through the trial to make us "mature and complete"—in fact, like God in character and ways. This is James's message: Christian, be astounded at your high calling to reflect and even participate in God's divine nature, and let your astonishment be your motivation then to "consider it pure joy . . . whenever you face trials of many kinds."

Our Response to Trials: A Theology of Suffering With the climax of the passage reached in 1:16-18, Christians can see how crucial is their response to trials. When servants of God meet trials (a loss, a setback, an attack, an injustice, a suffering), they can respond in either of two ways presented by James. They can respond out of evil desires, making the trial an occasion for temptation, leading to sin. Or they can respond out of faith, with joy that they are truly blessed. This response makes the trial an opportunity for testing instead of temptation, and this testing develops perseverance that causes the Christian to become more like God, mature and complete in Christ.

The purpose of reducing the passage to these simple terms is not to oversimplify the awful crises many Christians face, as if the response were easy or mechanical. The purpose is rather to illuminate the pivotal step in facing suffering. When you encounter a trial, such as unjust treatment from another, you may experience a temptation to retaliate by criticizing, gossiping, withholding love or inflicting injury. Instead, in the light of James's teaching, you can ask God to help you take several steps.

1. Deal with the *evil desire* in yourself. Repent of it, confessing that the temptation comes from your own evil desire.

2. Consider the trial *pure joy.* Thank God—not for the temptation, for that came from evil desire, but for the good gifts God will bring in the testing.

3. You may still go on to oppose the injustice and try to change the circumstances of the trial. Some Christians, when they encounter evil, regard it as sent by God and call it "the cross I must bear." From such a mistaken perspective, passive endurance is the only proper response, because resisting the trial would be resisting God. This is a misunder-

standing of Jesus' use of the cross image. When Jesus said his followers must take up their cross, he was describing the discipline they would need to persevere in the face of expected persecution. From James's teaching, the Christian does not have to leave circumstances untouched as "the cross" to be carried. God is not pleased by injustice; so the Christian will work to oppose injustice. At the same time, servants of God may consider it pure joy that they have opportunities to be tested for the development of perseverance.

The response of pure joy is, then, neither a passive acceptance of injustice (that would be unholy) nor an unrealistic escapism (that would be untruthful). James has shown joy to be an honest, realistic response to trials because of the truth of God's nature.

I recall again my dear friends Jim and Marie. It has been sixteen years since their son died. They did persevere then, but new trials have come. Marie was diagnosed with cancer. Months of chemotherapy followed; their financial burden was heavy with no insurance; Marie was confined to her home much of the time; loneliness and depression were frequent; pain was constant. Marie told me that at times it was difficult to feel confident about God's love for her. But she found her faith in God growing. She believed God's love for her through Christ to be real and sufficient to save her, deliver her and accomplish the blessing of her life in spite of the suffering. Marie set her heart on the crown of life.

Jim and Marie were not exuberant during those days; but they were persevering by faith. I prayed for the full blessing unfolded in James 1:1-18 to be fulfilled in them. For they are dearly loved by God, who unchangeably gives good gifts and who calls Jim and Marie to joy.

And now I have received news that Marie has died, and I have just talked with Jim. He said, "I tell people Marie is now in the best place she could possibly be, and that I will see her again. Some of them ask me, 'How do you know?' I tell them, 'I've staked my life on it.' " While that may not exactly answer their question, Jim's testimony is very proper. He has taken the stand of faith in Christ of which James the Just was writing. I weep for my friend, but I can rejoice for him as well.

☐ The Righteous Life That God Desires (1:19-27)

When King David faced his times of most intense persecution and danger, he frequently prayed a rather impressive request. On his heart was his need not merely for protection from his attackers but, even more, for protection from sin.

> Show me your ways, O LORD,
>   teach me your paths;
> guide me in your truth and teach me,
>   for you are God my Savior,
>   and my hope is in you all day long. . . .
> Guard my life and rescue me;
>   let me not be put to shame,
>   for I take refuge in you.
> May integrity and uprightness protect me,
>   because my hope is in you. (Psalm 25:4-5, 20-21)

> Set a guard over my mouth, O LORD;
>   keep watch over the door of my lips.
> Let not my heart be drawn to what is evil,
>   to take part in wicked deeds
> with men who are evildoers;
>   let me not eat of their delicacies. (Psalm 141:3-4)

It was a kind of praying we Christians need to learn: not just "Lord, keep me safe," but "Lord, keep me pure," because we abhor sin even more than suffering. This is the need the apostle James saw for the young Christians who had been scattered by persecution. He wrote in loving concern to strengthen them for clear-headed moral courage even when others were doing evil and even when that evil was being done against them.

But James is not merely a moralist. A moralist has a list of ethical guidelines by which to live a happy and respectable life. A Christian has a person, Jesus Christ, to whom the Christian owes everything, to whom the Christian surrenders everything, for whom the Christian lives in everything. Because of that relationship with Christ, the Christian becomes a person of deep moral commitment. That is how James writes— as a Christian of profound moral earnestness. Therefore what he writes now is not just a gathering of moralisms: "Be quick to listen and slow to speak, because it will help you get along better with people." James is writing about life in Christ.

He has just been telling his readers: When you face trials of various kinds, beware of the temptation to sin. It is not the suffering of the trial but the temptation to sin that is the most serious danger to you, because sin kills the sinner. Sin gives birth to death, whereas you have been given birth by the work of Christ to be delivered from sin and death. Because you have been given life in Christ, now live *the righteous life that God desires.*

There is both a grammatical and a textual issue to be decided concerning the first word. The textual uncertainty seems weighted in favor of the verb *iste,* "know" (as in the most ancient manuscripts and as agreed by most commentators), rather than the conjunction *hōste,* "wherefore" (in spite of Adamson's declaration that "*isto* is certainly wrong," 1976:78). The grammatical question is whether to render *iste* as indicative ("you know this") or imperative ("know this" or "take note of this"). Hiebert accepts the indicative as more probable (1979:123). Davids (1982:91), Laws (1980:80), Dibelius (1976:109), Lenski (1966: 557) and Ropes (1916:168) have preferred the imperative. This is the more likely intention, by the evidence of James's parallel construction in 1:16 and his predominant pattern of using the vocative *brothers* with an imperative verb. The result of these conclusions both textually and grammatically is to find 1:19 more forceful than in the other options. Apparently James does not simply pass on to his next thought with a connecting "wherefore" or a recognition that "you know this" or "of that you may be certain" (NEB). More than that, James urgently charges Christians to be sure to practice their faith by the specific behaviors listed in this section.

The urgency of this passage, then, is expressed (1) in his endearment *(my dear brothers),* (2) in his imperative *(take note of this)* and (3) in his inclusive application *(everyone, anyone, the man who).* It should be conveyed in exposition of this passage that all of this instruction is important, that it is for each individual reader and that it is for each reader personally to put into practice. The tone at the beginning of this passage is "Because you are very dear to me, I am urging all of you: be sure to do these things . . ."

Be Quick to Listen (1:19-21) Typically for James's literary style, he presents his instructions through pairs of complementary or contrasting ideas.

Quick to Listen and Slow to Speak (1:19) This is James's first assault on a major theme in his epistle: the immorality and destructiveness of an uncontrolled tongue. His first command regarding one's tongue is to silence it. Instead of talking, listen. His emphasis is not just on the quantity of listening (listen a lot) but on the promptness of listening (listen first): *be quick* to do it. The complementary command is to be *slow to speak.*

There is an important reason in the context of trials for making this the first instruction: trials make us do the opposite of what James says to do. The pressures of trials make us slow to listen and quick to speak—especially quick to speak in anger. The proverbial man who kicks the dog when he comes home from work does so not because the pet has wronged him but because he has suffered trials at work. It becomes even more serious when we "kick" other people. A married couple struggling financially is more likely to experience marital conflict. They may fight over the money or over other issues, but the financial trial has become the occasion for sinning against each other. With sensitive pastoral awareness of people's needs, James recognizes that their circumstances

___

Notes: 1:19 The parallel construction between 1:16-18 and 1:19-21 warns us not to interrupt the continuity of James's thought. Both of these paragraphs begin with an imperative, then offer identical vocative phrases and conclude with an emphasis on the redemptive effect of God's word. Dibelius ignores this parallel structure by treating 1:21 as the introduction to 1:22-25 (1976:112). Martin is also unconvinced by this parallel; his arrangement of the text is to place "Note this, my dear brothers" as the conclusion of the preceding verses rather than the introduction to the following verses (1988:29). Davids highlights the parallel construction between 1:16-18 and 1:19-21 (1982:91), even though he incorporates the first paragraph topically into 1:12-18, followed by 1:19-21 as treating a second topic. My own division between 1:18 and 1:19 is simply to emphasize James's transition from the worldview presented in 1:2-18 to the moral implication for practice in 1:19-27. In any case, for James it is all one fabric of thought.

The urgency of *My dear brothers, take note of this* is just as forceful whether one makes these words introductory to the following verses (as do most commentators) or in conclusion of the preceding verses (as does Martin), though the focus is obviously redirected in Martin's view. James's style is to employ the vocative frequently, including fifteen instances of *brothers* along with less affectionate addresses such as "you foolish man" (2:20) and "you adulterous people" (4:4). Though there are exceptions (such as in 3:10 and 3:12), James's general habit of thought is to introduce rather than conclude a section by addressing the

must present daily possibilities for relational conflicts.

James's instruction to them could apply to their conflicts with unbelieving persecutors; he would want Christians to maintain purity toward enemies as well as friends. However, there are indications later in the letter that he wanted especially to warn against impurity in relationships with fellow Christians (4:1, 11; 5:9).

The particular danger that James sees in these frequent relational conflicts should be defined from the preceding material in 1:2-18. James's argument does not appeal to a Pauline image of the body of Christ, in which he might have said everyone should be quick to listen because we are all members of one body (as in Ephesians 4), or later that we should look after orphans and widows because, if one part of the body suffers, every part suffers with it (as in 1 Corinthians 12). Nor does James write exactly with Paul's missionary argument of being light to a world in darkness (as in Ephesians 5). It is not that James would disagree with what Paul would later write, but that his context is the theology he has already written in 1:2-18. There he has explained that conflicts can be occasions for testing, which develops perseverance and leads to maturity; or they can be occasions for temptation, which promotes sin and leads to death. James is calling for purity in relationships because he sees the life-threatening danger of sin and the life-giving value of faith. The

---

people he has in mind. Martin seems to recognize this pattern in his division of paragraphs throughout the letter, even though he does render both 1:16 and the beginning of 1:19 as conclusions to their paragraphs (1988:29).

Careful inductive study of the letter as a whole should be employed to reach a conclusion about James's intended application here. Adamson believes James is instructing Christians to listen specifically "to the 'Word' of v. 18 preached or catechized" (1976:78); Songer (1972:112) and Hiebert (1979:121-126) agree with Adamson in seeing that connection between 1:18 and 1:19. Martin alludes to the possibility of a worship-service setting for this instruction but really emphasizes the broader application to ethical conduct as in the Wisdom literature (1988:47). Dibelius in general treats the epistle more as a series of sayings than as a coherently unified message. He denies the connection between 1:18 and 1:19, then finds James interpreting 1:19 "very unequally" and therefore concludes that James's real interest is in being "quick to listen," having included the references to speaking and becoming angry only because he is quoting a traditional threefold saying "handed down to him" (1976:111). Laws also tends to treat the epistle as somewhat disconnected sayings, but in this case she sees no problem relating 1:19 to James's elaboration on the themes of speaking and becoming angry later in the letter (1980:80). Davids generally assumes a coherent unity in the epistle, and he specifically refutes both Adamson's and Dibelius's alternatives (1982:92) regarding this verse.

danger in being slow to listen and quick to speak is in the sin aroused. As in 1:13-15, the trial becomes an occasion for death-dealing sin.

Almost daily as a pastor I see the value that good listening has for the church's purity within and the church's mission without. When disagreements occur in the church, over and over I have seen what great damage is done to people, to relationships and to the effectiveness of our ministries when we are quick to argue our positions, defend our views and push our opinions. I have also seen what great good is done when we discipline ourselves to postpone defending our own views and judging others' views while we concentrate on listening and giving a full hearing in order to understand the other side of the conflict. We usually find the conflict more easily resolved. Good listening is a protection against dissension.

It is not only the avoidance of conflict that James has in mind. This verse, when extended into verse 20, implies a ministry God wants us to have toward each other to promote the righteous life he desires. Good listening helps to administer God's love for others' healing and strengthening. The result is their greater ability to live the life of righteousness.

James expects people who have been given birth in Christ to begin changing habits and behavior. He tells us to become *slow to speak*. We have a problem, though. Listening is most difficult when we are angry. In fact, the underlying anger is a primary and root cause for our slowness to listen and quickness to speak. It is clear that James perceives a close connection between the speaking and the anger, for his instruction to be *slow to speak (bradys eis to lalēsai)* is followed by a further application in identical terms and structure: *slow to become angry (bradys eis orgēn)*. A major part of James's letter will be spent elaborating on this connection between sinful speech and selfish anger (in chapters 3 and 4), so that 1:19 is really a theme verse for the letter. James recognizes what trials do to us, that they stir our fear, self-pity, envy, confusion and especially anger. These result in behaviors of fighting, judging and attacking. He warns against these sins, and he writes about the ministry God wants us

---

1:20 Is *the righteousness of God* intended as a subjective genitive (referring to a quality of God's character), an objective genitive (referring to a standard God sets for human behavior) or a genitive of origin (referring to a righteousness that God gives, as in the Pauline concept of justification)? Even commentators who assign a later date to the writing

to have toward each other to bring about the righteous life that God desires.

Human Anger and Divine Righteousness (1:20) *The righteous life that God desires* is the NIV's lengthy translation of James's two words *dikaiosynēn theou*. This translation is an attempt to describe the active obedience desired by God rather than a static standard of righteousness, which is certainly in keeping with James's concern. The RSV stays closer to James stylistically, retaining his blunt grammatical contrast: "the anger of man does not work the righteousness of God." The Living Bible takes more interpretive freedom, but its terms convey too many questionable connotations: "anger doesn't make us good, as God demands that we must be." The TEV manages to include the idea of God's active purpose without diluting the concise and forceful contrast: "Man's anger does not achieve God's righteous purpose."

The contrast in this verse is made clear grammatically. The *anger of man (orgē andros)* as subject is positioned next to the *righteousness of God (dikaiosynēn theou)* as object, with the negated verb *does not accomplish (ouk ergazetai)* concluding the blunt sentence. Human anger and divine righteousness are typically at odds with each other. A person acting by the former does not carry out or produce the latter.

In spite of some commentators' depiction of James's epistle as a series of loosely connected thoughts, it should not be difficult to see the connection between 1:20 and the theological view of life that James has established in 1:2-18. The persecuted Christians have plenty of opportunity for anger in their trials. The one who desperately needs wisdom in his difficult circumstances (1:5) and the brother who needs help in his deprived economic conditions (1:9) are both urged by James to hold steady focus on the goal of real value: becoming mature and complete. Therefore they are to see their anger as tempting them to do evil and to recognize that such temptation is neither originating from God's will (1:13) nor (James now adds) achieving anything for God's will.

Again, we do not have to search long in Jesus' Sermon on the Mount

---

of James (e.g., Laws and Dibelius) properly reject the third meaning from the immediate context of this verse. The second alternative seems most fitting for the thrust of the passage, as agreed also by Davids (1982:93). Tasker's exposition of the verse makes use of both the first and the second meanings of the genitive (1983:50).

to find likely background to what James is thinking. The ones who are blessed are "those who hunger and thirst for righteousness" *(dikaio-synē)*, "the merciful," "the pure in heart," "the peacemakers" and "those who are persecuted because of righteousness" (Mt 5:6-10). Further, Jesus applied God's commandment against murder as a commandment also against hating, cursing or insulting—specifically being angry *(orgizome-nos)*: "anyone who is angry with his brother will be subject to judgment" (Mt 5:21-22).

In fact, the follower of Christ is commanded to carry out actions that are the opposite of anger: turning the other cheek to the one who strikes you, giving even more to the one who would take from you and loving the one who is your enemy (Mt 5:39-44). These are the kinds of application to be made from James's instruction.

The righteous life that God desires is the contrasting alternative. God has always stipulated holiness as the terms of being in covenantal relationship with the Holy One. The Lord appeared to Abram and said, "I am God Almighty; walk before me and be blameless" (Gen 17:1). James is writing from an awareness of this continuing command, made even more emphatic by the now fulfilled work of Christ.

The ministry to welcome from James is his unrelenting moral focus; he takes God's commands seriously, and he makes our unholiness clear and inexcusable. If one's goal is to "receive the crown of life," one will make moral choices accordingly. If I act in resentment toward the person who has greater comforts of wealth, I am not acting according to the righteous life that God desires. If I act in hatred toward the person who has injured me with spiteful attitudes or slanderous words or damaging actions, I am not carrying out the righteous life God desires. James is honest enough to face the choice clearly: Do I want revenge and comfort and avoidance of hardship, or do I want God's righteousness in my life?

If 1:19 pointed to the ministry that God wants us to have toward each other, now 1:20 points out our need for release from anger so that we can carry out that ministry and together learn the life of righteousness.

1:21 The term *kakia* has two senses as a term for moral wickedness. It can have a general sense, which Martin chooses when he translates it "evil" (1988:48). But the same term can refer to a particular kind of evil which we might translate as "malice." Davids prefers this second meaning, which is very possible from the theme of anger in the passage and from

That evokes the question "How can this happen in me?" The answer comes in the next verse.

The Prevalent Evil and the Saving Word (1:21) There are multiple contrasts in this verse. First, the sole imperative is *dexasthe* ("accept" the word), an act that stands in contrast to that of the modifying participle *apothemenoi* ("taking off" or "getting rid of" all moral filth and evil). Both are to be intentional acts for Christians: accepting the word while rejecting evil. Second, the evil to be put away is *prevalent (perisseian,* describing a surrounding presence in abundance), whereas the word to be accepted is *planted (emphyton,* depicting an internal presence of the word that has already been placed like a seed inside the Christian). Third, the implanted word is able to *save you (sōsai tas psychas hymōn,* "to save your souls"), implying a contrasting threat to your souls from the preceding moral filth and prevalent evil. This one verse is thus a marvelous window into the worldview from which James is writing. It is a worldview of complementary moral imperatives made urgent by their corresponding results.

get rid of	IS IN CONTRAST TO	humbly accept
the evil prevalent around you	IS IN CONTRAST TO	the word planted in you
which threatens you (implied)	IS IN CONTRAST TO	which can save you

By comparing other texts, James's worldview is found to be not an isolated thought but a genuinely biblical worldview. First, the prevalence of evil is a notion James would have found in Jesus' sermons. Jesus taught that the quantity of trouble *(kakia)* is enough in each day (Mt 6:34), so James can warn about the evil *(kakia)* with the quantitative term of *perisseian* (surplus, abundance). Jesus taught that one can store

the parallel emphasis in 1 Peter 2:1 (1982:94). Laws also chooses this meaning but gives it an even more specific focus as "malicious talk" (1980:81). This is probably more specific than the text warrants.
Compare these attempts at rendering the quantitative sense of *perisseia* as an abundance

up either good or evil in one's heart and that the abundance *(perisseu-ma)* in one's heart will direct how one speaks (Lk 6:45). James could be recalling that teaching now, both in the quantitative image of evil and in the application to one's speech.

Second, the need to put off this evil drives other New Testament writers. The force of the participle *apothemenoi* is properly translated as an imperative: *Get rid of . . .* This urgency is similarly reflected in 1 Peter 2:1, "Rid yourselves *[apothemenoi]* of all malice *[kakian]*." With the same verb, Paul will urge the Ephesians to put off the old self and to get rid of falsehood (Eph 4:22, 25).

Third, the emphasis on the ability of the word to save is also part of the fabric of New Testament thought. Again the origin is in Jesus' teaching—in Matthew 7:24. "Therefore everyone who hears these words of mine and puts them into practice is like a wise man who built his house on the rock." Christ's parable depicted a house surrounded by prevalent and threatening dangers—falling rains, rising streams, blowing winds. The inhabitants were saved through "words"—the words of Christ put into practice. Then James's theology in the first part of chapter 1 (specifically 1:18, concerning "the word of truth") provides the immediate context for his application here in 1:21. Finally, Peter again presents confirming parallel instruction in 1 Peter 2:2. The "pure spiritual milk" Peter has in mind is most likely the word of God, which he has just emphasized in 1:23-25. Thus Peter's line of thought runs parallel to James's:

---

or prevalence: Mayor's "overflowing of malice," Dibelius's "all that profuse wickedness," Laws's "great mass of malice." Readers may be confused, however, by three models of popular translations for this term. The NIV emphasizes the notion of abundance with *the evil that is so prevalent.* The NASB portrays the quantitative element as a remainder rather than an abundance: "all that remains of wickedness." Still others include a concept of quantitative increase, as in the RSV's "rank growth of wickedness" or the NEB's "malice that hurries to excess." The translator's dilemma is in the fact that *perisseia* normally means "abundance" and even "surplus" but that it would be unlikely for James to be telling Christians merely to get rid of their surplus amount of evil. Tasker is willing on this basis to conclude that James must be using *perisseia* with the same sense as *perisseuma,* "remainder," telling converted Christians to get rid of any evil remaining in them from their old life (1983:51). Martin accepts this meaning in translating it "every trace of evil" (1988:48). Davids too is attracted to this meaning as one that fits the context "admirably," but his endorsement is restrained because the definition is reached by speculation (1982:94). If it is true that the teachings of Jesus were guiding James's thinking in some detail, Matthew 6:34 and Luke 6:45 would seem to make "abundance" or "prevalence" the preferred idea.

1. God has given us birth through his word (Jas 1:18; 1 Pet 1:23).

2. Therefore it is imperative that we get rid of all evil (Jas 1:21; 1 Pet 2:1).

3. In place of the evil, it is the word of God that we must now accept and crave (Jas 1:21; 1 Pet 2:2).

Application is to be made based upon what we have seen of the meaning. First we found in this verse a worldview, seeing evil as both pervasive and life-threatening for us. This calls us to evaluate our own worldview by comparison. Do we see the world in the same terms? Minimizing the danger of doing evil is, in light of this verse, recklessly unrealistic. It is somewhat comparable to persisting in a heavy smoking habit while saying, "It's not as bad as they make it out to be" (that is, it's not really life-threatening) or "The cancer won't get me" (that is, the danger is not really prevalent). Unrealistic thinking leaves us insulated against the urgency for moral reform. This is one reason that our praying in crises is not like King David's: "Let not my heart be drawn to what is evil." We pray for safety instead of purity because we do not see impurity as dangerous.

Second, this verse calls for us to repent of all moral filth in our lives. It includes not only sensational crimes but also everyday evils like a complaining attitude, a jealous spirit, a deceitful or gossipy way of speaking, or a rebelliousness against authority. Like numerous other biblical statements, this one makes clear that repentance is not merely a sorrow

---

The term *logikos* used in 1 Peter 2:2 has only one other New Testament occurrence, in Romans 12:1, and means "spiritual" or "rational." It is possible that Peter intended even in this choice of terms a connection with the *logos* he had emphasized in 1:23, as asserted by Stibbs and Walls: "If the idea is milk 'consisting of word' rather than 'of liquid,' there is probably some intended connection in thought with the previous reference to the divine *logos* or 'word' (i.23)" (1959:96). Grudem lists six textual and logical reasons for concluding that Peter means the word of God by his reference to "pure spiritual milk" (1988:95).

The idea of *implanted* has received some attempts at interpretation as "innate" or "inborn" because the term *emphytos* is so used in Hellenistic literature. This would require a different identity for *the word* as something more like an inborn reason or capacity, rather than the word of God newly planted in James's readers, as I have portrayed it. (Cf. Knox 1945:14-15.) Davids refutes this with the observation from James's context that "something inborn could have nothing to do with receiving nor does it fit well with the context of hearing before and after this verse" (1982:95). James's evident contrast between *get rid of* and *humbly accept* supports the further understanding of *implanted* as employed to contrast with *prevalent.*

for one's sin but, more fully, a sorrow that moves one to make changes in one's life. Biblical repentance is a change of direction, a turning around, a choice to repudiate immorality and cry out to God, "I don't want to be like this anymore!"

The third area of necessary application is in the humble acceptance of God's word. It should not be confusing that James would tell us to accept what is already planted in us. The term *emphyton (planted in you)* indicates that the focus of the word's work is on changing the Christian rather than changing the circumstances of the trial. *Humbly accept* would then mean not only to believe teachably but to act upon that word—for example, to accept that being quick to listen and slow to speak really is the best course in the midst of the conflict. Anger is a stance of telling and demanding; James commands a stance of learning and receiving. It is the stance he has already prescribed and illustrated in 1:2-18 concerning trials. It requires a humble teachability to consider it pure joy when one meets trials because one knows, from God's word, that the trials will be used by God as tests to develop perseverance.

When I was directing an InterVarsity conference in Colorado one year, something the speaker said prompted a student to ask with evident intensity, "But what do you *do* when things are going wrong, and other people are hurting you, and you are hurt and angry?" The speaker answered, "Have your daily quiet time."

At first this made me angry; it seemed to be a simplistic answer that ignored the struggle expressed in the question. As I thought about it, though, the wisdom of the speaker's words came into focus. We need the word of God—we need to humbly accept it into our minds and hearts—because it really is able to save us from the destructive power of our own sinfulness. With this conviction, James goes on to explain how to use that lifesaving word of God.

Do What the Word Says (1:22-25) It would be natural for James, as a Jew, to refer to the Old Testament Scriptures as "the word," since this is a designation found within the Old Testament itself. We also find him using some distinct phrases *(royal law* and *the perfect law that gives freedom)* to express a new meaning which the word of God has assumed for him as a Christian. Add to this the fact that we find his letter permeated with references to the teachings of Jesus, and it becomes likely that when James refers to God's word he has in mind not only the Old Testament but also (in fact, especially) the teachings of Jesus which form the heart of the New Testament. It is appropriate, then, for us as Christians to take this as teaching about the proper use of Scripture, both Old and New Testaments.

For some people, reading the Bible is an unpleasant chore because their perception of the Bible's message is "Do this; do that; do this other. And do more of this and more of that and more of the other." The effect is only a building of stress and guilt. On the other hand, some people find Scripture to be indeed *the perfect law that gives freedom*. I recall a young man who was, by God's grace, taking some very large steps to walk more thoroughly according to Scripture. His humble acceptance of God's word was admirable to me; his resulting spiritual growth was exhilarating to him. One day in my office he said in amazement, "I am internalizing God's word so much more now; it makes me wonder how I could have called myself a Christian before. It's like it was all just head knowledge before."

It is that "internalizing" of Scripture that James describes now. As before, his style is to present two complementary images: do not be only hearers of the word; instead be doers of the word. To guide our inquiry here, we can ask three parallel questions of each image.

1. What is the pattern of the deception/blessedness?

2. What then is the nature of the word?

3. How would one be a hearer/doer of the word today?

Hearers of the Word: Deceived (1:22-24) The one fact James emphasizes about "hearers only" is that hearing the word without doing the word is an act of self-deception. The nature of the self-deception has received different interpretations that will make a large difference in personal or homiletical application about salvation. Martin's view illustrates one tradition, which says James is defining "the nature of true piety" (1988:49). Davids represents the other major tradition, which says the term means here "to deceive oneself as to one's salvation" (1982:97). In the former alternative, the passage is applicable as a warning to genuine Christians who are nevertheless not putting Scripture into practice seriously enough. The latter alternative makes this passage a warning against a false presumption of salvation in the first place.

The actual term for "deceive," *paralogizomai*, does not offer much help in this debate, as it is used only one other time in the New Testament (by Paul writing later in Col 2:4). However, James's own choice of analogy in 1:23-24 does provide material by which to interpret his intention. Here the text supports Davids's view that the passage is a warning against a false presumption of salvation.

1. What is the pattern of the deception? The hearer of the word is self-deceiving, like a person who looks in a mirror and then goes away without thinking further about his or her appearance. At this point the NIV's rendering is misleading by connecting 1:23 to 1:24 as a continuing clause with a compound predicate: "a man who looks . . . and . . . goes away," leaving the impression that the man's error is in going away while neglecting to change something that he ought to have changed about his appearance. If this were the case, then the analogy would be saying that the primary function of Scripture is to expose our faults and to tell us, "Do this; change that." While the word of God certainly does expose our sins so that we may repent, this is not the whole picture of Scripture's function.

The NASB more accurately captures James's grammatical stop at the end of 1:23 with a semicolon. This conveys that the analogy is complete at the end of 1:23. What James explains in 1:24 is additional, but not essential, information. The point is that the man does not need to keep thinking about his appearance; he can forget his appearance, because it is useless to him once he has finished looking. James's phrase *prosōpon tēs geneseōs* ("natural face" or "face he was born with") does not imply that the man is seeing something in his appearance that he ought to change. It speaks of the ordinariness of what the man is seeing; he doesn't need to think further about his appearance. His reflection in the

---

1:22 The ramifications of how one understands the nature of the self-deception are demonstrated in the debate stirred at times over "lordship salvation." John MacArthur's publication of *The Gospel According to Jesus* provided a modern occasion.

Laws finds it "unlikely" that 1:22 has any dependence on Jesus' teaching in Matthew 7 or Luke 6, because James makes no reference to Jesus' parable of the two houses in those passages (1980:85). Argument from omission, of course, is somewhat conjectural. Davids is satisfied with the probability that James would first have Jesus' own teachings in mind

mirror is useless for him in going about his daily business of life. This makes the application clear. If I hear the word of God but do not do what it says, I am treating the word as if it were useless. I am deceiving myself about the very nature and purpose of the word of God.

James's thought in the analogy is for the purpose of the word. If he has just stated a purpose of the word, that would most naturally be the purpose he has in mind now. When we look back at the text for such a statement of purpose, it is immediately before us at the end of 1:21: the word *can save you.*

The urgency of his message must be faced. He is warning us not to be self-deceived about our very salvation. James has emphasized that sin leads to death (1:15). We cannot claim a salvation from death while we carelessly persist in sin which kills. If sin is seen as our choice to run our own lives instead of submitting to God's rule, we cannot ask Christ to save us from sin and then go right on running our own lives; it is self-contradictory. To think we can so live is to practice self-deception. The core of accepting salvation is accepting Christ as Savior and Lord. If I am saved, I will give myself to the doing of my Lord's word. It is not that I will attempt to save myself by obeying commands; rather, because I am saved, I will set my heart on doing the will of God who is my Savior.

This is consistent with the teachings that James had learned from Jesus and that are expressed later by Paul just as clearly, that the follower of Christ will die to self-will and live unto the Lord's will. James is earnest about specific moral issues in this letter because he is earnest about the lordship of Christ.

2. *What then is the nature of the word?* James's analogy places emphasis on the usefulness of God's word for our salvation in daily living. Unlike our useless reflection in a mirror, the word of God is to be taken into our daily decisions and actions. For the analogy of the mirror to be

---

here; he even recalls, as an unprovable but possible theory, Origen's belief that 1:22 is an unrecorded saying of Jesus (1982:97).

1:23 I agree with Davids (1982:98) that James's phrase *prosōpon tēs geneseōs* (translated "face" in NIV) means simply "natural appearance," and that it is an overinterpretation of the text to see in this a deliberate contrast between physical and spiritual appearance as in Adamson (1976:82-83) or between human birth and rebirth as in Laws (1980:86). Martin's later suggestion of an intended contrast between what we are and what God intends us to become in Christ should be treated with similar caution.

appropriate, James must have believed in both the perspicuity and the applicability of Scripture. He believed the word of God to be clear and understandable, comparable to a mirror that gives an accurate reflection rather than one so clouded or distorted that the viewer would gain no real understanding from looking at it. James believed also that the word of God reveals matters upon which the readers should take some appropriate action; the word is relevant in application to our lives. People who are hearers only are deceiving themselves because they ignore these two features of the word of God. They treat the word as if it were useless because of being either unclear or irrelevant.

3. How would one be only a hearer of the word today? By the description James has given of God's word, at least four approaches to Scripture that are common today should be repudiated as examples of merely listening without doing and so deceiving oneself.

Relativistic. The scholarly study of linguistics and literary criticism during the past few decades has been characterized by an increasing skepticism regarding the possibility of absolute truth. Formalism, structuralism, phenomenology and deconstruction have some diversity of forms, but they have led to some common philosophical assumptions, including the impossibility of objectivity, the relativity of truth, the subjectivity of meaning and the resulting primacy of experience (since ultimate meanings are regarded as indeterminate).

Relativism as a worldview now pervades contemporary thought and even pressures many Christians. A common assumption today is that Christianity is an alternative that has already had its day. This is so persuasive precisely because modern culture has adopted the notion that everything changes and anything becomes passé, whether fashions or automobiles or religion or, ultimately, truth itself. One perceptive businessman in the church I pastor commented to me, "I find the persuasiveness [of this view] very sophisticated and tugging at my elbows *every day!* And I consider my faith reasonably strong."

The impact of relativism is to undermine exactly what James prescribes for our study of Scripture. We say the Bible is the word of God; then we contradict that belief by conceding a cultural relativity to points of doctrine that are presented in Scripture as transcending culture. We say we believe in the authority of Scripture; but we have so often been told "It may be right for you, but not for me" that we begin to believe this relativism in our own hearts. Then, when we read the word of God, it falls on ears that hear but do not respond with action.

Superstitious. In 1 Samuel it is recorded that the Israelites were defeated by the Philistines. The elders of Israel conferred and decided to bring the ark of the Lord's covenant from Shiloh "so that it may go with us and save us from the hand of our enemies" (1 Sam 4:3). When they next went into battle, this time with the ark of the Lord present, Israel was again defeated, and the ark was captured.

What went wrong with their plan? They treated the ark of the covenant as if it were magical, as if *it* could save them. Instead, they should have sought the Lord. Doing so, they would have realized that they could not expect salvation from a holy God while persisting in wickedness. They would have to do what James says to do: act on God's word.

This is not far off from the way some people treat Scripture still. The Bible is revered as an object, as if *it* would bring blessing on one's life. The Bible may be read often; prayers may be said frequently; church services may be attended; yet there may still be a self-satisfied overlooking of gossip or lies or irresponsibility or emotional abuse of one's spouse. This amounts to a superstitious use of Scripture.

James is insisting that the words of Scripture are of no value unless put into practice. If you study the word of God and begin to see a picture of true justice or genuine love or real holiness, then start practicing what you are discovering. This is the passion on James's heart.

Emotional. The word of God is certainly intended to affect our emotions. Jesus himself told his disciples that he spoke his words to them so that they might not fear but instead have joy (Jn 14:1-2; 15:11). The misuse of this is the employment of the word of God only for emotional comfort while avoiding obedience. By James's instruction, one should not be satisfied with a superficial devotional reading merely for emotional satisfaction. He demands a reading of the word with the goal of doing the will of God found there.

Theoretical. James's instruction also repudiates the merely theoretical use of the word of God, in which a person may study the word in exhaustive detail but then use the word only as material for philosophical or theological debate. The result is an abundance of doctrinal correctness but a scarcity of biblical godliness. The ones who are "hearers only" after this pattern tend to build a reputation for holding proper theology while leaving behind a trail of divisiveness and damaged relationships.

Doers of the Word: Blessed (1:22, 25) The better alternative of being "doers" (RSV) is introduced in 1:22 and then described further in 1:25. The initial imperative in 1:22, *Do not merely listen to the word. . . . Do what it says,* probably again recalls parts of Jesus' own sermons, such as Matthew 7:21-27 and Luke 6:46-49. Instead of a relativistic, superstitious, emotional or theoretical approach to the word of God, James urges a practical approach. Do what the word says. The chief fact which James emphasizes about doers of the word is that they will be *blessed.*

1. What is the pattern of the blessedness? The phrases flow from James's heart, dramatizing the pattern of being blessed and making his appeal more emphatic. Forms of the verbs *do* and *forget* are repeated from 1:23-24, maintaining clear contrasts with the pattern of deception. The pattern by which one is blessed is stated in four successive terms rather than portrayed through an analogy.

Looks intently. This is a participle *parakypsas* which continues the image of a person looking into a mirror. Now, however, the person is looking into the word of God itself, which is worthy of an intent look because it is *the perfect law that gives freedom.*

Continues. The looking is now augmented by a second participle, *parameinas,* for James means we should not only look intently but also persist in looking.

Not forgetting. Still not satisfied with the emphasis, James further adds, literally, "being not a hearer of forgetfulness."

But doing. The full participial phrase makes a striking contrast of images: "being not a hearer of forgetfulness but a doer of action."

1:25 The participle *parakypsas* is from the verb *parakyptō,* which is used by Luke and John in their resurrection narratives with the verb's literal sense of bending over to look more closely (Lk 24:12; Jn 20:5). The only other New Testament instances of this verb are here in James 1:25 and in 1 Peter 1:12, both using the verb figuratively to imply an intensity about looking into something. Hence the NIV inserts the adverb *intently.*

See the introduction concerning James's use of *law* as referring especially to the teachings of Jesus. Paul, writing in a different time and context, perceived similar implications from the Old Testament and the teachings of Jesus, as pointed out by Davids (1982:100). Laws

After this piling of phrases for emphasis, the conclusion of the sentence is like a climax reached within this one verse. This is the crowning goal of looking intently, continuing to do so and not forgetting but doing: *He will be blessed [makarios] in what he does [poiēsei]*. The statement recalls two dramatic scenes in Jesus' teaching ministry, once again revealing how studiously James has learned the teachings of his half-brother who had become so thoroughly his Lord. The first, of course, would be the Beatitudes, in which Jesus repeated the same term "blessed" *makarios*. That scene exhibits how the term *makarios* took on a particularly Christian and eschatological content in the New Testament, where the Greek term occurs fifty times and forty-four of them are beatitudes. Jesus based blessedness specifically on the coming of his kingdom, and the blessedness was often identified in paradoxical contrast to the world's usual standards for happiness. Jesus made it a point to declare "blessed" those who were poor, mourning and persecuted. Now James is writing to Christians who are often poor, mourning and persecuted, and his promise of blessedness carries this Christian content. True blessedness—the joy of Christ's kingdom—comes not by escaping trials but by doing the word of the Lord.

The second scene would be the Last Supper, at which Jesus washed his disciples' feet, instructed them about servanthood from his example and concluded, "Now that you know these things, you will be blessed *[makarioi]* if you do *[poiēte]* them" (Jn 13:17). It was not enough for Jesus that his disciples "know these things." Likewise, it is not enough for James that his readers be hearers of the word. Blessing is found in the doing of God's will through a life of active obedience.

2. What then is the nature of the word? In contrast to the hearer who is deceived, the doer is blessed. What is the nature of the word that makes it something which brings blessing? It is, literally, *the perfect law*

---

cites references in Jewish, Stoic and Pauline writings and concludes that James is simply "reiterating a familiar idea, probably in a familiar phrase" (1980:87). Dibelius similarly argues for an influence from Stoicism in James's text (1976:116-20). But the notion of such a connection is speculative, figured to have been easy in the setting of a late dating of the epistle in Diaspora Judaism. Much clearer is James's dependence on his Old Testament background and his knowledge of Jesus' own words. The earlier dating for the letter is argued in my introduction.

of freedom. The phrase is unique to James in the New Testament, occurring only here and in 2:12. The primacy of *freedom* in the nature of the word is significant in two regards.

First, this is one of the phrases in James indicating that he is using the term *law (nomos)* with a connotation different from Paul's in Galatians or Romans. Paul would write about the law as an avenue by which one might attempt to attain a standing of righteousness before the holy God. In this respect, law would have to be treated in contrast to faith. James, however, is speaking of moral law as the deeds of *the righteous life that God desires.* The teachings of Jesus would especially be *the perfect law* to which James refers. As discussed in this volume's introduction, there is no need for the book of James to be read as a response to the Pauline letters. It is entirely clear and appropriate as a pre-Pauline encouragement by James for scattered, persecuted Christians to remain true to the word of God. By living according to this word, or law, they could live in true freedom in spite of their oppressors, for they would have the freedom to enter the kingdom of heaven and to live righteous lives. This theme in James can be seen to flow readily from Jesus' teachings in the Sermon on the Mount in Matthew 5:17-20 and 7:21, 24.

Second, the emphasis on freedom shows James's integration of his Old Testament Jewish tradition and the teachings of Jesus. The Old Testament certainly emphasized the blessing inherent in obeying God's laws. Jesus then emphasized his commitment to fulfill the law (Mt 5:17) and to give freedom (Jn 8:36). For James now, *the perfect law that gives freedom* is the very *word* of which he has been speaking. His warning against being "deceived" (with two different verbs in 1:16 and 1:22) is motivated by his assurance that we have, in contrast to deception, a real "word of truth" from God. This word of truth is a "perfect gift . . . from above," for it gives us birth, it saves us and it gives us freedom. So it is again described as *perfect* in 1:25. Especially for people who tend to think of God's word as a collection of burdensome, guilt-producing demands, James is a marvelous corrective model. He exhibits the admiration for the perfection of God's will and the delight in doing God's will which are to be normative for God's people according to both the Old Testament (Ps 19:7-11) and the New (Mt 7:21; Jn 14:15).

3. How would one be a doer of the word today? What we believe about the nature of Scripture affects how we use Scripture. Some people, believing Scripture to be a list of performance demands, use it to see how to perform more and more instead of looking into Scripture for truly biblical standards of how God wants us to live. Others, with a more relativistic belief, use Scripture selectively; they accept what they feel comfortable doing while simply ignoring the more difficult steps of faith commanded in the Bible. Often this selective approach comes from fear of the demands of Christ's lordship; we simply do not fully believe that his word is *the perfect law that gives freedom.*

To find the freedom promised here, one would have to take the four stages in the pattern of blessedness and put them into practice. These are not to be four more steps added onto other humanly devised performance standards. Rather, these are the steps to take first with Scripture, so that Scripture can then reorder the rest of one's life.

Looks intently. We will search the Scriptures. We can go beyond a superficial devotional reading. We will bother to learn sound principles of inductive study so that we can dig deeply into the word and feed ourselves from Scripture.

Continues. We will stay in Scripture. We can learn to be regular and habitual, rather than occasional, in our Bible study.

Not forgetting. We will learn Scripture. We can study it so as to know its content and to remember it in our daily lives. Memorizing Scripture passages is an excellent discipline for the practice of this third step.

But doing. We will apply Scripture. We can afford to leave our mirrors behind because our reflections are useless. But Scripture is another matter. We need it in our daily lives. We will take Scripture into our thinking, submit our minds to it and formulate our beliefs by what it says. We will make decisions by Scripture—about how we will respond to trials, what goals we will pursue, how we will spend time and money, how we will use our tongues. We will dare to live by the word of God.

The church is much weakened today by the defective approaches to Scripture that I have mentioned. In one verse James has spread out the blueprint for how Christians can equip themselves with the word of God for freedom and blessing.

Practice Pure Religion (1:26-27) James now supplies examples of this life of active obedience. With these examples, he again poses two contrasting alternatives in two kinds of "religion." Both as an adjective *thrēskos* in 1:26 and as a noun *thrēskeia* in 1:27, the term especially refers to the outward observance of worship—for example, attending worship services, praying and fasting. James's initial proposition is that even among people who perform these outward observances, there are some who practice a deceptive and worthless religion and others who practice a pure and faultless religion. The examples he gives are so practical that they may make these verses pointed and uncomfortable reading for us.

Deceptive and Worthless Religion (1:26) The first example James chooses is a negative one—failure to control one's tongue. This is not the first time he has brought it up (cf. 1:19). It is far from the last time. In 3:1-12 he will discuss the huge evil done by the tongue; in 4:1-12 he will give further examples of impure speech (e.g., quarreling and slander); in 5:9 and 5:12 he will tell his readers not to grumble or swear. The repetition of the theme shows that it has great importance in the message of James's letter. Sinning in the way we speak cannot be regarded as a minor matter.

James's imagery here gives a second clue as to why he sees one's speech as deserving such attention. The participle *chalinagōgōn* is properly translated *keep a tight rein on,* because it is indeed an equestrian term. James is the only New Testament writer to use the word, and he employs it again significantly in 3:2. He sees the control of one's tongue as decisive in the control of one's entire behavior, much like the decisive control of a horse's direction by means of the rein and bit.

The conclusion James reaches within this one verse appears to have two parts in the NIV. Actually, the first part, *he deceives himself,* stands as a contrast to bridling one's tongue. More literally, it reads, "If anyone thinks himself to be religious, not bridling his tongue but deceiving his heart . . ." To neglect controlling one's tongue while still considering oneself to be a religious person is self-deceiving. The actual conclusion is that such religion is *worthless (mataios,* meaning idle, fruitless, use-

---

1:27 The term *pure (kathara)* is used in the Gospel teachings of Jesus to refer to the purity of heart God desires in people (Mt 5:8), the religious cleaning of cups and dishes applied figuratively to the moral purity lacking in the Pharisees (Mt 23:25-26; Lk 11:39-41), and the cleansing that Jesus provided for his followers (washing their feet in Jn 13:10-11

less). This term makes emphatic James's rejection of a disobedient faith as a false faith. Genuine, saving faith will produce actions in the believer's life which are obedient to the word of God.

From James's repetition of emphasis throughout the letter, from his imagery of a horse's rein and bit, and finally from his conclusions of self-deception and worthlessness, the implications are inescapable. Readers who affirm biblical authority and so seek to submit their views to the biblical view will give priority attention to their speech as they seek to purify their behavior. Immoral ways of speaking simply cannot be excused biblically as somehow of secondary importance. Further instruction concerning specific forms of impure speech will come later in James's letter.

Pure and Faultless Religion (1:27) James's further examples illustrate a religion of positive value. The first portion of this sentence is like a public introduction of two important persons: James is announcing facts about two examples of active obedience so that we will know why these two are to receive our careful attention. The introductory facts should therefore be noticed first.

1. The two reasons for active obedience. In the Greek sentence structure, the initial introductory fact is that these examples of behavior will demonstrate religion that is *pure and faultless.* The first of these two terms *(kathara)* is used in the New Testament to refer to purity of heart as well as a ritual cleanness of objects. The second term *(amiantos)* means "undefiled." Together, the two terms hold up a standard of purity, complementing the standard of worth raised in 1:26. The terms emphasize that the examples of active obedience about to be presented are to be desired and practiced by all who seek a genuine, uncorrupted religion before God.

The second introductory fact is the identity of the one who raises these standards. He is none other than God, who (James is deliberate in stating) is the Father. This emphasis recalls the theological context shared in 1:2-18: God gives generously, without finding fault, to those who ask in faith; God gives the crown of life to those who love him; God is pure, neither tempted by evil nor tempting anyone to do evil. All of this

and washing them by his word in Jn 15:3). It is also used several times by Paul, both in his letters and as he is quoted in Acts. The term *faultless (amiantos)* occurs in only three other instances in the New Testament, always describing something held high and sacred. It occurs in Hebrews 7:26 referring to the purity of Christ as our high priest, in Hebrews

culminated in James's description of God as "the Father of the heavenly lights" who does not change, who is the giver of every good gift and who has given us the gift of birth through the word of truth. He gave this gift specifically with the intent that we might be "a kind of firstfruits." This Father of the heavenly lights has thus become *our* Father. For James, that fact makes it automatic and imperative that we should practice religion in a way that is pure and faultless in the eyes of this God.

The phrase *that God our Father accepts* is the NIV's rendering of a prepositional phrase that envisions our practice of religion as being "before" God our Father. This sense is worth preserving when one teaches or preaches from this verse. Envision your own practice of religion as taking place before the glorious God and Father who has given every good and perfect gift, including his own Son to save you, and you will gain a sense of why James writes about these matters with such moral earnestness. What matters is that which is pure and faultless specifically before God (or in his "sight" in the NASB).

2. The two examples of active obedience. With this introduction, the two examples are presented. The first directs our attention toward needy people with acts of love; the second directs our attention toward ourselves for maintenance of purity.

The instruction *to look after orphans and widows in their distress* can be examined in three parts. First, the verb *to look after (episkeptomai)* is a compound verb in which the prepositional prefix *epi-* places an emphasis on the act of looking. The basic act "to look" becomes intensified for a possible meaning of "looking at observantly" or "examining," though this meaning would not fit the present context. It is used elsewhere to express the awe with which one describes a visitation from God himself (Lk 1:68, 78; 7:16). In the context of James's instruction, the verb would carry the connotation of giving active care or help. Here, then, it is proper to translate this verb not merely as "visit" (KJV, RSV, NASB) but as "look after" (NIV). It is the same verb used by Matthew in Jesus' warning about the future separation of people for blessing and cursing.

13:4 referring to the purity of the marriage bed and in 1 Peter 1:4 describing Christians' inheritance.

Both the NIV and the NASB supply the word *our.* This certainly reads more comfortably than "before God and the Father" in the KJV and RSV. The contextual justification for

When the Son of Man comes in his glory, some will be welcomed into blessing because "I was sick and you looked after me," while others will be sent into the eternal fire because "I was sick and in prison and you did not look after me" (Mt 25:36, 43).

Second, in specifying *orphans and widows* James is prescribing nothing new or innovative for the church. He is recalling an explicit theme in God's Old Testament revelation of his will, so that there should be no disputing that this is indeed what God accepts as pure and faultless religion. Psalm 146:7-9 describes God's commitment to care for the needy such as the fatherless and widows. Jeremiah 7:1-8 warns against placing trust in the presence of the temple while oppressing the fatherless and widows—an example of religion that is "deceptive" and "worthless."

Third, *in their distress* refers literally to a pressing or a pressure, or figuratively to an affliction or oppression. In keeping with the Jeremiah passage, James has regard for the powerlessness of these people, their inability to protect or care for themselves.

Altogether this is a biblical view, not just James's own thinking. Scripture says that God is committed to caring for the powerless and defenseless, including the poor, the alien, the fatherless and the widow. Since the needs of such people are on God's heart, he expects that same heart to be in us. Further, Jesus himself so identified himself with needy, oppressed people that when we care for one of his people in need, we do it unto him. Any practice of Christianity that does not exhibit this concern in action is deceptive (it misrepresents the truth about God's own heart) and worthless (it is of no value before God). We have to conclude, then, that this first example of pure and faultless religion is a matter of serious obedience required of the church.

The second command is *to keep oneself from being polluted by the world*, and it too has three parts to be examined. First, it directs our attention to ourselves. In the two examples of active obedience in 1:27, James is certainly not trying to give a comprehensive list of all acts that

supplying *our* is in the review of what James has said about God in 1:2-18.

Examples of Old Testament instruction to look after orphans and widows in their distress: Deuteronomy 14:29; 27:19; Job 31:16-17; Psalms 68:5; 94:6; 146:9; Isaiah 1:17, 23; Jeremiah 7:6; Zechariah 7:10; Malachi 3:5.

make up pure and faultless religion; rather, these are just two examples of the kinds of acts needed. We would probably be reading a notion into the text to suppose that James's two examples are intended to encompass outward acts and inward purity (as in Hiebert's commentary); more likely the continuation of the text in the next chapter gives an illustration of what James means by the pollution of the world, and if so it has much to do with outward actions. By strict observation of the text, however, there is a complementarity to be identified between the two commands. The first command sends the Christian with acts toward others; the second command directs one's attention toward oneself. The first command prescribes positively certain acts of love, while the second warns negatively against the pollution of the world. This is the nature of the balance James is urging in the Christian life.

Second, the term behind *polluted* is *aspilon*, literally meaning "without blemish" or "spotless." Like other terms and concepts in James, it is a term familiar to Peter, as in 1 Peter 1:19 (referring to Christ as a lamb without blemish) and 2 Peter 3:14 (referring to Christians' striving to be spotless). We can see the term, therefore, being used in the church of James's time in a literal way that drew upon the Old Testament sacrifices of lambs without blemish and in a figurative way applied to Christians' moral purity.

The third important term in this command is *world*. This is the first of five times James will use the term *kosmos* in this short letter (in 1:27; 2:5; 3:6 and twice in 4:4), each time with a negative connotation. James, in keeping with other New Testament writers, calls Christians to be morally distinct from *the world*. This is the course charted for Christians by Jesus himself at the very beginning of the Sermon on the Mount, which might be summarized in this way: Blessed are those who become so different from the world that they come to be persecuted by the world; only so can they become "the light of the world" (from Mt 5:3-16).

Conclusion In this first chapter of the biblical text we have found the thrust of James's entire letter: calling upon Christians to live with moral urgency, serious holiness and unconditional obedience to the word of God. By putting the two halves of the chapter together we also establish the context for the moral earnestness of the entire letter: complete confidence in and reliance upon the grace of God. James is so earnest for moral purity in 1:19-27 because of the theology he has taught in 1:1-18. It is the thorough purity of God (never tempted, never tempting, never changing) that calls us to holiness; it is the generous giving of God (giving wisdom without finding fault, giving the crown of life, giving every good and perfect gift, giving us birth) that moves us to holiness. Furthermore, going back to the very beginning of James's message, this pursuit of holiness is not an oppressive burden but a task of joy, because of the great worth of the goal that God's grace has made possible. God has called Christians to become mature and complete, as firstfruits of all he created. This is so high a calling and so valuable an attainment that we may consider even trials along the way pure joy!

□ The Integrity of Faith (2:1-13)

I remember my son asking, "Why do you let him do that when you don't allow me to do this?" It is one of the more humbling experiences of parenthood to be caught in an inconsistent treatment of one's children. They are so quick to notice the injustice! And many adults are still wounded by the feeling that they were (or still are) on the short end of their parents' favoritism. Our sensitivity to partiality is an evidence of our desire for justice to be real. It is no small matter to us.

Nor is it a small matter to God. Through Moses he charged the people of Israel to believe and to remember his divine purity on this issue: "For the LORD your God is God of gods and Lord of lords, the great God, mighty and awesome, who shows no partiality and accepts no bribes" (Deut 10:17). That is why the oppressed could trust him, for it follows immediately that he "defends the cause of the fatherless and the widow, and loves the alien, giving him food and clothing" (Deut 10:18).

The persistent, inescapable principle of being related to God as his people is that his character and ways are binding upon us as well. We are to be holy as he is holy. So God equally charged the people of Israel to care for the fatherless and the widow and the alien and to appoint judges who would "judge the people fairly" and "not pervert justice . . . show partiality . . . [or] accept a bribe" (Deut 16:18-19). Partiality is *an* issue for James because God's righteousness is *the* issue for James. God does not show partiality; therefore we must not show partiality.

Eusebius's account of James's martyrdom gives us a vivid example of impartiality (1890:125-128). James was held in such high regard as one who "does not respect persons" that when the Jewish authorities in Jerusalem were alarmed by the numbers who were believing in Jesus as the Christ, they appealed to James to make a speech to calm the crowd! When they presented James to the crowd, the speech he gave was hardly what they wanted, for he declared Jesus to be the Christ in such strong terms that many became believers then. According to the account in Eusebius, it was this incident that led to James's death. The authorities were so angered by his speech that they cast him to the ground and stoned him to death—while he prayed for God to forgive them.

Thus James's reputation as "the Just" is quite appropriate as he follows a very familiar line of Old Testament thought about justice. The chapter division in our text should not be allowed to disguise the continuity from 1:27 to 2:1. James says *Don't show favoritism* because that would be an instance of "being polluted by the world." Impartiality is binding on us because of the same standard of justice that compels us to "look after orphans and widows in their distress." If James were speaking this as a public address, we would expect a slow, deliberate and emphatic pronunciation of each word: My brothers! Don't . . . show . . . favoritism! Do not compromise purity, because God himself is pure.

James's term for "favoritism" *(prosōpolēmpsia)* is not used in either secular Greek literature or the Septuagint. The problem was, however, apparently a common concern in the New Testament church. With the use of James's identical term or a derivative, God's impartiality is asserted in 1 Peter 1:17, Acts 10:34, Ephesians 6:9, Colossians 3:25 and Romans 2:11. We can see something of the reason for this concern by what James makes of the issue.

We will not grasp accurately the thrust of James's message if we fail to see that the continuing, underlying issue on his mind is to encourage the integrity of faith in the lives of his readers. James is approaching that central passage of his letter in which the most frequent occurrences of the term *faith (pistis)* will be concentrated. The following outline of his use of the term exposes the flow of his message about faith.

1:3. The goal: to treat trials as testings of faith in order to develop perseverance and to become mature and complete.

1:6. An illustration: that those needing wisdom in their trials should ask God, but ask in faith.

2:1. An application of genuine faith: that we are not to hold faith in Christ with favoritism in our treatment of people.

2:5. The matter of true value: to be rich in faith, not rich in money.

2:14-26. The theological unity: faith and deeds (with the term *faith* used eleven times in this section).

5:15. The concluding emphasis: that we are to pray in faith.

Seeing this, we can now follow James's teaching on favoritism toward the rich in 2:1-13 in terms of two arguments related to faith. First, favoritism contradicts faith (2:1-7). Second, favoritism breaks the law that people of faith follow (2:8-13).

Favoritism Contradicts Faith (2:1-7) As James states the basic instruction of this paragraph in 2:1, the imperative is, literally, "Do not have [or hold] the faith of our Lord Jesus Christ." The idea of favoritism comes in a prepositional phrase preceding and qualifying the imperative verb: "in [or with] favoritism." The structure implies a contradiction between faith and favoritism: "Do not hold faith in Christ with partiality toward persons." It is a common problem for us, a prevalent form of "being polluted by the world." To help us with this, James mentions in 2:1 three factors that call us away from favoritism and into a life of faith. He will elaborate on the implications in the subsequent verses.

Who We Are: "Brothers" James begins with his previously used term of address, *my brothers.* The earnestness of the whole letter should lead us to expect that this address is more than an unintentional habit. The "high position" that his readers hold specifically as "brothers" is already on James's mind in 1:9-11; it is a high position even if they are in humble circumstances. So they do well to persevere even under the trial of poverty, because when they have "stood the test" they will receive "the crown of life" (1:12). What is being tested? Their faith, according to 1:3. Their sense of identity, then, should be in their position as people of faith rather than in their status as people of wealth or poverty.

In 1:9-11 James has thus applied faith to self-image. Now he applies faith to Christians' treatment of others. The term *brothers* is a reminder of the high position they already have on the basis of faith. If they were to show partiality toward certain people because they are rich, these Christians would be acting as if high position came by wealth instead of faith. In that sense, favoritism is a clear contradiction of faith.

James elaborates on this fact of our faith-brotherhood with an illustration of favoritism in 2:2-4. His term for favoritism is plural in 2:1, implying "acts of partiality" to include the variety of ways in which favoritism could be shown (Hiebert 1979:147). The specific example now cited does not appear to be written in the manner of Paul's instructions in 1 Corinthians, addressing actual events in the church. Judging from James's conditional phrasing ("for if") and from the drawing of exact contrasts in the style of the narrative, he is presenting a theoretical occurrence.

However, even in choosing a hypothetical situation, James does reveal facts of the early Christians' cultural setting. We have found it to be the frequent lot of James's readers to be in economic hardship, even poverty, because of persecution. (See commentary on 1:9 and the appendix on the identity of the rich in James.) Now we find, though, that it was not out of the question for rich people to be found in the gatherings of Christians. The possibility of preferential treatment toward the rich was a realistic issue for James to address.

Two questions have intrigued students of this passage. What is the hypothetical meeting in view, and what is the reason for the rich and poor persons' presence? The traditional understanding has been that the meeting is a gathering for worship. Since the rich and poor individuals seem to be unfamiliar with procedures, they would be visitors who are either interested non-Christian observers or new converts to be instructed in the Christian faith. A second and more recently advocated possibility is that the meeting is a judicial assembly of the church, and that the rich and poor individuals are both members of the believing community who are involved in a dispute to be adjudicated.

The attractiveness of the first alternative is that it seems a natural understanding of the scene and of the term James uses for "meeting"—*synagōgē*. The term *synagogue* would be a recognizable term for a place of worship, and even later Christian writers in the first and second centuries used the term to refer to Christian gatherings. Far more common in the New Testament, though, is the term *ekklēsia*, which James himself uses in 5:14. In fact, 2:2 is the only New Testament use of the term *synagogue* for a Christian assembly, which has led some to question why James would have used the term here. Perhaps he had in mind a Jewish synagogue with Jews and Jewish Christians still worshiping together as in the early chapters of Acts, but James's description indicates a Christian ownership of and authority over this assembly.

In 1969, R. B. Ward argued that James is describing a judicial assembly rather than a worship service. This is certainly a possible use of *synagogue*. There are two major arguments in favor of this alternative. First, it makes the subsequent references to judges and courts (2:4; 2:6) more consistent with the context. Second, it rather neatly resolves the questions some have had about this illustration in a worship setting. Why would Christians coming to worship need to be told where to stand or sit? Or if they are non-Christians, why would James cite the unlikely event of a wealthy non-Christian visiting a church? Why would some stand and others be seated? In Ward's judicial setting, procedures of standing or sitting might well be unfamiliar to the participants, and clothing might be a factor that would unfairly impress the judges.

The case for the judicial setting of James's illustration is intriguing but not conclusive. Why wouldn't a worship setting be a proper context for concern over seating and posture? In Jesus' parable of the Pharisee and the tax collector who were praying in the temple (Lk 18:9-14), where and how one stood were choices made with strong moral implications. Especially if the rich and poor persons were new converts, they could have experienced uncertainty about the matters raised in James's illustration. In addition, making the reference to judges in 2:4 consistent with the context is attractive, but it is not necessary to the logical flow of thought. James could simply be using the term for "judge" *(kritēs)* as a figure, drawing upon the primary message in the verb *discriminated (diekrithēte)*, which is directed more broadly to the community of Christians: you have *discriminated among yourselves*.

An additional source of insight into James's thinking may be found in comparison with the Lord's Sermon on the Mount. Because of James's emphasis on judging, the obvious place to begin looking is Matthew 7:1, where followers of Christ are commanded not to judge *(krinō)*.

Except for James's omission of Jesus' emphasis on asking and believing (which James included in 1:5-8 and which does not really fit his primary purpose in this section), the parallels between the two passages are extensive.

Matthew 7		James 2	
1-2	Prohibition against judging	1	Prohibition against judgmental favoritism
3-5	Illustration of removing one's own faults so that one can help remove others' faults	2-4	Illustration of removing one's own partiality so that one can judge or instruct others
6	Warning not to despise what is sacred in favor of dogs or pigs that will harm you	5-7	Warning not to despise brothers who are rich in faith in favor of others who harm you
7-11	Encouragement to ask and to believe		
12	Summary of the law as doing to others what you would want for yourself	8-11	Summary of the law as loving others as yourself
13-14	Summary admonition to follow the narrow way that leads to life	12-13	Summary admonition to follow the law that gives freedom
15-23	Warning against false prophets, with the true test presented: deeds	14-19	Warning against dead faith, with the true test presented: deeds
24-27	Parable to illustrate putting Christ's words into practice	20-26	Examples to illustrate putting faith into practice

Christ's teaching recorded in Luke 6:37-49 follows a similar order, with some sections omitted but with one notable addition in verses 39-40. The emphasis there is on getting rid of one's own blindness in order to be able to teach others. It fits into the same place as Matthew 7:3-5 and James 2:2-4 in the scheme outlined above, and it is immediately followed by Luke's parallel to Matthew 7:3-5. If Christ's teaching recorded in Matthew 7 and Luke 6 is the background for James 2, it is a clue that in the illustration of 2:2-4 James is thinking of the rich and poor individuals as ones who come needing to be instructed in some way. James's illustration fits the pattern in Matthew 7 and Luke 6 if the favoritism is seen as disqualifying the Christian community from being able to instruct the ones who come into the assembly.

Overall, these considerations seem to indicate more strongly the setting of a Christian assembly for worship and instruction, with the rich and poor persons coming as recent converts needing to be taught. It would then provide a picture of the early church as a consciously teaching community. However, the judicial setting, in which the rich and poor men would be coming with complaints to be settled, is not impossible. The passage would then be an early portrait of church discipline, with its proper focus on instructing rather than punishing. What should be foremost for us, however, is that in either case what James has in mind is much weightier than merely how our modern church ushers escort visitors to their seats. The passage calls us to consistent love, not just polite ushering. People of low income are to be fully welcomed into the life of the church. The passage calls us to be blind to economic differences in how we offer our ministries. The poor person is as worthy of our discipling and pastoral care and love as the person who has the means to rescue our church from its budget crisis.

Either understanding of the setting for 2:2-4 provides some cultural information about the dispersed church. Persecution and scattering did not cause the Christians to meet hesitantly and fearfully. They were holding organized assemblies with deliberate instruction or discipline. Although Christians were commonly persecuted by the rich, evidently the gospel was spreading among rich as well as poor people, or else it would be unrealistic for James to suppose a rich person would be present at either the worship or the judicial assembly. Christians were encountering the moral issue of discrimination, and they were struggling with the relationship between rich and poor.

It is on this point that James draws his conclusion in 2:4 to show that favoritism contradicts faith. The verb translated "discriminated" has already been used in 1:6, there translated "doubt" but also used in contrast to faith. Note the parallel between the two passages:

1:6   Ask for wisdom in faith, not doubting.
2:1, 4 Hold faith in Christ, not discriminating.

The common idea between the two instances of the verb is that of division, which is the essence of judgment. Doubters asking for wisdom are divided internally, because they hold doubts at odds with faith. Christians who practice favoritism are divided relationally, because they hold materialistic values at odds with faith. Doubters are discriminating, or making a judgment, whether God will or will not give what is needed; Christians who practice favoritism are discriminating, or making a judgment, between the value of the rich person and the value of the poor person. The corrective for both is to be single-minded, not divided, in faith.

Who Christ Is: "Glorious Lord" For the second element in 2:1, James reminds them of the one in whom their faith resides: *our glorious Lord Jesus Christ.* The phrase has been a point of controversy in the study of this epistle; some have argued that it is a later addition to the original text. Expunging such references to Christ from the text is part of some scholars' portrayal of the remainder of the letter as a Jewish work written in pre-Christian time and later adapted for the Christian community. The theory is advanced on the basis of the unusual structure of the phrase *our glorious Lord Jesus Christ* as a genitive phrase modifying *faith.* However, the awkwardness of the structure can be used just as well as an argument *against* a deliberate interpolation, and the extremely specula-

---

Notes: **2:1** Dibelius, Davids and Martin, for example, all reject the interpolation theory as too extreme, lacking textual evidence and unnecessary to account for the successive genitives in the last part of this verse. All three provide helpful consideration of the interpretive options, and they agree in preferring the translation *our glorious Lord Jesus Christ.* See Dibelius (1976:126-28), Davids (1982:106), Martin (1988:59-60).

2:2 Adamson (1976:105) and Hiebert (1979:150) accept the traditional understanding of

tive nature of the theory must be faced. In the absence of any textual evidence, there is no real reason to reject this affirmation of Christ as Lord. Coming from Jesus' own brother James, this is a strong confession of faith. It reflects a high Christology, even if James's concern here is only to declare the doctrine, not to develop it in detail.

There remains an interpretive question regarding the term *glory* in the genitive case coming at the very end of James's sentence in 2:1. Does it modify *faith* (as "the glorious faith" or "faith in the glory of")? Does it modify *Lord* (as "the Lord of glory") as chosen in the KJV, LB and RSV? Does it stand in apposition to *Jesus Christ* (as "our Lord Jesus Christ, the Glory" or "the Lord Jesus Christ our Glory")? Or does it describe our Lord Jesus Christ (in the sense of "our glorious Lord Jesus Christ")? This last option seems the most natural and least forced of the readings, and it is the one chosen in the NIV and NASB.

In any of these options, the contradiction between faith and favoritism is strong. Even if *glory* modifies *faith*, the faith is made glorious because of the object of faith—our Lord Jesus Christ. James sees clearly how a partiality toward people because of their wealth treats their wealth as more valuable than Christ. It is unthinkable that this should be tolerated in the lives of people who are believers (ones who "have faith") in the glory of Christ.

What We Have: "Faith" The third element in 2:1 is "faith," unfortunately obscured in the NIV as *believers*. Again, the heart of James's plea in this passage is the complete contradiction between faith and favoritism. When he elaborates in 2:5-7, his argument is the utter disparity of value between faith and wealth. That is why he is moved to adopt the phrase *rich in faith*—meaning that faith is the wealth of true value. It becomes unthinkable then that believers, of all people, should insult the poor and favor the rich. If they do, they are acting as if they do not know the value of faith.

The details in 2:5-7 explain his argument. First, James writes with a

---

synagōgē as referring here to the Christians' gathering for worship. Martin acknowledges the credibility of this but finds the judicial setting more likely (1988:61). Davids is persuaded that Ward's judicial setting is the most likely solution (1982:109). Laws, on the other hand, is convinced that the rich and poor persons are depicted as visitors, and that Ward's theory is therefore unworkable because it requires the two to be members of the believing community (1980:101).

sharp contrast between the rich *(plousioi)* and the poor *(ptōchoi)*. James would surely remember Jesus' warning of how hard it is for a rich man to enter the kingdom; it astonished the disciples when he said it (Mt 19:23-25). Why would wealth have this effect? The implication in James 1:10-11 is that wealth leads one to become poor in faith because it gives one a false sense of security. James's assertion in 2:5 makes sense in this context, with no need to read it as a theological statement that God eternally elects all poor people because they are poor. Rather, James is observing that God does choose many poor people to be rich in faith and so to inherit the kingdom. He probably has in mind the teaching of Jesus (as in Lk 6:20), the Old Testament tradition of God's care for the poor (as in Deut 10:18) and the prevalent economic situation of his readers. The fact that James could speak so broadly of God's choosing of the poor of the world to be rich in faith is evidence that poverty was the common economic status of believers. Probably many Christians had lost wealth because of the persecution, and probably the gospel was spreading especially among the poor.

Second, the value of faith is placed in uncompromised opposition to the value of riches by the transferring of the very term *plousioi* to the believing poor. They are the ones who are truly rich, by being *rich in faith*. This phrase refers not to an abundant quantity of faith (as if that were their wealth instead of the kingdom) but to the value of faith, as confirmed by the parallel in 1 Peter 1:7. With *faith* set grammatically in contrast to *the world*, this is a denial that the world's material wealth constitutes true riches at all. There is even a disclosure of what constitutes the enormous wealth and investments of the poor: they inherit the kingdom!

Third, James provides some detail of how rich unbelievers are treating Christians. He reminds his readers of three common offenses against them, and each one has particular significance for people of faith.

2:5-6 R. B. Ward argues that James deliberately places the two terms *ptōchoi* and *plousioi* in opposition (1969:96). He notices that James avoids using *plousios* in reference to the rich individual in the illustration of 2:2-4, and that James now resumes this term as he leaves the illustration and returns to a more general discussion of Christians' life situation. The indication is that James reserves *plousioi* for rich non-Christian oppressors of the Christians and does not apply it to the occasional wealthy convert.

2:5 The dative *tō kosmō* is placed in antithesis to the prepositional phrase *en pistei*. Since

1. The rich are exploiting (oppressing or dominating) them. This verb *katadynasteuō* occurs only one other time in the New Testament, in Peter's message to Cornelius's household recorded in Acts 10. That message begins with Peter's affirmation that God does not show "favoritism" (Acts 10:34), for Christ came to deliver all who were oppressed or dominated by the devil. God's impartiality is binding on Peter, who therefore realizes that he must accept Gentile believers as brothers. Here James is showing the complementary side of the same principle. To show favoritism toward the rich is to join sides with those who perpetuate oppression. Davids puts it this strongly: "They have, in effect, sided with the devil against God" (1982:112).

2. The rich are dragging them into court. The exploitation of the poor is being carried out even through formal legal action against them. The verb here is properly translated "dragging" to convey the forcible tone. It is not a polite settling of disputes that is occurring, but a harsh treatment. In response, James does not urge revenge by the Christians when a rich person appears in their assembly. But he does expose the senselessness of favoring the rich, as if their wealth made them more valuable in the kingdom. It should be obvious from their treatment of Christians that it is not so.

3. The rich are blaspheming the name of Christ. Their treatment of Christians is religious persecution; that is, harsh treatment is directed at the Christians explicitly because they bear the name of Christ. This is implied in the concluding words of 2:7, where the rich are said to be blaspheming the name that, literally translated, "has been called upon you." The modifier for *name* is stronger than *agathos* "good"; it is *kalos* "noble, beautiful, excellent." Bearing this name implied a relationship; hence the NIV's rendering *of him to whom you belong.* Therefore "abuse of Christians is abuse also of the name they bear" (Laws 1980:106). The rich are treating that noble name of Christ as worthy of contempt upon

---

James is clearly not referring to an abundant quantity of faith, it would seem that the dative *tō kosmō* would also identify not a quantity of things of the world, but rather the sphere of reference, reflected in the NIV's translation *poor in the eyes of the world.* So argue Dibelius (1976:137-138), Davids (1982:112) and Martin (1988:64). This view has James's emphasis on the world's view of what is valuable rather than on material wealth itself.

2:6 Cf. the verb *helkō* in John 21:11 and Acts 21:30.

2:7 *Of him to whom you belong* is more literally "that has been called upon you." The

those who bear it. If Christians now practice favoritism, they are agreeing!

James has written about the integrity of faith; there are things Christians must do because of what they believe. This was capsulized in 1:22, "Do what [the word] says." Now, by applying that principle specifically to economic impartiality, James calls the church to a lifestyle and a mission that confront economic prejudice. Martin calls this passage James's announcement of his commitment to a "theology of justice" (1988:73).

For the church today confronted with this message, the role of material wealth becomes a major spiritual issue. It demands address within the church (with pointed sermons and thorough courses of instruction) as well as action by the church (in a lifestyle and outreach that abhor economic favoritism). The need for confrontation is urgent; "you cannot serve both God and Money" (Mt 6:24). James makes clear that integrity of faith places Christians in opposition to the roles that money, across the centuries, has played in human society. An application of James 2:1-7 in the church's preaching and practice will confront these roles of money.

1. James confronts the role of money as *status*. He employs the phrase *our glorious Lord Jesus Christ* deliberately at the beginning of this passage. It places before our eyes the standard that should control our response to people. We are not to respond to the glory of people's wealth or dress, for this relative glory is exposed as insignificant compared to Christ's glory. Churches and parachurch organizations that are informed by the message of James will preach the glory of Christ, will be enamored of the glory of Christ and will therefore not be impressed by wealth. We will not pander to those with money. In selecting people for positions of leadership, we will look for godliness and spiritual gifts instead of bank accounts.

2. James confronts the role of money as *value*. He exposes the destructiveness of wealth. According to his description, money has the power to make us exploitative, abusive and blasphemous. We must accept this as a warning that the more wealth we accumulate, the more

---

verb is *epiklēthen*, aorist passive participle of *epikaleō*. The NASB renders it "by which you have been called." The phrase is drawn from Amos 9:12 and was evidently an important concept in James's mind, since he quoted it in Acts 15:17. It is not certain whether this would

likely we are to fall into these sins. Far from being valuable, material wealth is actually dangerous! No wonder that it is so hard for a rich person to enter the kingdom of heaven.

Christians taking heed to James's warning will be all the more watchful for signs of these dangers in themselves. We will be watchful to repent of exploitative actions, abusive thoughts and attitudes toward people poorer than we, and blasphemous religious talk and jokes.

In this there are also important implications for the church's mission. *Has not God chosen those who are poor in the world to be rich in faith and to inherit the kingdom?* We have already assessed this statement in 2:5 to be an observation of common fact, based on Scripture and actual circumstances, rather than a theology of preferential eternal election. It would be a distortion of the text to conclude that God loves the rich less than he loves the poor, or that the poor are less in need of Christ's atoning work than the rich. The very foundation of the passage is that God does not show partiality. However, as a matter of mission strategy, if wealth does hinder people's receptivity to the gospel, and if God does commonly choose poor people to inherit the kingdom, then the church should invest heavily in evangelism toward the poorer levels of society.

Donald A. McGavran's thesis pushes today's church on this matter. "Missions from the wealthy West usually overlook the Bible at this point. Missionaries customarily place a high value on the educated, the wealthy, the cultured—in a word, the middle and upper classes" (1980:281). Instead, if we truly want to save as many lives as possible, McGavran urges a focus on the masses by the strategy of "winning the winnable" (1980:291).

3. James confronts the role of money as *power.* It is not that he denies the power of wealth. On the contrary, he sees quite clearly that it powerfully endangers people's spiritual end (1:10-11) and that it empowers people to abuse others and to blaspheme the Lord (2:6-7). The church must not take lightly the power of wealth. Jacques Ellul warns that money in the biblical view is not a neutral object but rather a power "that acts

indicate a use of the name *Christian* as at Antioch in Acts 11:26 (as Adamson claims, 1976:112). However, Peter does make explicit use of the name *Christian* in a context about suffering because of bearing the name (1 Pet 4:14-16).

by itself, is capable of moving other things, is autonomous (or claims to be), is a law unto itself, and presents itself as an active agent. . . . It is oriented; it also orients people" (1984:75-76). So he concludes, "We absolutely must not minimize the parallel Jesus draws between God and Mammon" (1984:76). The church, then, must confront and oppose this dangerous power of wealth explicitly and urgently.

James has fixed a spotlight on the dangerous role of wealth. Christians who seriously desire to be doers of this word will be all the more earnest in practicing the law that is higher than the law of economic power. The law of economic power enables people to practice exploitation and abuse and blasphemy. We who are people of faith will adhere passionately to another law: the royal law, which commands impartial, unconditional love.

Favoritism Breaks the Law That People of Faith Follow (2:8-13)
This passage about breaking the law does not include the word *faith*, but the central violation of the law on James's mind is still the sin of favoritism (2:9). Therefore this passage is still in reference to the command with which he began in 2:1, where favoritism was declared to be in conflict with faith.

What is the *law* to which James refers in this passage? One possibility is that he means only that one commandment he quotes in 2:8 from Leviticus 19:18. It would be consistent with the whole passage to see this as James's central focus: favoritism is a violation of this Levitical command. However, questions are raised about this conclusion when we notice that James uses the more inclusive term *nomos* for "law" rather than the more specific *entolē*, which could be translated "commandment." Furthermore, his earlier reference to the law in 1:25 was broader, not specifying this one command; and that reference to *the law that gives freedom* is repeated now in this passage (2:12). It would appear that James is making a primary reference to the command *Love your neighbor*

2:8-11 James's argument is very simple: that a violation of one commandment makes the violator a lawbreaker even if he or she is keeping other commandments. Dibelius attempts to draw conclusions from this which simply are not required logically: that only this one Levitical commandment could be under discussion here, that this one commandment must be of equal rank alongside others, that therefore Jesus' quotation of Leviticus 19:18 as one

as yourself, but that he has in mind a larger body of law as well.

Therefore a second possibility is that James is referring to the body of Old Testament Mosaic laws, in what amounts to an anti-Pauline requirement of lawkeeping. I have argued in the introduction (section on "The Law") that this understanding should be rejected. James consistently focuses on moral law, with no trace of controversy over circumcision or any aspect of the ceremonial law. And James's unusual phrases *royal law* and *law that gives freedom* indicate that he has something distinctive in mind.

A third alternative therefore needs to be defined from the content of James's own writing. The first clue is in the striking term *royal law.* The designation that the law is *found in Scripture* reveals James's awareness that he is quoting the Old Testament, but he adds the adjective *royal,* which is normally used in recognition of a king's ownership—as in a king's country, a king's robe or a king's official (Jn 4:46, 49; Acts 12:20, 21). The reference James the Christian would most likely be making would be to Christ as king. Then the phrase *law that gives freedom* (2:12), especially augmented as "the perfect law" (1:25), conveys the sense that James is describing a special law with new significance, beyond that law with which he spent most of his life in Judaism. There is no suggestion that this law contradicts the Old Testament moral law; in fact, James affirms the Old Testament moral commandments in 2:11. But he believes there is a law to lead his readers to the goal he has set before them: being "mature and complete, not lacking anything" (1:4), being "a kind of firstfruits" (1:18) and living "the righteous life that God desires" (1:20).

What would that law be? This is answered by the third clue, which is our finding that James's thought is thoroughly saturated with the teachings of Jesus. These teachings are clearly on James's mind throughout the letter, and they would be the natural referent of his terms *royal* and *perfect law that gives freedom.* The teachings of Jesus have become for

---

of the two most important commandments could not be on James's mind at all, that there is no reason then to take *the royal law* as a reference to the commandment of love and that *royal* could not be a reference to Christ (1976:142). It is a multiple non sequitur. Davids, in contrast, has sound basis for calling James's law the "law of love" and for asking, "Is it not most natural to see a reference to the whole law as interpreted and handed over to the

James this new law, not repudiating but rather fulfilling the Old Testament law, not replacing the Old Testament law but rather claiming Christ's authorship of it as his own *royal law.* That makes it legitimate to conclude that, even with the command from Leviticus 19:18, James is probably remembering Jesus' own quotation of the command, as in Mark 12:31.

The Content of the Royal Law James begins with the Old Testament command *Love your neighbor as yourself* because it is the specific command being violated by favoritism, and because Jesus used it to summarize the Old Testament teaching regarding our treatment of each other. The law for people of faith is the law of love, taught in the Old Testament and now delivered personally by Christ as his royal law for his followers. Favoritism is sin because it violates Christ's law of love.

James would have us look carefully at the content of this law. Loving your neighbor as yourself requires an openness to friendship with any neighbor—regardless of that neighbor's wealth, position, status, influence, race, appearance, attractiveness, dress, abilities or personality. Every Christian operates in some social group—a school, a neighborhood, a workplace. And most social groups have their social misfits—the ones who are looked down upon, ostracized or neglected. The royal law absolutely prohibits the Christian from joining in the favoritism. The follower of the royal law will reach out to any neighbor.

Loving your neighbor as yourself means treating others' concerns as important as your own. Therefore followers of this law will seek the common good rather than personal good. Imagine a church committee meeting in which one person presents an idea of what should be done about a particular issue. A second person disagrees. The first person, because she is a follower of the royal law, responds not by arguing her own idea but by helping the group fully hear and understand the other person's proposal. Love brings a desire to protect each other's interests.

Loving our neighbors as ourselves means treating others' needs as

---

church in the teaching of Jesus?" (1982:114).

2:9 This is the only New Testament use of the verb *prosōpolēmpteō* ("to show favoritism"). James is repeating from 2:1 the same root as in the noun *favoritism.* The only other New Testament uses of this root are in Romans 2:11, Ephesians 6:9, Colossians 3:25 (all noun forms) and Acts 10:34 (adjective form).

needs we have in common as neighbors—and so caring for others' needs in unison. Americans during World War II tasted that sense of neighborhood. My wife's father was in Europe for the first two years of her childhood. There were long stretches of those two years during which my mother-in-law had no word from her husband and did not know anything of his safety. When she shares memories of those difficult days, people sometimes ask her, "How did you stand it?" Her answer: "Everyone had someone over there in the war, so we were in it together." That is the help we give when we love each other as ourselves, and there should be that strong sense within churches that keep the royal law. When one person is in trouble, "we're in it together."

The Status of the Royal Law The point of emphasizing *the whole law* is that the whole law is to be kept. The status of the royal law, then, is that it is indispensable. If we are believers in Christ (that is, "ones who have faith in Christ," as stated in 2:1), then we must follow the teachings of Christ. We must bring our relationships under the lordship of Christ. That is why, in 2:8-11, James elaborates with repetition on the fact that favoritism makes one a lawbreaker. The message is, Don't think you are keeping the law of Christ while you are practicing favoritism. It is as much a contradiction as if you claimed you were keeping the law just because you were not committing adultery even though you were practicing murder. James's language is stark and emphatic in 2:9: *If you show favoritism, you sin.*

The Result of the Royal Law James's first intention in 2:12-13 is to make a summary application, as indicated by his return to the more general terms *speak* and *act.* These terms are reminders that the issue of favoritism is but one application of the principles of speaking and acting by what the word of God says, as expounded in 1:19-27. "Do what [the word] says" (1:22).

But James's second intention is to warn his readers of this result: they will be *judged by the law.* He has already warned against discriminating

---

2:10-11 These two verses state a principle (2:10) and an illustration (2:11) of what has been called the unitary nature of the law (Hiebert 1979:168; Davids 1982:116; Martin 1988:69). It was a Jewish as well as Christian concept of the law (Mt 5:18-19). We should not see in it a threat to the concept of grace. Adamson, for example, seems moved to defend the principle of grace against the "ruthless legalism" of this passage (1976:116). The unitary

against the poor and so becoming evil judges (2:4). Now he reminds them of the danger that they will in turn be so judged, if that is the standard they adopt. This seems a clear application of Jesus' words in Matthew 7:1-2. Judgment requires meeting a standard, living up to a law. Christians are covered by the blood of Christ and so will receive mercy instead of condemnation in the final judgment. Nevertheless, Scripture speaks of the divine judgment as a reality that should deter all people, most of all Christians, from sin. For all people, including Christians, will give an accounting of what they have done. Specifically, we will give an accounting of whether we have lived by this royal law, *Love your neighbor as yourself.*

There is a third intention to see: James is directing his readers toward *freedom.* The emphasis on freedom here would have to make an impression on the readers by its contrast to their exploitation and oppression by the rich (2:6). Believers are not to act as if they will be judged according to a law that condones oppression—which is what favoritism toward the rich would imply. Rather, they are to act as ones who are obligated to live up to a standard that frees from oppression. Our relationships are corrupted by the sin in our character that leads us to approach people with fear, calculation, judgmentalism and manipulation for our self-interest. These really are burdens upon our relationships. Christ would free us from the sin of materialism, so that we can be freed from economic favoritism. He would free us from the sin of racism, so that we can be freed from ethnic favoritism. The royal law of loving one's neighbor as oneself brings freedom to forgive the neighbor's wrongs, freedom to ask forgiveness for our own wrongs, freedom to accept differences among us and freedom to open ourselves to others. It is freedom from the selfishness that is at the heart of favoritism.

The Essence of the Royal Law When James prohibits favoritism, he would not replace it with a legalistic consistency, as if righteousness consisted merely of giving everyone identical treatment. What James has

---

nature of the law is, instead, the very fact that establishes grace. The unitary authorship of God's moral law (asserted in 2:11) makes any violation a sin against God himself; any violation makes us convicted as sinners before God; we are all then in need of grace, equally unable to save ourselves by any comparative keeping of God's law.
2:13 The same verb *katakauchaomai* ("triumphs"), used positively here, is also used by

in mind as the opposite of favoritism is *mercy*. Mercy is the essence of the royal law. Instead of favoring the rich, believers in Christ are to have mercy on the poor. So mercy is the trait we must learn if we are to be rid of favoritism, and mercy triumphs as a far better way over the judgmentalism described in 2:4.

If we are going to be motivated to practice this, it is critical that we see why mercy is essential. In the divine judgment, we are freed from condemnation by God's show of mercy. Far from treating us with contempt, God has mercifully covered our sin and made us his own honored people. Now in relationships with others, we absolutely must practice mercy ourselves, or else we show that we have not accepted God's mercy. The principle of mercy in Matthew 6:14-15 and the parable of the unmerciful servant in Matthew 18:21-35 provide the forceful teaching from Jesus. James is only applying that teaching of his Lord. Mercy must and will replace discrimination as the way of life for people of faith.

This again verifies that James's underlying concern is for a life of genuine faith. Looking back over the entire argument in 2:1-13, we find James to be saying: My brothers, as believers in our glorious Lord Jesus Christ (and as believers therefore in a salvation by the mercy of God), do not be unmerciful to others. If you practice favoritism instead of merciful love, you are denying the very principle of our faith—which is belief in God's mercy through Christ. If you deny your faith by such actions, then your faith is not genuine (in fact, it is dead, to use the term James will employ in 2:14-26). And if you have no genuine faith, then you can expect only *judgment without mercy* from God.

It has been by now repeatedly evident that James's emphasis on the law is thoroughly Christian. His moral earnestness is rooted in redemption. For the law he prescribes is emphatically Christ's law. And that law requires mercy in us, because we who are believers in Christ look in faith for mercy from God.

The application of James's message should be made explicit by the

---

James negatively with condemnation as "boast" in 3:14 and 4:16. The common element among James's uses of the verb is the idea of exulting in being able to prevail over something or someone else. In 2:13, mercy is said to prevail exultantly over discrimination as the superior law by which Christians shall live. James's line of thought about judging and mercy will be drawn together in the discussion of 4:11-12.

church today, certainly in regard to the materialism that results in economic favoritism, as described at the end of the commentary on 2:1-7. However, as James presents the issue in more general terms in 2:8-13, the applications broaden. The racism that results in ethnic bigotry is an obvious area for application today. But there are others. Favoritism is the sin of extending special favor to some people for self-serving purposes, and we have a multitude of ways to be so "polluted by the world" (1:27).

We experience poor substitutes for Christian friendship all week, and it is hard to change our patterns when we gather with other believers at church. We learn to treat relationships as merely opportunities to get business done; then we come to church and waste our sabbath rest getting church business done. Instead of making contact with fellow Christians in love and then experiencing worship as celebration, we take care of self-serving agendas.

Professionalism pollutes our friendships. We work in contexts that honor self-motivation, self-reliance, achievement and success. That context pulls us with tremendous force. We learn to impress others with our success, and we become attuned to the marks of success in others. We learn to size people up by the way they speak, the way they dress, the way they act.

We also subject ourselves to our standards of favoritism and so inject our fears and insecurities into our relationships. We abhor exposure of our failures and weaknesses; we are internally driven to compete and outdo.

All of this is favoritism in modern dress. The result: self-serving relationships, the heart of favoritism. It pollutes the church. It keeps the church from being a fellowship of love in which our lives are refreshed and healed by the taste of God's love in each other and by a wonderful celebration of God's love in real worship.

James has shown us the solution to our problem of self-serving relationships; it is to bring our relationships under the government of *the royal law*. Douglas Webster captures the biblical vision excellently in his chapter on this passage. "The church should be a competition-free zone" where "instead of courting one another's favor we rejoice in God's favor" (1991:69-70). "Instead of maneuvering for the best possible advantage, we give ourselves to one another for the sake of Christ" (1991:75).

□ Faith and Deeds: The Theological Unity (2:14-26)

As an InterVarsity area director and now as a pastor, I have often been asked to fill out recommendation forms for people who are candidates for positions with various Christian ministries. Some of those forms omit the question that I always find the most revealing: How have you observed the candidate's faith affecting his or her lifestyle? I try to imagine James at the head of any of these mission agencies or parachurch organizations, and I expect he would insist on including that question. Why would he want to hire someone in whose actions there was not good evidence of faith?

We have already found James insisting that genuine faith must be put into practice. He began speaking of faith right away (1:3), and he was blunt in telling his readers to do what the word says (1:22). His letter thus far could be broadly outlined as follows:

1:1-18	Maintaining faith in the midst of trials
1:19-27	Putting faith into practice by being doers of the word
2:1-13	An example of practicing one's faith: impartiality

It is a natural flow of thought for James now to draw this together by explaining the theological unity of faith and actions. He argues his case first with logic (2:14-18) and then with examples (2:19-25). But he "sustains a single, theological argument throughout" concerning the issue that "lies at the very heart of James' concern" (Moo 1985:99).

James's Central Concern: Faith That Works (2:14-18) The works James requires are not done apart from faith but done in faith, not done instead of faith but done because of faith. Faith is the underlying stance of Christian life; deeds are the way of life; becoming mature and complete is the goal of Christian life. James cannot be charged with opposing deeds to faith, since he does not say, "I will show you deeds instead of faith." Rather, he contends for a showing of both faith and deeds: *I will show you my faith by what I do.* He does not object to faith; he objects only to faith *not accompanied by action.* Simply stated, he wants Christians to have faith that works.

James's logical argument in 2:14-18 can be outlined in four parts, so that conclusions can be drawn about his meaning.

Rhetorical Questions About Faith Without Deeds (2:14) The two rhetorical questions about faith without deeds are (1) "What good is it?" (answer: none) and (2) "Can it save?" (answer: no). The first question implies a general lack of any usefulness for a faith without actions. The second question specifies a particular use that is lacking— salvation itself. The combined impact is to declare a thorough uselessness of faith without deeds and, to make it absolutely clear, also to declare its particular uselessness in regard to salvation, which would be the primary point of having faith in the first place. "In a Christian context such as this, . . . the 'use' takes on serious consequences, for it is salvation which is at stake" (Davids 1982:120). In the subsequent example in 2:15-16, there is no "good" for the needy person who receives no help. Here in 2:14, however, it is explicit that the good lacking is for the person who claims to have faith. James asks not if such faith can save "anyone else" but if such faith can save *him.*

An Example of Faith Without Deeds (2:15-16) The situation in James's illustration is technically hypothetical ("If . . . ") but probably one he considered quite realistic. James's specification of *a brother or sister* (not just "someone") reflects an envisioning of real action toward real people. We already know many of his readers were living in economic hardship. His illustration does not imply that all Christians were living in poverty, but that in their midst they would be encountering cases of hardship as severe as a lack of sufficient clothing and even "the day's supply of food" (Adamson 1976:122).

The hypothetical response to the need is good wishes without any actions, for the needy ones are merely "dismissed with friendly words" (Davids 1982:121). The response to the needy ones begins literally, "Go in peace." The verbs "be warmed" and "be filled" could be either pas-

---

Notes: 2:14 The same phrase *What good is it* is repeated at the end of 2:16 and is used one other place in the New Testament, by Paul in 1 Corinthians 15:32. Jesus posed a question in similar form in Matthew 16:26, using a verb of the same root. In each case, the force is to expose a complete uselessness.

What James teaches here can be compared to Jesus' teaching in Matthew 7:21. The deeds Jesus went on to identify in 7:22 (miraculous works done while neglecting the will of the Father) can be contrasted to the deeds James goes on to emphasize in 2:15-16, the necessary actions of helping those in physical need.

sive or middle. Though Davids disagrees (1982:122), Adamson (1976: 123) and Laws (1980:121) take them in the passive voice, which allows a religious overtone to the wishes. The person would be saying not just the secular-sounding translation of the NIV but the more pious "Go in peace. May you be warmed and filled" as an expectation that God would provide for the needy one. This would certainly suit James's context, objecting to "faith" that has pious words but no actions. The uselessness of this response is so obvious and offensive that James needs only to repeat his first rhetorical question: *What good is it?* James expects that faith will surely lead to actions to meet others' material needs.

Conclusion About Faith Without Deeds (2:17) In fact, his expectation is so strong that he concludes with the most severe condemnation of faith without deeds: it is *dead.* The last words of his sentence are *by itself,* referring back to *faith.* Placed here, these words emphasize the focus of James's concern, which is faith by itself—that is, faith without the authenticating actions. It is not that he is promoting deeds as an alternative to faith. He obviously knows the value of faith, for he called those who have faith "rich" in 2:5. What James is rejecting is the notion that one can have faith *by itself,* without the accompanying actions.

An Anticipated Objection and Its Answer (2:18) The objection that James anticipates presents a problem. We would expect him to propose the statements "You have deeds; I have faith" as a potential retort spoken to him; but what he writes is a reversal of these statements. Some have supposed a loss from the original text; but with no manuscript evidence to support it, this theory must remain a last resort. Others (e.g., Ropes 1916:208-14; Dibelius 1976:155-56; Laws 1980:123-24) have simply accepted James's reversal of these statements as a carelessness about how he formulates them; his primary point is to confront the false

---

2:15 James's term for "without clothes" *(gymnoi)* can refer to a total lack ("naked," as in Mk 14:52), a lack of the outer garment considered a necessary part of one's dress (Jn 21:7) or a condition of being dressed in rags. In any of these, James is following Jesus' teaching about the importance of acting to help a person in such need (Mt 25:36). James's word "for the day" *(ephēmeros)* is used nowhere else in the New Testament or LXX.

2:16 The NIV obscures James's literal requirement that Christians "give" the things needed. James's term *epitēdeia tou sōmatos* ("what is necessary for the body") is general to include the range of *physical needs* (NIV).

theology of separating faith and actions, regardless of which party holds which alternative. Such an explanation is possible but dangerous with any text; the first course must be to seek a reasonable explanation for a deliberately worded text. Laws, for example, admits the solution is not entirely satisfactory (1980:124). Mayor (1897:95-96) and Adamson (1976:124-25) try to solve the problem by extending the quotation through the end of 2:18 and rendering the whole verse not as an anticipated objection to 2:17 but as a further confirmation of it. This requires an understanding of *will say* in 2:18 as "someone may well say" and the rest of the verse as the person's argument, which James is commending to his readers.

A paraphrase of James's thought would then be: "Faith by itself is dead. In fact, someone could properly say, 'You have faith, and I have deeds. Show me your faith apart from deeds, and I will show you my faith by deeds.' " This solution is possible grammatically and attractive because of the consistency it provides for James's use of the pronouns. However, it is too forced, not only because of the sense it requires of the verb *will say* but also because it attempts to reverse the whole first phrase *(but someone will say),* which in all other cases in Greek literature introduces a contrast or objection to what has preceded. Davids (1982:124) and Moo (1985:105-6) finally choose the solution accepted by Ropes, Dibelius and Laws as the most likely, acknowledging that all of the solutions to this passage have their difficulties. This does seem the best option.

In other words, James is not particular about whether any hypothetical questioner believes in faith alone or in deeds alone. Instead, James is repudiating any separation of faith and actions as if they were contradictory or even equal alternatives. He is insisting on the theological unity of the two. In 2:18 he challenges anyone to be able to claim genuine faith without the authenticating works, and he declares the only way to have genuine faith is to carry it out with deeds. He affirms the necessity of both faith and actions and says he will show the former by the latter.

With these observations of James's logical argument, we are in a po-

---

2:18 The NASB is a good example of Mayor's and Adamson's approach, and the LB reflects the same influence. The NEB smooths out the difficulty in the text by actually changing the first- and second-person pronouns into the third person, apparently trying to

sition to draw interpretive conclusions.

1. What does James mean by *deeds?* First, we can state the theological content of *deeds.* James consistently speaks of deeds as actions that are taken because of one's faith and that therefore demonstrate and authenticate one's faith. The primary, earnest and repeated point he makes is "not that works must be *added to* faith but that genuine faith *includes* works" (Moo 1985:99). It is the very nature of genuine faith to express itself in works. Though he uses the same term for deeds *(erga)* as Paul does in Galatians and Romans, James is not writing in the same context. It is not just that Paul and James discuss different times in the Christian life (as Barclay presents it, 1976:74); they are addressing different issues at any stage in a Christian's life. Paul uses the term to refer to works of the law (not only rituals but any act of obedience to God's commands, as Moo rightly contends, 1985:101-2) intended as a basis for standing as righteous before God. In that context, such works are a false alternative to faith in which one would rely on one's own works instead of relying (by faith) on God's redemptive works. James is referring to moral actions flowing naturally from genuine faith, so that the faith and deeds are not a dichotomy but a unity. Paul agrees in Ephesians 2:9-10: we are not saved "by works" *(ex ergōn),* but we are saved "for works" *(epi ergois).* (See the section on "Faith and Deeds" in the introduction to this volume.)

Second, we can state some of the practical content of deeds. James's illustration calls for the active giving of material help for people lacking clothing and food. The deeds James especially has in mind for a life of faith, then, are not the keeping of religious ritual but the acts of love commanded in Christ's "royal law." We also find in James a conviction that Christians are responsible to care for each other. He pictures fellow believers (a needy brother or sister) in his example, and it is *one of you* who speaks the good wishes without taking the practical actions.

2. What does James mean by *faith without deeds?* James has used three important terms by which to assess *faith without deeds.* First, such faith is of no *good.* We found this term to mean of no use or benefit. Second,

---

reflect Ropes's, Dibelius's and Laws's view that James is unconcerned about who holds faith and who holds deeds in separation from each other.

such faith does not *save,* and we found this to refer to the lack of salvation for the one who has this kind of faith. Third, such faith is *dead.* James chose this third term for summation and climax in 2:17, even as he will employ it again at the very end of this passage in 2:26. There he will explain his analogy: faith without deeds is dead as a body without a spirit is dead. The force of his meaning thus builds and intensifies. Faith that does not result in deeds is a faith that is utterly useless, ineffectual for salvation and in fact dead. With such terms in the text, we are finally forced to conclude that he is talking about a "faith" that is no genuine faith at all. Even when James depicts a Christian in the example of 2:15-16 *(one of you),* this does not mean that he expects a person of genuine, saving faith actually to ignore the poor. The point of the illustration is that such an outcome is unthinkable.

This biblical truth needs to be forcefully preached and taught for the social conscience of the modern church. It must become unthinkable for us, too, that our faith would leave us content to ignore needy people. Our churches are failing to supply the channels of ministry for a life of faith if they are not providing ways for Christians to minister to needy people. As churches plan their priorities, it does not matter whether church growth can occur through outreach to the poor; it is a question of whether we have genuine, saving faith. This point is a message to convict and to motivate those who would be people of "faith."

3. What does James mean by *faith?* A life of faith *(pistis)* is the unifying theme of James's letter. He strongly emphasizes that faith is a stance of belief and trust toward God—for example, trusting God even in the face of trials. But with equal strength James emphasizes that genuine faith is "working faith" (Moo 1985:107). It is the stance of belief toward God by which one endures trials, asks for wisdom, resists temptation, controls one's tongue, looks after orphans and widows in their distress, keeps oneself unpolluted by the world, avoids favoritism, loves one's neighbor as oneself, gives physical necessities to the poor and, in short, lives as

---

2:19 Davids: "Significantly [James] indicates an intellectual commitment on his interlocutor's part to a creed *(pisteueis hoti)* rather than the distinctively Christian personal trust and commitment which would include obedience *(pisteueis* plus dative, *en* or *eis). . . .* In this he is indicating something far different from the Pauline concept of faith and thus not addressing the Pauline doctrine at all" (1982:125).

a doer of the word.

We can affirm all of this with James's passionate earnestness but without distorting his view into an unrealistic expectation of sinless perfection. Of course Christians fail to live up to this perfectly; that is why James bothers to write about it. But the meaning of real faith is still to be embraced and practiced. If the works of faith are not present, the authenticity of one's faith is in serious question. Genuine faith, faith that does result in salvation, must acknowledge the lordship of Christ and so respond to Christ's word with actions of obedience. Thus 2:14 recalls the emphasis on that "which can save you" in 1:21. Christ is both Savior and Lord; he cannot be separated into two persons. Genuine, saving faith necessarily includes both a trusting of Christ as Savior and a following of Christ as Lord.

Three Examples (2:19-26) James now supplies a series of three examples to confirm the necessity of submission to the lordship of Christ in any saving faith.

Demons (2:19) The first example is devastating. What could there possibly be from which people of "faith" would want to distance themselves farther than demons? *You believe (pisteueis)* leaves the continuity of the theme of faith *(pistis)* unmistakable. But it is a doctrinal belief (believing that something is true) rather than genuine Christian faith (believing in Christ with trust and obedience); therefore it is hardly a rebuttal to what the apostle Paul wrote about faith. For the particular point of doctrinal belief James chooses the fundamental affirmation of Judeo-Christian monotheism from the *Shema* of Deuteronomy 6:4. This is devastating again, for no one claiming to have Christian faith could dismiss this as a trivial example. Even the demons believe in the sense of recognizing the truth, and they at least realize that it leaves them cause to shudder in fear rather than rest in confidence that they are saved. James may well be remembering the monotheistic fear that demons

---

A textual uncertainty results in some varying translations ("there is one God," "God is one"). The variation in meaning is not great, however, and the point of James's argument remains unaltered.

This is the only New Testament use of the term *shudder (phrissō)*, though it was used in both Jewish and later Christian literature.

exhibited when confronted by Christ, for it made a powerful impression on observers (Mk 1:23-28; 5:1-20). The point is that believing the truth without obeying the truth does not save us at all, any more than it saves demons. In fact, the comparison to demonic "faith" implies that belief without obedience is even worse than useless.

Abraham (2:20-24) If the first example provided devastating irony, the second example gives biblical authority. The importance James sees in the issue is reflected in his hypothetical addressing of a *foolish man*— using a term meaning "empty," probably referring to the man's lack of understanding about this issue of faith. In other words, it is senseless to think that faith without actions is a genuine, saving faith.

Interwoven throughout this paragraph are three components to James's argument. One component is the credentials of the chosen model. The patriarchal standing of Abraham *our ancestor,* the explicit affirmation of his faith (quoted in 2:23 from Gen 15:6) and his title as *God's friend* (reference to 2 Chron 20:7 and Is 41:8) all make Abraham an indisputable precedent.

The second component in James's argument is the illustration of his point with an incident from Abraham's life. The incident James chooses is a revealing narrative to confirm what we have already argued, that James is not attempting to refute Paul or even to correct a distortion of Pauline teaching. James's illustration is Abraham's offering of Isaac—an act of supreme obedience carried out in faith, exactly suiting the context of what James is encouraging his readers to practice. Paul's illustration will be Abraham's confidence in the promise of God in Genesis 15— an act of trust in God's grace to provide what was beyond human ability, exactly suiting the context of what Paul would be encouraging his readers to practice. James's illustration here is not a refutation of Paul but an independent (and prior) addressing of a different issue.

Third, James describes faith and actions as inseparable by identifying

---

2:20 The textual variation "dead" should be rejected as apparently an attempt to harmonize the language of the passage. The reading "useless" commends itself as probably a play on words by James with *ergōn* (works) followed by *argē* (useless). Moo captures it well: "faith that has no works does not work" (1985:107).

2:21 *Our ancestor Abraham* is literally "Abraham our father" and could have been written to Gentile as well as Jewish Christians, reflecting Christians' sense of being the true Israel (Gal 3:29; Rom 4:16).

three ways in which they operate together. In 2:22, faith and actions work together as part of one reality—"faith was working with his works" (a literal wordplay by James, *synērgei tois ergois*). Then faith is said to be *made complete* by what Abraham did. The verb *eteleiōthē* means "perfected" (or "brought to maturity," Davids 1982:128). This describes faith as a reality that grows and matures in a Christian's life, and it gives strong motivation for doing the works, because becoming "mature" *(teleios)* in faith is the goal to which James directed us in 1:4. Finally, in 2:23, even the scriptural promise of justification through faith is said to be fulfilled by actions. James would not have meant that Abraham was left unjustified until he offered Isaac; James knew that Abraham was credited with righteousness before he had offered Isaac (just as Paul would argue in Rom 4 that Abraham was credited with righteousness before he was circumcised). But James means that Abraham's belief in God's promise and the consequent crediting to him of righteousness in Genesis 15:6 were proved to be real and were carried out in deed when Abraham offered Isaac in Genesis 22.

These three ways in which faith and actions operate together make faith a dynamic factor in a believer's life, not a static condition. James has insisted on the union of belief and actions, so that he clearly wants neither faith nor deeds neglected; he is insisting on the inseparable union of the two. The imperfect tense of *were working* emphasizes that what James expects is a continuing life of deeds done by faith; the aorist verb *was made complete* describes his expectation of the final result. Faith "leaves evidence of its occurring" in the form of works, and "so 'perfect' faith is produced through successive acts of obedience" (Moo 1985:112).

Finally, in 2:24, James's summarizing conclusion of the paragraph is that *a person is justified by what he does and not by faith alone*. The verb *justified* is a repetition from 2:21, now in present tense instead of

---

2:21, 24 Adamson (1976:129) sees the moral sense of *justified* as dominant in James over the judicial sense used by Paul. Davids agrees (1982:127). Moo sees the judicial sense dominating in James but describes the difference between Paul and James with Wesley's "initial justification" (Paul) and "final justification" (James). Thus Moo summarizes, "Paul wants to make clear that one 'gets into' God's kingdom only by faith; James insists that God requires works from those who are 'in' " (1985:109-10).

aorist. Together, these two verses are instances of James's use of identical terms with Paul *(works* and *justified)* but with a different emphasis appropriate to his different context. James is speaking of moral deeds flowing naturally from genuine faith and showing the doer to be righteous. James's emphasis on faith *alone* shows that he affirms the necessity of faith; what he is opposing is a faith that denies the obligation to obey Christ as Lord. (Again, see the section "Faith and Deeds" in the introduction.)

James's meaning is not particularly clarified if we decide whether *justified* carries a demonstrative sense (with works demonstrating a person's righteousness) or a declarative sense (with works securing a person's righteousness). The probable background for James at this point is in Jesus' teaching on recognizing trees by their fruit in Matthew 7:15-20 and 12:33-37. There it is emphasized that a tree will demonstrate its quality by the kind of fruit it bears, but the judgment in a declarative sense is also strong in the verb "acquitted" *(dikaioō)* in 12:37. James's point is this: faith is the initial and continuing context for one's relationship with God; the genuineness of one's faith will be demonstrated in actions; and this genuineness will provide the basis for whether one is declared righteous before God.

Rahab (2:25-26) The third example is intended as further biblical precedent, but of a complementary sort. Abraham was the respected patriarch. Rahab represents the opposite extreme, both because she was a prostitute and because she was a comparatively minor figure in Old Testament history. Yet *even Rahab* had to carry out her faith in the true God by actions of obedience. It would not have been enough for Rahab to have said to the spies, "I hope you don't get caught"; that would have been comparable to the pious but useless wishes in 2:16. On the basis of her actions to help the spies, the identical verb is applied to her in 2:25 as to Abraham in 2:21, translated "justified" (NASB) or "considered righteous" (NIV). Thus Rahab's example demonstrates the universality of the principle.

This leads James to a summarizing conclusion about Rahab and about

---

2:26 Proper inductive study will be careful not to press James's meaning beyond what

the entire discussion in 2:14-26. He states his conclusion by the analogy of a body without a spirit, enlarging on his labeling faith without actions as *dead* in 2:17. It is an apt analogy at this point. As final as death, it brings an end to the hypothetical debate in which James has engaged. It also conveys meaning along with emphasis. If faith without actions is dead like a body without a spirit, again faith without actions is no genuine, Christian, saving faith at all. It is a meaningless, useless, powerless, lifeless impostor.

Applications for the Church Today If we take seriously this section of James's letter, there will be important ramifications for various aspects of our life together in the church.

The church's gospel. Some churches will have to reevaluate their fundamental understanding of the gospel, for James does not endorse a two-stage relationship with Christ in which a person trusts Christ as Savior at one point in life and then submits to Christ as Lord at a later stage. In James's assessment, faith without submission to Christ's lordship is no genuine, saving faith at all. The biblical truth can be taught this way: If sin is our act of managing our own lives instead of giving God his place of rule, then we cannot legitimately ask Christ to save us from sin and then go on managing our own lives; it is self-contradictory.

The church's discipline. Many of us will have to upgrade our practice of church discipline. First, discipline needs to permeate relationships throughout a local church, for church discipline is the discipling of church members. Though church officers properly carry special authority for discipling, nevertheless discipline is a ministry to be owned by all church members. We need to do for each other exactly what James does in his letter—hold each other accountable for a life of faith. Second, our discipline should not dilute the standard of Jesus' call for anyone to "deny himself and take up his cross and follow me" (Mk 8:34). This was not just a call for actions that come easily according to one's personality or temperament or circumstances. It was a call for actions that may be painful and sacrificial (like Abraham's), or risky and frightening (like Rahab's), or uncomfortable and inconvenient (like getting to know poor

---

he says. James's analogy simply says that the body without the spirit is dead; he is not entering debate about whether humans are bipartite or tripartite beings.

and homeless people face to face by spending nights helping at a homeless shelter, or by building friendship with a poor family for long-term help out of a lifestyle of poverty).

Third, in our exercise of discipline, church members need to be hearing faith and deeds as a unity instead of a dichotomy. The unifying of belief and actions will help our discipline of each other to accomplish both of its intended purposes: *restoring* and *purifying* people's lives. When the church neglects faith in favor of deeds, we burden people's lives with expectations to do more, and we fail to give the assurance of God's grace; then discipline no longer accomplishes restoration of the sinner. When the church neglects deeds in favor of faith, we tell people to believe God's forgiveness, but we omit the appropriate acts of faith; then discipline no longer accomplishes purification of the sinner's life.

The church's balance. James obviously condemns the pattern of dead orthodoxy. His illustration of demons inescapably shows that reliance on one's correct grasp of theology will not save. At the same time, James equally rejects a pattern of faithless humanitarianism. From the earliest verses of the letter, he has affirmed the necessity of faith and the importance of believing the word of truth. In 2:14-26 we have found him to be pressing not deeds *instead of* faith but deeds *in completion of* faith. The example of Abraham's deed suits James's intent precisely because Abraham was a man of faith; he *believed God.* So the church will maintain a complementary balance of orthodox doctrine and orthodox practice. We will teach correct doctrine and pursue social justice, and we will do both energetically and aggressively.

The church's activities. James's teaching helps us avoid being driven by guilt and fears and demands, as is so common even among Christians in our society. It is important to acknowledge now the definition that James has implied for deeds. They are not actions such as making the dean's list, scoring goals in a soccer game, publishing a research paper, reaching a high income level or getting a promotion. Those are achievements, but they are not what James means by *deeds.* He does not even mean having large numbers of people come to one's Bible class or other Christian ministry. That may be success, but even when success is experienced in a Christian ministry one is not necessarily performing what

James means by *deeds*. The unity of faith and deeds means that deeds are simply actions taken because of one's faith.

Therefore the message of this passage does not demand that we drive ourselves to do *more;* it calls us to do *differently.* James calls us to live by faith. What deeds will we do when we understand that the necessary deeds are those done specifically because of our faith?

First, we will do deeds of *devotion*—prayer, Bible study, worship and sacrifice. Abraham's action in sacrificing Isaac is an example; he placed that which was dearest to him in this world on the altar, because he loved God more than he loved his own son. Deeds of devotion are to be done because God is worthy of them. They are also done because we have a need for them; they keep us in touch with God and nourished by God, so that we have the resources for carrying out the other two kinds of deeds. We must not allow the achievements of life, or even the deeds of ministry, to leave us with only a pittance of time for the deeds of prayer, Bible study and worship.

Second, we will do deeds of *morality*—doing what is right to purify our speech, thoughts, attitudes and behavior. Rahab's action in this passage is an example of morality. It was not that she had been praying about the needs of homeless spies and decided to start a shelter ministry. She was simply confronted with a situation and responded by doing what was morally right, because she had heard about the God of Israel and had faith in him (Josh 2:8-11). Helping the needy is a deed of morality incumbent on all Christians simply because it is right to do.

Third, we will do deeds of *ministry,* but this is where we get into trouble with being driven. Every Christian needs to do the deeds of devotion, and the biblical moral standards are prescribed for all believers. All Christians are also called to ministry, but Scripture says we have diverse spiritual gifts and therefore diverse ministries. The application of faith as the source of deeds will help us pursue appropriate deeds of ministry. We do those deeds of ministry to which we believe by faith that we are called; we do the deeds of ministry relying by faith on God's power rather than our ability; we do deeds of ministry seeking God's glory and surrendering our desires for success and achievement; and we persevere in deeds of ministry by faith, obeying the calling God gives.

The church's mission. That James's illustration in 2:15 involves fellow

Christians does not limit its application to the church's internal discipline, for his burden is the essential unity of faith and deeds. Even if the needy people were non-Christians, all of James's arguments would still apply: the faith of the one withholding help would still be offensively useless, ineffective for salvation and as dead as a body without a spirit. Therefore James's message can be properly applied to the church's mission to people outside the Christian community.

James's synthesis of belief and actions must be the model that holds the church on course with evangelism and social action. John Stott has outlined the church's three historical attempts at holding evangelism and social action together by treating social action as: a means to evangelism, a manifestation of evangelism or a partner of evangelism. Stott finds the first two insufficiently biblical and argues for the partnership model between evangelism and social action: "For each is an end in itself. Both are expressions of unfeigned love" (1975:26-27).

The essential unity of belief and practice, especially as applied by James to acts of charity, means that it is not yet genuine faith to have good wishes or sympathetic attitudes toward the needy. We can make statements in all sincerity of mind and emotion: "I feel sorry for the poor; I don't condone racism." But James will say, "What good is that if you aren't doing something to help the poor or to heal the distrust and injustice between races?" Some Christians attempt a stance of personal belief without personal action, saying, for example, "I personally disagree with abortion, but I won't try to change others' minds." James persists in asking us: What are you doing to protect the victims—both the victimized baby and the victimized mother?

Answers to the social problems are not easy, but the biblical message requires individual Christians and local churches to get busy setting definite goals for specific actions with mercy ministries as well as evangelistic messages.

□ Controlling What We Say (3:1-12)

Years ago I visited a college friend at his home. On campus we had

Notes: **3:1-12** Some commentators see James quoting or paraphrasing popular proverbs and common phrases throughout the letter. Especially in this passage, many of the statements certainly have a proverbial sound to them, and some parallels can be found in

enjoyed a significant sharing of personal values and philosophies, much of it through discussion of literature, history and music. When we met at his home, he wanted me to hear a certain Mahler symphony that expressed some of his aspirations toward the attainment of love and peace. We listened together in silent pleasure, caught up in the music and our high ideals—until, at a particularly moving point in the symphony, my friend's mother broke the spell by entering the room and asking a mundane question about supper. Her innocent interruption received a fierce verbal rebuke from her son. How dare she spoil the exquisite music! Startled and embarrassed, she retreated from the room, but the damage to our mood had been done.

The damage to our illusions had also been done. My friend and I talked about the incident. What good were ideals of love and aspirations to "self-actualization" if we could not control our tongues enough to speak respectfully to other human beings? The spirituality was only a feeling, an illusion, if it could not purify our behavior in the practical matter of what we said.

Exactly so, writes James. He returns now to a theme he introduced in 1:19 and emphasized in 1:26, to provide his most complete explanation of this issue—controlling our tongues.

The General Theme: Humility (3:1-2) With his now familiar and kind address *my brothers,* James begins with a specific instruction that not many should become teachers. His concern is not to give career counseling. Rather, he is addressing those who aspire to positions of authority in the church. Church leaders are his primary focus now. And what is on his heart is a sin to which leaders are vulnerable—the sin of pride. The NIV reflects this emphasis by rendering the words "become teachers" as "presume to be teachers." James's point in the last half of 3:1 (that teachers will be judged more strictly) is driven home in the first part of 3:2 (reminding them that everyone is vulnerable because we all stumble in many ways). It is a warning not to think one has attained an unassailable spirituality. It is a serious reminder to be humble.

biblical and other literature. At the same time, the deliberate unity and the cohesive line of thought by James should be acknowledged.

Further discussion of the role of teachers in the church will begin in 3:13. The fact that James mentions teachers here but does not specifically return to the topic until so much later does not have to mean this is a later addition to the text, as Davids allows (1982:135). A continuing flow of thought makes sense here. James has been prescribing humility implicitly and explicitly in 1:5, 1:9-11, 1:13-15, 1:16-18, 1:19, 1:21, 1:26 and 2:13. Nor is this to be the end of the matter. The reader can glance over chapters 3—5 and find, in the diverse applications, the unifying intent to warn against arrogance and instruct in humility. James evidently saw those in authority to teach as being particularly in danger of spiritual arrogance, which would be expressed in impure speech. He therefore introduces his address to teachers and then proceeds to develop his message with care and detail.

All of this is immediate confirmation that in his emphasis on deeds in the preceding passage James is still realistic about the persistence of sin and is not expecting perfection in holiness. It is also confirmation that the theme of humility, especially as expressed in speech, is fundamental to James's teaching about Christian living. Humility is a trait we must examine, search out and cultivate if we claim to take this book of God's word seriously.

As the foundation for this particular character development, James confronts us with two inescapable facts of life: judgment and failure. These are the two facts, therefore, that an expositor of this passage should establish in order to disciple young Christians in humility. James has already warned that we are not to judge (2:4) and that we will be judged (2:12). Now he adds these two points.

First, there is a greater strictness of judgment for ones who teach. This could be based upon Jesus' statement in Matthew 7:2. It means that a teacher is obligated to teach what is true and then to live up to what is taught. God expects more from church leaders and holds them accountable for what they teach his people. This biblical principle is exemplified in Ezekiel 34:1-10, where the unfaithful leaders of the nation are condemned for being neglectful and abusive shepherds of God's people, and God declares that he will "hold them accountable." See it again in Matthew 5:19 and 18:6, where Jesus gives warning to anyone who teaches others to sin. See it repeated in Luke 12:42-48, where Jesus' parable is about a manager "whom the master puts in charge of his servants to give them their food allowance at the proper time." The Lord's instruction culminates in this principle: "From everyone who has been given much, much will be demanded; and from the one who has been entrusted with much, much more will be asked."

Second, there is failure by all of us. This failure James describes with the verb *stumble (ptaiō,* used before in 2:10). This verb has the literal meaning of "stumble" or "trip," but it is used as a figure for making a mistake or sinning. (James will repeat the verb in the last half of 3:2; Romans 11:11 and 2 Peter 1:10 are the only other New Testament uses of this verb.) James is saying, "Remember, you are subject to judgment even more if you try to teach others; and you are highly vulnerable in that judgment because we all sin in many ways."

The Focused Theme: Decisive Influence of the Tongue (3:2-5)
Now James applies the broad theme of humility to the specific theme of the tongue. The unity of these verses as a paragraph is supported by stylistic features reminiscent of other passages in the letter. The paragraph is introduced with *if anyone* (as in 1:5). It is tied to the preceding verse with repetition of the verb *stumble (is at fault* in NIV). And it concludes with the *likewise* statement in 3:5 *(houtōs* as in 2:17, 2:26). James makes application specifically to the tongue because he sees the controlling of one's tongue as a decisive matter, influencing the entirety of one's life. He explains this fact first, before instructing his readers in the specific errors of an uncontrolled tongue.

To explain this, first James states his basic principle: If you control what you say, you can control the rest of what you do. The intent seems twofold: to prove that we all stumble in many ways (for we fail even in the simple everyday matter of speaking) and to motivate us to diligence in speech (because it is so influential over the rest of our lives).

Second, James illustrates his principle with two analogies—the horse's bit and the ship's rudder. Both images have to do with steering, and so refer to the directing of one's whole life. Both images emphasize the size of the accomplishment *(the whole animal* and the ships *so large . . . driven by strong winds)* and so emphasize the magnitude of the tongue's influence.

Third, James concludes the analogies with the summarizing principle in 3:5. Thus far his emphasis is largely positive, describing the tongue's potential for good, in keeping with his intent to motivate us to diligence in this matter of speech. Positive application should be made: that learning godly ways of speaking will help us learn godliness in other ways. Therefore the issue of speech should not be put off while one works on other areas of behavior. If you want purity and Christlikeness to characterize your life, here is a valuable secret of strategy: start with your tongue!

The Specific Dangers of the Tongue (3:5-12) However, James's predominant emphasis in the passage is more negative: warning that judgment is real and that we all stumble, intending that we should humbly repent of our impure speech. He dwells then on the potential for evil rather than the potential for good with one's tongue. Three dangers are specified.

The Tongue Spreads Evil (3:5-6) We have found James's style to be full of imagery, previously using a wave of the sea (1:6), a wild flower (1:10), a crown (1:12), childbirth (1:15), lights and shadows (1:17) and a mirror (1:23), and already using a horse's bit and a ship's rudder in the current passage. Now he adopts a new image appropriate for his topic: fire. The effect of this choice of image can be shown by comparing it to another possible image. If he had compared the tongue to an ax, he could have portrayed quite vividly a destruction of a large tree by a small tool. Instead of such an isolated act of destruction, however, James chose to portray a spreading destruction. An ax destroys one tree at a time; with our tongues, one act of evil starts a destructiveness that spreads beyond the initial act.

What kind of spreading does James have in mind? It is easy to envision the spreading of evil through a church family because of gossip, slander

---

3:6 The beginning of this verse is a series of terms and phrases lacking a tidy grammatical structure but conveying vivid pictures (e.g., speech as *fire,* as in Prov 16:27; *a world of evil*). The middle part of the verse repeats the subject "tongue" and says, literally, that it "is set among our members corrupting the whole body." All three NIV verbs *corrupts, sets on fire, is set on fire* are feminine present participles describing the feminine noun *tongue.* The phrase *the whole course of his life* is used nowhere else in Scripture; its origin is uncertain and probably removed from James's current usage anyway. Commentators have labored over

and criticisms. If Paul had written this passage, we might expect him to employ his image of the church as the body of Christ to describe the injury done to other lives by one person's impure speech. But James's reference to the body appears to be in the Jewish sense of the whole person rather than a figure of speech for the church. His focus is more on the destruction of the impure speaker's own life.

We can envision how this might be so. Spread gossip, and people will not trust you. Speak with sarcasm and insults, and people will not follow you. Yet what is especially on James's mind is not the reaction of others to your speech but the spreading of sin from your speech to the rest of your life. Be hateful with your tongue, and you will be hateful with other aspects of your behavior. If you do not discipline and purify your speech, you will not discipline or purify the rest of your life.

A true exposition of this text should be severe, uncompromising and authoritative in its condemnation of this evil, faithful to James's language, which is neither mild nor restrained. With a rapid succession of images prompted by the devastation he sees, James says the uncontrolled tongue

□ is *a world of evil*—a whole world of wrongdoing and wickedness, "a vast system of iniquity" (Hiebert 1979:215). The phrase implies a multitude of forms that our impure speech may take.

□ *corrupts the whole person*—an image of a staining and defiling spread of sin from wicked speech into all other behavior. The contrasting pattern, using the same term in the form of a negative adjective, was in 1:27—keeping oneself unstained or unpolluted by the world.

□ *sets on fire* the course of one's life—now depicting the tongue's wickedness as a conflagration spreading through the time span of one's life as well as the diversity of one's behavior. But this is more serious even than the length of time involved: the fundamental direction of one's life is affected. James refers to this with a phrase that is unique in

the difficulties of the grammar and figurative expressions in this single verse (Mayor 1897:109-14; Adamson 1976:158-64; Laws 1980:148-52); some have conjectured a corrupt text or gloss (Ropes 1916:233-34; Dibelius 1976:193-95). Davids is wise to keep the expedient of changing the text as a last resort (1982:142) and finally reaches the simplest and most sensible conclusion: that James has piled up phrases which may be "a mixture of metaphors and grammar but which would have impacted upon the original readers with rhetorical clarity." He adds, "The same is often true of modern sermons" (1982:144).

all of biblical literature: *ton trochon tēs geneseōs.* Its literal meaning would be "wheel of existence" or "wheel of human origin." James uses it as a figurative expression to mean *the whole course of his life.* The phrase emphasizes the thorough and far-reaching destruction wrought by the uncontrolled tongue.

□ *is itself set on fire by hell*—taking the same verb that described the action by the tongue and now applying it to the tongue in passive voice, to expose the true origin of the tongue's blazing power to destroy. James picks up the term *gehenna* ("hell") which Jesus often uses in the Synoptic Gospels. It is hard to imagine a more condemning way to conclude this description of the uncontrolled tongue.

The images thus build in a progression. The first phrase points to the multitude of evils contained within and prompted by impure speech. The second phrase warns that the whole person becomes corrupted by the uncontrolled tongue. The third adds to corruption the picture of destruction and extends it to the whole course of the person's life. The fourth phrase provides the climax by exposing the tongue's source of evil: hell itself. It is altogether a devastating denunciation.

The Tongue Is Impossible to Tame (3:7-8) The sight of a rapidly spreading fire is terrifying; James has used the image to stir people to swift and radical action. If we come to the realization that the fire's source is unquenchable, the effect is more sobering; James now uses this fact to call for sustained and disciplined action. For this second warning about the tongue, James changes his imagery and speaks of wild animals. He repeats the verb *tame* in present and perfect tenses so that we make no mistake about how commonplace it is for human beings to tame wild animals. Yet no human being can tame the tongue.

Why is that so? To explain, in quick succession James adds two phrases referring to the tongue. First, the tongue is a *restless evil,* untamable because it is inherently unstable and therefore, even when brought un-

---

3:7-8 This verb *tame* is used only one other place in the New Testament, in Mark 5:4 to characterize the inability of anyone to "subdue" the demon-possessed man. James's meaning should be understood more broadly than "domesticate" to include "overpower" or "control." Cf. commentators' common dissatisfaction with the single term *tame* (Adamson 1976:145; Laws 1980:153; Hiebert 1979:220).

3:8 *Restless:* This adjective is used only by James in the New Testament. See 1 Corinthians

der some control, always prone to further evil. This requires that we be continually watchful over our tongues, never thinking we have successfully altered the nature of our speech.

James used the same adjective *akatastatos* in 1:8 to describe the "unstable" man; he will use the related noun *akatastasia* in 3:16 to refer to the "disorder" that prevails where humility and wisdom from above are missing. We are left with a picture of this instability as characteristic of unspirituality; it stands in contrast to the peace *(eirēnē)* emphasized in 3:17-18.

Second, with a sudden change in imagery, the tongue is *full of deadly poison.* Again we are compelled to be continually watchful—to keep the lid on the poison, to keep the discipline of our speech in place, because we know the power to destroy with our tongues is present as often as we speak.

From all three images—wild animals, restless evil and deadly poison—the application is the same: discipline. Self-discipline is to be practiced actively and diligently, in recognition of the constant danger. It takes discipline to be "quick to listen, slow to speak and slow to become angry" (1:19). And, looking ahead to the next verse, it will mean controlling what one says to stop verbally abusing people who are made in God's own image.

The Tongue Makes Us Liable to Judgment (3:9-12) Judgment is not mentioned in 3:9-12, but it is the unspoken implication still being explained from the beginning of the passage in 3:1. What James does describe explicitly in 3:9-12 is the product of one's tongue: the contradictory product of praise and cursing. If we treat this as a relatively superficial matter which he wants cleared up merely for the sake of consistency, we have dodged the force of this paragraph. James's specific language drives us to the serious issue of facing divine judgment. The three phases of this paragraph make this evident.

14:33 and 2 Corinthians 12:20 for Paul's use of the noun form with emphasis similar to James's. Adamson's translation "irreducible to order" reads awkwardly but attempts to capture the concept of persistent instability. The KJV's "unruly" is based on an inferior textual variant.

Poison: See Psalms 58:4 and 140:3 (also quoted in Rom 3:13) for biblical precedent for this image. The adjective *thanatēphoros* ("deadly") occurs only here in the New Testament.

First, the literal example he gives in 3:9 involves our relationship with God himself. If we praise God and then curse our neighbors, our praise to God is contradicted. James's logic is important to trace.

1. The one we praise is no less than *our Lord and Father.* This is a phrase not repeated anywhere else in the Bible; James is deliberately bringing into focus the greatness of God with respect to these two terms.

2. The one we curse is made in the likeness of that Lord and Father.

3. Therefore, to treat people with contempt is to treat God's own greatness with contempt.

This principle has huge implications in our day, requiring just and honorable treatment of the unborn, the poor, the sick and the elderly. James's application here, however, is to our speech. He refers to a praising or blessing *(eulogeō)* of God—a common Old Testament theme with this same verb in the Septuagint (e.g., Ps 103:1-2). He is exposing the hypocrisy of speaking praise to God with the worshiping church or in private prayer while abusing people with ridicule, insults and attacks through the rest of the week.

Second, the effect of 3:10 is to declare such inconsistency unthinkable for Christians. The tone of James's summary in the first part of the verse is amazement that such praise and cursing should come from the same mouth. This evokes immediately the negated verb in the last part of the verse, as if to say: "Praise and cursing from the same mouth? It can't be!" This also happens to be the only New Testament instance of the impersonal verb *chrē;* it conveys the most earnest and blunt emphasis. Adamson describes James's language as "the strongest possible Greek . . . spoken with all the force of protesting condemnation" (1976:146-47). The contradictory speech of praising and cursing "makes moral and logical nonsense from James's theological standpoint" (Davids 1982:146).

Do we today have this same, intense reaction—this sense that praising God and cursing people is utterly unthinkable, abhorrent nonsense? Consider the habitual verbal abuse that occurs in our churches—how

---

3:11-12 The example of water in 3:12 may be a rephrasing of the similar example in 3:11, but a series of distinct pictures from nature appears more likely as James's intention. The type of water contrasted to fresh is "bitter" *(pikros)* in 3:11 and "salty" *(halykos)* in 3:12, and the verbs refer to different actions. Davids thinks James uses *pikros* deliberately instead

commonplace it is for us to speak of others with ridicule or with cutting remarks, how quickly we accuse others of evil motives when they do things we don't like and how easily we can have angry fights in our churches. Where is our biblical sense of shock at all of this?

Third, the examples from nature in 3:11-12 are intended to describe situations that never happen. These are not to be allegorized, and oddities of nature do not negate James's point. He is stating the obvious, normative facts that one spring does not pour forth two kinds of water; a plant of one kind does not produce fruit of another kind; a salt spring does not produce fresh water. The implication is that a true Christian will not make a practice of unchristian speech; and the practice of unchristian speech is evidence that the speaker is not a Christian and is therefore in danger of hell.

This implication is reinforced when one considers James's possible reliance on Jesus' teaching for example, in Matthew 12:33-37, where the image of a good tree bearing good fruit and a bad tree bearing bad fruit is applied specifically to speech as the fruit of one's inner character. "For out of the overflow of the heart the mouth speaks." Jesus made the divine judgment explicit: "Men will have to give account on the day of judgment for every careless word they have spoken." Similarly in the Sermon on the Mount in Matthew 7:15-23, the trees bearing bad fruit will be "cut down and thrown into the fire" and the ones who praised Jesus saying "Lord, Lord" will be sent away as impostors who are not genuine Christians at all: "Then I will tell them plainly, 'I never knew you.' "

James insists on purity of speech if one's faith is genuine. He recognizes that Christians fail in this; he is willing to identify himself with sinful speech—it is something "we" do. But to accept it or to tolerate it, instead of being horrified at it and repenting of it—this must not be! For we, like springs and plants, produce according to our true nature. The production of good fruit is an evidence of genuine faith and therefore salvation itself. James says to each one of us: Purify your speaking, or show yourself to be an impostor and therefore under judgment.

---

of *halykos* in anticipation of his use of the same term in 3:14 (1982:148), but it is more probable that James uses it here at face value to mean "bitter water" and then picks up the term for its moral connotations when he arrives at his point in 3:14.

He will not let us avoid this issue with excuses or delays. He writes conscious that his readers worship together and then have fights and quarrels among themselves (4:1). How often do Christians sing "Praise to the Lord, the Almighty" and then leave the worship service with angry complaints about others with whom they have worshiped, or fight with each other at a church committee meeting later in the week? James tells us this must not be! Remember, he is writing to Christians who are facing trials of many kinds, including unjust treatment from rich pagans. Nevertheless, James will not condone participation in worship which is contradicted by a cursing of people, even a cursing of persecutors. He would remember Jesus' saying "Bless those who curse you" (Lk 6:28). People violate this today by singing praise to God on Sunday and then complaining and attacking neighbors, coworkers or employers on Monday.

To the person who speaks praise to God in the worship service and then abuses people verbally at home or at work, James commands, "Purify your speech through the week." With the person who says, "Oh, I know I talk too much," and laughs it off, James is not amused. He insists, "Be quick to listen, slow to speak." By the person who boasts, "I always speak my mind, no matter who gets hurt," James is not impressed. He commands, "Discipline your speaking." Of the person who says, "I know I gossip too much, but I just can't help it," James still requires, "Control your tongue." Of the person who is in the habit of speaking with insults, ridicule or sarcasm, James demands, "Change your speech habits." He expects discipline to be happening in the life of a Christian. Any Christian can ask for the grace needed, for God gives good gifts (1:17) and gives them generously (1:5). There is, then, no justification for corrupt habits of speech in our churches today. We simply must repent.

☐ Spirituality from God (3:13—4:12)

One of the saddest phone calls I have ever received came from an elder at another church; he barely knew me but was searching for help. His church was without a pastor at that time. The board of elders had interviewed a man and had voted to recommend calling this candidate. Only one elder had dissented, and he had asked his fellow elders to postpone action for one week of further consideration and prayer. The elders had agreed to this reasonable request. However, now it appeared that the one dissenting elder had used that week to begin a campaign of criticisms against the pastoral candidate within the congregation. The church became deeply torn with fears and passionate opinions. By the time the issue came before a larger meeting of church members, there was such rage and shouting that the elder who was phoning me, and who had moderated the meeting, said to me painfully, "I found myself wondering, 'Are these Christian people? Are these believers?' " He was agonizing over his divided church and asking for counsel.

Suppose this elder could call a meeting of the congregation to receive spiritual counsel from the apostle James. The people of the church would find him a tough realist. We like to think of ourselves as wise, and we are quick to justify our own role in conflicts. But James is exactly the kind of counselor we need—one who will not let us deceive ourselves and who will bring clarity to the complex issues. For Christians who want to learn true spirituality, James cuts to the heart of the matter.

We will miss the point if we do not recognize the continuity of thought between the previous section and this one. James has just given his readers a sobering picture: the certainty of judgment and their vulnerability in that judgment because of the terrible evil they do with their speech. It leads to one of the most fundamental questions of life anyone must face: How can I hope to purify my behavior (such as my speech) when it flows from my corrupt inward character? How can my heart be changed from its selfishness? Is there any hope?

James writes now about this hope: that there is a spirituality available from God. This is to be distinguished from Paul's focus in Romans 3. Paul would write about the impossibility of attaining a righteous standing before God by self-reliant observance of the law—and then about "a righteousness from God, apart from law" through Jesus Christ. James is writing about the impossibility of living the Christian life (for example, controlling our tongues) by our own resources—and then about a spirituality that comes from God. Aspects of this spirituality will include gaining wisdom from God, asking for provision from God, living in friendship with God, drawing near to God and being lifted up by God. It is all from God; it is all attained by reliance on God; it is a spirituality that comes because God "gives us more grace" (4:6). Though his focus is different from Paul's in Romans 3, James's message is just as much a message of God's grace.

James develops this message by asking a series of three questions, which introduce the three sections of this passage.

Who Is Wise Among You? (3:13-18) When James invites people who are (supposedly) *wise and understanding* to step forward and identify themselves, he is returning more explicitly to the topic of "teachers" addressed in 3:1. Especially for those who think they are wise enough to teach others, James wants his readers to know what true wisdom means. What he gives is more a description than a definition of wisdom. In fact, he has been describing it all along, with his talk of believing God, relying on God's goodness, doing what God's word says and living the righteous life that God desires. Now he will label this as wisdom and describe it further as a humble submissiveness to God which results in a life of goodness, purity and peace toward other people. To explain this, James analyzes three aspects of wisdom.

The Nature of Wisdom In regard to the nature of wisdom, first the impact of the question in 3:13 must be faced: *Who is wise and understanding among you?* For those who do not care about true wisdom but only want the status of being thought wise, the question is a challenge; James's answer will expose them for what they are. For those who honestly aspire to being wise, the question is an invitation; James's answer will divulge the way to attain their aspirations. James is saying, "I am about to tell you the nature of true wisdom; treasure this." Let all readers, then, first examine their own hearts before reading beyond the question posed in 3:13. Do you really want to be wise?

Then we must submit to James's answer about the requirement of true wisdom. Consistent with his previous instructions, James again requires actions that authenticate words. Who claims to be wise? *Let him show it by his good life.* Today the phrase *good life* has taken a connotation of

Notes: 3:13 Who can argue with Dibelius's assertion that contentiousness "exists in the most diverse of human situations" and that James's teaching here is "useful and necessary *for all situations*" (1976:208-9)? Yet Dibelius overstates this general applicability of the passage and denies any deliberate connection with James's reference to teachers in 3:1. It is a more natural and likely understanding of the text to see a connected flow of thought between 3:1-12 and 3:13-18, "as directed generally to all believers, but especially to those

a prosperous, pleasurable life. James, of course, is talking about quite another matter: moral goodness. His phrase is *kalēs anastrophēs,* "good conduct" or "good behavior." He elaborates: *Let him show it . . . by deeds.* James is thinking with the same verb *deiknymi* and noun *ergon* as in 2:18; his point must be very close to that earlier verse. Genuine wisdom, like faith, is a practical matter; it shows up in how one lives. Literally James says, "Let him show by good behavior his deeds in the humility of wisdom." Wisdom, then, is not something I will merely possess in my head; if I am wise at all, it is something I will demonstrate in my conduct.

Finally, the personality of wisdom should be taken to heart: the wise deeds will be done in *humility.* Humility is the character trait underlying the Christian behavior described in the entire letter; this is the trait to cultivate if one would take James's teaching deeply into one's life. James would have approved of what Calvin wrote quoting Augustine, "When a certain rhetorician was asked what was the chief rule in eloquence, he replied, 'Delivery'; what was the second rule, 'Delivery'; what was the third rule, 'Delivery'; so if you ask me concerning the precepts of the Christian religion, first, second, third, and always I would answer, 'Humility' " *(Institutes* 2. 2. 11).

Therefore James's notion of humility is worth exploring. His term *praÿtēs* is variously translated as "meekness" (KJV) and "gentleness" (NASB), but the NIV's "humility" is much to be preferred. "Meekness" today connotes a touch of weakness and passivity, which are not at all true in James's requirement of active obedience. "Gentleness" is appropriate in reference to our relationships with each other (and should be brought out in an exposition of 3:17-18); but James has a larger concept in mind as humility.

The terms *praÿs* and *praÿtēs* ("humble" and "humility") do not occur in the Gospel of Mark, in Luke's Gospel or Acts, in Hebrews, or in the Johannine writings of the New Testament. This reflects the Christology of those writers, who place their emphasis on Christ as powerful Son and

who pride themselves on their superior understanding" (Moo 1985:132).

3:14 James's term for "bitter" has a literal meaning which he used for the unfit water in 3:11; now he uses the same term in its figurative sense to describe envy. The term for "envy" *(zēlos)* refers to a zeal that in this context has a clearly negative sense. Davids prefers "harsh zeal" (from Ropes 1916:245) or "rivalry" over "jealousy." James's term *eritheia* is also found in Paul's lists of sins in 2 Corinthians 12:20 and Galatians 5:20, meaning "selfish ambition"

Lord. In Matthew the adjective *praýs* is used three times, as a significant, characteristic trait of Jesus himself and of his followers. In Matthew 5:5, when Jesus pronounces the "meek" to be blessed, he is calling people to enter his kingdom with this stance of humility. In Matthew 11:29, Jesus invites people to come and learn from him specifically because he is himself "gentle." In Matthew 21:5, Matthew identifies Jesus as the "gentle" messianic king promised in Zechariah 9:9. Paul uses the noun *praýtēs* several times, notably as a fruit of the Spirit (Gal 5:23) and a trait of Christ (2 Cor 10:1) to be exhibited by all Christians toward other people (Eph 4:2; Col 3:12; Tit 3:2). This Christian virtue of humility is modeled after the ministry of Christ, who served others, sacrificed himself and placed himself wholly at the Father's disposal in perfect trust and obedience.

This seems to be very much James's own concept of humility, as observed in three applications within his letter. Humility is, first, the teachability by which we are to accept "humbly" the word of God in 1:21. But James emphasizes there that humbly accepting God's word entails doing the word. Therefore humility is, second, a submissive readiness to do what the word says with *deeds done in . . . humility*. Third, James shows in our current passage that in humility toward God we will become humble (and gentle) to live at peace with each other. The opposite of humility is an unwillingness to learn and a refusal to yield: the *bitter envy and selfish ambition* that will result in *disorder*. For James, *humility* is a yielding of oneself in ready teachability and responsiveness to God's word, resulting in a good and unselfish life of peace with other people.

Compare the two terms James employs when talking about humility. In 1:9-10 he used *tapeinos* to refer to the poor person's "humble circumstances" and *tapeinōsis* to mention the rich person's reduction to a "low position." James used that term when thinking of circumstantial station in life. When speaking of the spiritual stance of teachability before God (as in 1:21 and here in 3:13), however, James uses *praýtēs*. Davids ex-

---

as distinct from the more general term for "strife" *(eris)*, also found in those lists.

The last phrase of this verse is literally "lie against the truth," as in NASB. Davids' paraphrase is "claiming to be wise when in truth one is foolish" (1982:151). Mayor is concise: "your profession therefore is a lie" (1897:123).

3:15 Though there is no literary dependence on Paul here, it is helpful to compare the Pauline usage of the same terms: *earthly (epigeios)* in contrast to *heavenly* in 1 Corinthians

plains the awkwardness of the phrase "in the humility that comes from wisdom" as due to "a preference for the Semitic-influenced genitive construction" (1982:150). But the phrase is prompted by more than a grammatical preference. James is talking about a foundational element in a person of faith.

The problem James is addressing, then, is not that there are teachers spreading false doctrine (as would often be the concern in Paul's letters). James is addressing the problem of arrogance, which can be present even when correct doctrine is being taught. His warning should bring all teachers to an abrupt halt for self-examination. I can be correct in my doctrine down to the most esoteric details; I can attain a consistency in my orthodoxy which surpasses others'; I can gain a reputation for my thorough grasp of theology and be regarded as a protector of the faith; and my teaching may still be *earthly, unspiritual, of the devil,* resulting in *disorder and every evil practice* by stirring up suspicion, slander, distrust and contention within the Christian community.

James puts the critical issue to me: Am I teaching from humility or from selfish ambition? If it is the latter, then I am even failing in the matter about which I am most proud: my grasp of truth. For then my claim to be wise is itself a falsehood. That is the sense of James's conclusion, *Do not boast about it or deny the truth.*

The Source of Wisdom The wisdom James wants his readers to seek is said to come *from heaven* (adverb *anōthen).* The term can have a local sense ("from above") or a temporal sense ("from the beginning" or "for a long time"), and it is the term used in John 3 to describe being born "again" or born "anew." In the present passage, the local sense is indicated by the verb *come down* and by the contrast to the adjective *earthly.* This sense is also consistent with James's use of the same term in 1:17, where every good and perfect gift was stated to be from above and then explicitly from the Father. Wisdom is now declared to be one

---

15:40, and *natural (psychikos)* in contrast to *spiritual* in 1 Corinthians 15:44, 46. James's third term, *daimoniōdēs* ("of the devil"), is used only here in the New Testament. Dibelius claims a Gnostic background for the term *psychikos;* but, lacking any definite Gnostic reference in the epistle, he must admit no direct relation to Gnosticism and concludes that James must be using a technically Gnostic term without adopting its technical sense (1976:211-12).

of those precious gifts that come from above.

But that divine origin makes the issue more important than mere location. James explains this by the series of three adjectives at the end of 3:15. The adjectives build upon each other in "an ascending scale of wickedness" (Mitton 1966:139). Earthly origin, in frequent New Testament usage, implies inferiority to heavenly origin. James then makes this more specific: *bitter envy and selfish ambition* are also unspiritual, denoting a natural source devoid of the supernatural Spirit of God. Finally, to leave no doubt about the evil source of the envy and ambition, James says they are literally demonic: *of the devil.* His investigation of false wisdom uncovers the same source as his investigation of the uncontrolled tongue in 3:6—they are both from hell. This is evidently the reason for the NIV's translation of *anōthen* as *from heaven* in 3:15 and 3:17 rather than "from above" as in 1:17. James's intention is to point us to a wisdom from heaven in contrast to the wisdom from hell, a wisdom far superior to any wisdom we find in ourselves naturally, and certainly superior to that which comes from demons.

Since true wisdom comes from outside ourselves and from God himself, we have to examine where our reliance is placed. It makes sense of what James has already prescribed for a life of faith. It requires of us an active prayer life—to ask for wisdom as 1:5 commands. It requires a conscious dependence on God—in the humility prescribed in 3:13. True wisdom can be had only by people who live in active reliance on God.

The Expression of Wisdom Here James gives particular content to the *deeds done in the humility that comes from wisdom.* What will genuine wisdom look like in a person's life? James describes both the false wisdom and the true, and in each case he lists identifying attitudes and actions.

Regarding the false wisdom, we can understand why *bitter envy and selfish ambition* are the characteristic attitudes: they are the opposite of the humility entailed in admitting one's need and relying on God for the wisdom one lacks. The adjective *pikros* ("bitter") describes a harsh stance of demanding to be recognized as wise, instead of being willing to learn.

3:16 Dibelius at this point analyzes the author of the passage as one who would shortsightedly renounce all intellectual controversy in order to avoid tensions in relationships (1976:212). This is a surprising assessment, given James's very forthright engaging in intellectual debate throughout the letter. It also misses the depth of James's spiritual insight. Cf.

The noun *zēlos* ("envy") reveals the motivation as jealousy. The second noun, *eritheia* ("selfish ambition"), exposes the sinful desire for personal glory—wanting the status of a teacher so that others will have to learn from me. At this point it is valuable to remember that James has been addressing people who gather in Christian assemblies and who function as teachers in the church. His words shine a spotlight on the craving for self-glorification which moves even much of our work in "Christian ministry."

The resulting actions of false wisdom are also identified: *disorder and every evil practice*. James ever sees the connection between inward stance and outward practice. Genuine faith will manifest itself in deeds, and the same principle holds true in the contrasting demonic realm. The false wisdom that is of the devil will manifest itself in practices of disorder and evil. This is simply the application of the principle James learned from Jesus: by their fruit you will recognize them. When self-glorification is at the heart of Christian ministry by church members, those Christians will eventually become sowers of disorder, contention and other evil practices in the church.

Finally, the expression of true wisdom in the church is presented with the characteristic attitudes and resulting actions listed in 3:17-18. Three emphases stand out in the way James states this contrast with false wisdom.

First, in 3:17, James is deliberate to state a foremost characteristic of the wisdom from above: it is *first of all pure* and only then the other qualities. His term *pure* speaks of holiness and provides the immediate contrast to *every evil practice*. It reflects the high moral sensibility that we have found in James all along; he does not descend from it now. It is never a sentimental humanitarianism or an amoral pragmatism that motivates James; it isn't just that bitter envy hurts people or that selfish ambition does not work. The first and foremost reason for valuing wisdom is that it will lead people to do what is morally right. Today's popular relativism makes it all the more urgent that Christians learn James's passion for purity. Will we do what is wise *first of all* because it is right?

James's noun *disorder* with the adjective of the same root translated "unstable" in 1:8 and "restless" in 3:8. In contrast to this pattern, the humility of true wisdom will lead to peace in 3:17-18.

Second, in 3:17, James lists other attitudes and behavior of the wisdom from above. *Peace-loving, considerate, submissive, full of mercy and good fruit, impartial and sincere* fill out a picture of humility put into practice. The first three of these traits are terms that James uses only here in his letter; they describe people who can yield status, who care for others and who are willing to submit and learn from others—all in contrast to the bitterness, envy and selfish ambition of false spirituality. The remaining traits weave some of James's earlier instruction into this picture. *Full of . . . good fruit* is reminiscent of the recent imagery in 3:12. *Full of mercy* reminds James's readers of his urging to be merciful in 2:13. The terms for *impartial* and *sincere* are both built upon the root for *judge* (verb *krinō*, noun *kritēs)*—an important concept already in the epistle.

Third, James summarizes in 3:18 (literally): "The fruit of righteousness is sown in peace by those who make peace." This connects peacemaking and righteousness (cf. Jesus in Mt 5:9-10) and suddenly reveals why the *disorder* in 3:16 is so abhorrent to James. The opposite of the disorder is not a morally neutral order but a morally significant peace. James wants peace for the church because peace is the context in which right-eousness can flourish. This is the positive side of what James said in 1:20, that human anger does not bring about the righteous life that God desires. Again, James writes out of a passion for righteousness.

What Causes Fights Among You? (4:1-3) The false wisdom that comes from envy and selfish ambition produces disorder (3:16). To put it bluntly, it leads to fighting. James therefore carries his argument forth-rightly to this next issue: *What causes fights and quarrels among you?* The term for *fights* is *polemos;* in other contexts (as in Heb 11:34), it refers to actual armed conflict and so carries a violent image. The term for *quarrels* is *machē;* it is used in other literature only for battles without material weapons and so refers more to angry disputes. James uses the terms as a pair to make his question inclusive and pointed. It is not to be avoided.

3:17 *Impartial:* Because this verse's focus is wisdom's effect on how we treat each other, the NIV's "impartial" is preferred over the NASB's "unwavering" (though both meanings are otherwise possible for the term).

The fighting among Christians which James is addressing is an outrageous evil. Yet I have seen it accepted complacently; one church member who saw a church breaking into factions even commented cheerfully, "Oh, I love a church fight!" In reality it is a tragedy which can cripple a church's internal ministries and external witness for years before a measure of healing and purification becomes evident.

James is not talking about disagreements—the healthy conflicts that should be expected in a church whose ministries are expanding. He is writing about fighting, which is "earthly, unspiritual, of the devil" in origin, and he will call its perpetrators "you adulterous people" (4:4). So serious a crime calls for a serious response. When we Christians find ourselves embroiled in fights with each other, we should examine what we are doing in the light of this paragraph. James gives us great help by answering three questions that are hard for us to face.

What Is the Fighting Really About? (4:1) Honestly facing what James says here is one of the most decisive steps of faith in all of a person's life. For it requires tearing oneself away from self-justification and redirecting oneself toward self-examination. This is a violent uprooting of our selfishness. We try to justify our role in fights in terms of the high ideals, the critical issues and the injured rights we are supposedly defending. James does not entertain any such talk. He drives right to the fact that the fights are, at bottom, about personal *desires*. His point is reminiscent of 1:14, where he refused to allow excuses for temptation. People are tempted when they are enticed by their own "evil desire." There the term was *epithymia;* now in 4:1 the term for "desires" is *hēdonē*, which speaks more distinctly of pleasures. We get into fights because of pleasures we desire for ourselves. An important self-examining question for Christians in conflict is "What personal desire am I trying to protect or to gain?"

James does not specify examples of the desires. What he does say could refer to conflict in group relationships, such as within a church: inflexibility about issues (from a desire to have one's own way), maneu-

---

3:18 Most commentators agree with this understanding of the genitive *of righteousness* as denoting the definition of the *fruit,* so that the *fruit* does not refer to something that springs from the righteousness, but rather consists of righteousness. Therefore, peacemakers provide the context for righteousness to happen.

vering for position of authority (from a desire for status and admiration within the community) or criticizing others (from a desire to make oneself look good). It is equally applicable in individual relationships, such as a marital conflict: constantly exchanging hurtful words (from a desire to get even) or carrying out sexual infidelity (from a desire for selfish pleasure or simply a desire for another spouse). All of these happen in Christian churches and Christian marriages; they are all immoral.

James says the desires *battle within you* (with the verb in participial form, for we have a continuing problem here). Against whom are they battling? We should not be too quick to assume that James means our good and evil desires are battling against each other. Peter's parallel use of the same verb depicts the evil desires as warring not with each other but against the Christian's own soul (1 Pet 2:11). It is likely that this was the common apostolic concept and is James's own notion here. It means he is not sympathizing with the readers' internal conflicts but warning that those who fight are cooperating in their own self-destruction.

How Do the Desires Lead to Fighting? (4:2) A second way we justify our role in fights is by rationalizing the moral impurity of our actions. James's point in 4:2 is, quite simply, that our desires lead to fighting because of our immorality in trying to grasp what we want. The verb "you want" *epithymeō* at the beginning of this verse does not automatically signify evil desires; with the same verb Luke has Jesus desiring to eat the Passover with his disciples in Luke 22:15. But the surrounding context here in James is clearly negative, and the verb recalls James's theme of "evil desire" *epithymia* in 1:14. Thus the NASB translates it "you lust."

What is complicated about this verse is the determination of the correct punctuation and the resulting structure intended by James (since the ancient manuscripts have no punctuation to guide us). One tradition perceives James to be thinking in a series of clauses coming in pairs with contrasting positive and negative verbs. This is reflected in the KJV as a series of three such pairs:

4:2 There is some manuscript witness to support Dibelius's and Davids's addition of *kai*

Ye lust, and have not:

ye kill, and desire to have, and cannot obtain:

ye fight and war, yet ye have not, because ye ask not.

The NIV follows the same pattern. A more comprehensive version of this structure is advocated by Dibelius (1976:218) and Davids (1982:157-158) as a series of four pairs extending into 4:3. It could be outlined (translating literally):

You want,

 and you do not have.

You murder and covet,

 and you cannot obtain.

You quarrel and fight,

 [and] you do not have because you do not ask.

You ask,

 and you do not receive because you ask wickedly. . . .

In either variation, this view focuses on the pairs of verbs, a positive verb followed by a negated verb, as the guiding thought in James's meaning. If so, then James's intent is to describe the pattern of frustrated desires. The chief grammatical difficulty with this view is that it requires a key role for *kai* ("and" in an antithetical sense, similar to "but") to form each of the contrasts and therefore has to overcome the absence of *kai* from the third pair. Dibelius is willing to conclude that a *kai* must have been in the original text (1976:218), and Davids considers this a real possibility (1982:158).

A second way to punctuate the verse (preferred by Mayor 1897:131; Mitton 1966:147; Laws 1980:169; Moo 1985:140; Kistemaker 1986:131 and others) is reflected in the RSV, TEV and NASB. This view recognizes the first two contrasts of positive and negated verbs but ends the series where the text lacks the *kai* to continue the grammatical pattern. This view discerns two parallel statements, each asserting a cause and effect:

You want and do not have: (so) you murder.

And you covet and cannot obtain: (so) you quarrel and fight.

If this is James's meaning, then his intent is to draw a definite connection

to the verse. The evidence is far from conclusive, but it is at least "respectable" (Dibelius 1976:218).

between desires and behavior. This has James making a clearer moral exhortation, warning that Christians' covetous desires lead to murderous fighting. It leaves the remainder of 4:2, with 4:3, as James's further exhortation on the matter of asking God for what they want.

This second rendering of 4:2 is to be preferred for two reasons. First, it avoids the grammatical difficulty of the missing *kai.* Second, the questions in 3:13, 4:1 and 4:4 are setting the outline of this section of the epistle, and the clear moral exhortation fits the context perfectly as James's answer to the question posed in 4:1. The conclusion, *you quarrel and fight,* is even stated with verbs sharing the same roots with the two nouns (in opposite order, *fights and quarrels)* in the initial question of 4:1.

Many commentators have found the verb *kill* (more precisely "murder") in 4:2 incongruous—too extreme for the context, especially when followed in sequence by the less violent sin of coveting (as in the rendering adopted by Dibelius and Davids, above). As a result, some have agreed with a conjecture dating back to Erasmus that the verb *murder (phoneuete)* is a textual error that was *envy (phthoneite)* in James's original text. (Cf. Mayor 1897:131; Dibelius 1976:217; Adamson 1976:168.) This makes the reading more acceptable to our hearing, but that is not sufficient reason to conclude that the text is corrupt; it is better practice of inductive study to see if sense can be made of the text and to adjust our hearing to the message. In the first place, there is no manuscript evidence for the theory of a textual error here. In the second place, this is not the only time James warns his readers about the sin of murder; he mentions it (with this same verb) in 2:11 and 5:6. Third, the frequent parallels we have found with Jesus' teaching in the Sermon on the Mount make it not at all improbable for James to be thinking with Jesus' categories, as in Matthew 5:21-22 where sins of hatred and insult are treated in the same category as murder. It is very likely, then, that *murder* did not strike James as incongruous at all. Moo wisely rejects the attempts to change or to dilute the term and counsels that "it is simplest to take 'murder' straightforwardly and to regard it as that extreme to

---

4:2-3 Many have tried to discern distinct meanings in James's shifting of the verb *ask (aiteō)* from middle voice to active voice and then back to middle. It has proven difficult to make a case; Adamson (1976:169) and Moo (1985:142) reject such attempts. On the other

which frustrated desire, if not checked, may lead" (1985:141).

The purpose of 4:2, then, is to explain the answer James has just declared in the second half of 4:1 to the question he posed in the first half of 4:1. By the parallel structure James implies that quarrels and fights are like murder, and he draws a direct connection between unfulfilled coveting (the cause) and murderous fighting (the effect). James is laying bare the immorality of the motivation for our fights. We fight because we are coveting and are not able to get what we covet.

What Is It That Is Going Wrong? *(4:2-3)* Even with the origin of the fights identified as our own desires, and even with the immorality of certain actions exposed, there is yet a third way in which we justify our role in fights—by claiming necessity. "I had to do that, or else _____ would have happened!" This last justification is rendered indefensible by the availability of another course of action: prayer.

James makes his point in two stages, and each stage reflects a theological premise he has asserted in chapter 1. First, in 4:2, *You do not have, because you do not ask.* (The NIV adds *God.*) The theological premise is that God is graciously generous (stated in 1:5), by which James is convinced that one may ask God and rely on him for what one needs. This emphasis on prayer is another manifestation of James's consistent reliance on God's grace (refuting the portrayal of James as self-reliantly focused on works).

However, God is also pure, and he will have nothing to do with evil (as asserted in 1:13, 17). This is the basis for the second part of James's point, stated in 4:3: a warning that one may not expect God to answer prayer when one's motives are wicked. He warns against asking *kakōs*, wrongly or wickedly, which the NIV paraphrases as *with wrong motives.* Adamson considers it stronger language than the KJV's "amiss" and paraphrases it "Your praying is corrupt" (1976:168). Then James explains the wrong motives: they ask in order to spend on their *pleasures,* emphasized by the same noun *hēdonē* translated *desires* in 4:1.

The conclusion for us is that our fights reveal a wrong relationship with God which is manifest in our prayer lives. Either we do not pray,

hand, the shifting voice may be more than merely stylistic balance. It may be the result of deliberate reference to the teaching of Jesus in Matthew 7:7. See comments by Adamson (1976:169) and Davids (1982:160).

because we do not trust in God's grace, or we pray with wrong motives, because we do not follow God's purity.

In all this, James is again taking his Lord at his word and applying it in full belief to a practical situation of life. Like the references to judgment in 3:13-18, James's flow of thought parallels that of Jesus in the Sermon on the Mount.

Matthew 7:1-12	James 3:13—4:3
Do not judge.	Do not practice false wisdom (which includes judging).
Example: humility to see one's own faults, in contrast to hypocrisy.	Examples: humility and not hypocrisy.
Ask (instead of judging).	Ask (instead of fighting).

Don't You Know the Choice to Be Made? (4:4-12) As James poses (in 4:4) the third question of this section, I paraphrase it in order to display the heart of the matter. James has placed the problems of selfish ambition and fighting under his spotlight in 3:13-18 and 4:1-3. Now he addresses what to do about the problems. In light of the preceding paragraphs, a choice must be made between friendship with God and friendship with the world.

The Significance of the Choice (4:4-6) The presentation of this choice extends the parallel with Matthew 7 one step further. After inviting his hearers to ask the Father for what they needed, Jesus confronted them with a choice between wide and narrow ways leading to opposite ends—destruction and life (Mt 7:13-14). Now James's thought runs in

---

4:4 *You adulterous people* is a feminine noun here; hence the NASB's "you adulteresses." A textual tradition with much inferior support added the masculine noun *adulterers* in an attempt to make the address more inclusive. This was unnecessary, since James was probably not trying to address only women at this point. The most likely explanation for James's choice of the feminine noun is that he was employing the Old Testament imagery of the people of Israel as God's bride in the covenant, which made them adulteresses in their

the same direction; his purpose in this paragraph is to impress on his readers the importance and urgency of the choice.

First, the importance of the choice is clarified by the simplicity of the alternatives. It becomes a matter of whether we want friendship with the world or friendship with God. This use of *world* to encompass the patterns of human life contrary to God's will was apparently common enough in Christian circles for James to expect his readers to understand; Paul would use the term in a very similar sense. James thereby cuts through the complications and subtleties of our secondary goals and defines the matter in terms of primary values. Whether we will be described more accurately by 3:16 or by 3:17 will be determined by whether we want the world or God.

Second, the seriousness of the one alternative is made clear with shocking terms: *you adulterous people, hatred toward God, an enemy of God.* It all sounds so offensive that we are tempted to think he must be addressing non-Christians rhetorically (similar to his address of the rich oppressors in 5:1). Here, however, he must be addressing his Christian readers, for his immediate message is still too closely connected to the hypocritical wisdom and the fights and quarrels *among you* from 3:13 and 4:1. But he is again warning those who call themselves Christians that they may be false Christians who are really enemies of God.

James simply writes with a stronger conviction of the seriousness of sin than most of us are willing to hold. In fact he writes with a sense of moral outrage. Consider Davids's rendering of the beginning of this paragraph: " 'Adulteresses!' the author cries" (1982:160). We should accept James's terms, learn from his acute sense of moral right and wrong, and apply it to ourselves in fear of the judgment that comes to any who are not true Christians. Harboring bitter envy and selfish ambition, with the actions of fighting and quarreling, makes us adulterous people who are treating God with hatred and enmity.

---

unfaithfulness. There may also be another reference to Jesus' teaching, as he adopted this same image (Mt 12:39; Mk 8:38).

4:6 Cf. 1 Peter 5:5-11, which quotes the same proverb and includes several of the themes in James 4—5: humbling oneself before God, being lifted up by God, trusting God for what one needs, resisting the devil, enduring suffering and receiving grace from God. The more common scholarly conclusion is that Peter was drawing from James's epistle rather than the reverse. Cf. Guthrie 1990:797.

Third, the powerful reality of the other alternative is offered so that we will not miss it by indifference. The point of James's references to Scripture in 4:5 and 4:6 is to persuade his readers to choose God unreservedly instead of the world because God himself is jealous that they make this choice and is furthermore gracious toward them to welcome their humble commitment. Contrary to the NIV, *God* should be understood as the subject of the clause in the scriptural reference of 4:5 as well as 4:6.

However, 4:5 is one of the most problematic verses in the letter. We would be helped in determining the meaning if a definite Old Testament origin could be identified, but there is no verse like the last half of 4:5. In the absence of a definite reference by which to establish the meaning, two major understandings have been proposed.

One possibility is reflected in the NIV. Here the subject of the clause is *spirit, pneuma,* taken to mean the human spirit which God *caused to live in us* from creation. This is the spirit that *envies intensely,* so James is reminding his readers that human nature tends toward the envy and jealousy about which he has been warning since 3:14. The arguments in favor of this rendering are as follows.

1. Linguistic. James says literally that this spirit "yearns to jealousy." This verb *epipothei* is never elsewhere applied to God, and the noun *phthonon* is consistently negative in other instances.

2. Contextual. A reference to human envy would be consistent with what James has been emphasizing in the larger passage.

3. Logical. The next scriptural reference, in 4:6, would provide logical contrast by stating that God gives more grace to overcome this human tendency toward envy.

While these are worthy arguments, an alternative reflected in the NASB and the NIV margin is preferable. Here the subject of the verb is the understood *he,* referring to God. The object of his yearning is *the spirit he caused to live in us.* This spirit could be either the created human spirit or the Holy Spirit given to Christians, though the former seems more likely because it is consistent with James's only other reference to "spirit" in 2:26. In either case, the meaning is that God jealously desires us to belong wholeheartedly to him. (Even if one takes the Jerusalem Bible or Living Bible rendering with "spirit" referring to the Holy Spirit as the subject of the clause, one is left with the same meaning: that God jealously desires us.)

The arguments making this understanding of 4:5 preferable are the following.

1. Linguistic. Two terms for "envy," *phthonos* and *zēlos,* are sometimes interchangeable, and *zēlos* is used elsewhere of God. James would be choosing this more unusual use of *phthonos* simply for stylistic contrast, since he recently used *zēlos* negatively of human envy in 3:14 and 3:16.

2. Grammatical. It is more natural to have the same subject for the two verbs *yearns* and *caused to live.*

3. Contextual. An emphasis on God's jealousy for righteousness in us is equally consistent with what James has emphasized in the letter.

4. Logical. A reference to human envy here would be awkward, because it would seem to ignore the point to which James has come in 4:4 and would instead return to his point in 4:1-3. On the other hand, a reference to God's jealousy fits the flow of thought well. The point of 4:4 logically raises the objection "How does friendship with the world make me an enemy of God?" James would be answering this in 4:5 by reminding us of God's jealousy. Then 4:6 would follow as a reminder of God's grace to the humble, which protects us from being overwhelmed by God's jealousy.

If this second alternative is the correct understanding, then the Old Testament Scripture James has in mind is probably a theme rather than a particular verse—the frequent theme of God's jealousy for undivided devotion from his people (e.g., Ex 20:5). The reference in 4:6 is more specific and definite, quoting Proverbs 3:34 about God's personal stance in regard to the choice before us. He is neither passive nor indifferent but quite active in opposing the proud and giving grace to the humble. The proverb is also reflected in Jesus' teaching in Luke 14:11 and 18:14. It fits James's context perfectly here, as it reminds the readers succinctly of the two alternatives James has taken trouble to portray since 3:13— pride and humility.

Altogether, the paragraph of 4:4-6 emphasizes God's requirement of Christians: "a total, unreserved, unwavering allegiance" to God rather than to the world (Moo 1985:144). It equally emphasizes that this requirement is not an achievement by which the proud can earn God's friendship, for the call to devotion is based on God's extension of *grace to the humble.* Grace is what opens the way for the steps prescribed in the next two paragraphs.

Steps to Be Taken Toward God (4:7-10) James has a problem: his readers are being corrupted by *bitter envy and selfish ambition* leading to *fights and quarrels.* He has a goal: to help them learn to live in love and at peace with each other. Therefore he has a prescription for them: repentance. That is what his ten imperatives provide—a forceful call to repentance as the requisite to love and peace in the community.

There is a clear structure to this paragraph. *Submit yourselves to God* states the theme, which is indicated by the insertion of *then* to be an application drawn immediately from the preceding Proverbs 3:34. *Humble yourselves before the Lord* is also drawn from Proverbs 3:34 by repetition of the term for *humble* in verb form. These first and last of the ten imperatives are intended to be synonymous, the former introducing and the latter summarizing the theme. In between, the imperatives flow in three couplets.

Resist the devil, and he will flee from you.
Come near to God and he will come near to you.

Wash your hands, you sinners,
and purify your hearts, you double-minded.

Grieve, mourn and wail.
Change your laughter to mourning and your joy to gloom.

James's description of becoming humble or submissive before God, then, begins with a willful rejection of and opposition to the devil, complemented by a deliberate choosing of God instead of the devil. It reflects the biblical worldview of God's enmity with evil and the choice this requires of us. God opposes or resists *(antitassō)* the proud in 4:6; now in 4:7 we are to oppose or *resist (anthistēmi)* the devil. The verb *anthistēmi* has the middle sense of "set oneself against" and so emphasizes the Christian's deliberately chosen personal stance. The contrasting action that we are to take toward God is to *come near.* Thus James has put this entire section in terms of knowing the choice to be made: friendship with the world or friendship with God, opposing the devil or opposing God.

Along with the presentation of this choice comes a pair of promises to encourage James's readers. *The devil . . . will flee from you.* Meanwhile, *God . . . will come near to you.* Just as there is a continuity between God's stance toward the devil and our own (opposing him), so now there is a continuity between our reverse action toward God and his action toward us (drawing near). The same verb *engizō* identifies our act and God's act of drawing near, to make definite that God will not give himself to us any less than we give ourselves to him. This is an assurance of God's readiness and availability.

The middle couplet requires a sincere purifying of one's life, since both verbs *(katharizō* and *hagnizō)* emphasize a moral and ceremonial cleansing, and since the two objects *(your hands . . . your hearts)* complement each other for external and internal cleansing. The essential connection between external washing and inward purifying is already an Old Testament theme in James's background (Deut 10:16; Is 1:15-17). James may also be prompted by Jesus' own teaching on washing of hands and purification within (Mk 7). An evidence of the unity of thought in James's letter is his reference to the *double-minded* in 4:8. It is the same term as in 1:8, where the double-minded man is condemned as "unstable," *akatastatos.* This is the evil James abhors in 3:16 as the "disorder," *akatastasia,* resulting from selfish ambition. From the very beginning of the epistle, James is giving a consistent picture of authentic Christian faith in practice.

The third couplet describes deep and acute sorrow—not merely regret over mistakes but actual grieving, mourning and wailing over one's sin. The three verbs, in order, make vivid impressions: *talaipōreō,* a state of being miserable or wretched; *pentheō,* the great sadness of mourning; and *klaiō,* a vehement or bitter weeping. Again James is calling for what Jesus prescribed in the Sermon on the Mount (Mt 5:4, using a participle of the verb *pentheō).* The seriousness of sin is unmistakable here, and Christians today who lack that sense of seriousness about sin are weakened and corrupted. Tasker sees the importance of this application: "When the Christian compromises with the world and is *double minded,* it is a sure sign that his sense of the gravity of sin has become blunted" (1983:95). James is unapologetic and authoritative in his command to such a person: *Change your laughter to mourning and your joy to gloom.* We should not be afraid today to call for such deeply felt repentance.

The whole paragraph (not just the third couplet, as in Davids 1982:167) is a portrait of repentance. Repentance is an act of humble submission to God which includes a choice to resist the devil and to draw near to God, a commitment to moral purity both externally and internally, and a genuine remorse for one's sin.

I would love to know how James's message was received in his day. James is properly described as a "prophet-pastor" (Webster 1991:22), and I wonder whether he sounded too much like the Old Testament prophets to be very popular. He may be recalling passages like Amos's prophecies of wailing and mourning (5:16; 8:10). Amos was ordered to go away and stop prophesying. James's message is not the kind of spiritual direction most people want to hear today; the church is being pressured to rely on counsel that is only affirming, programs that are merely entertaining and music that is always upbeat. Yet the problems James has addressed require a submission that is humbling, a resistance that is demanding, an attitude that is sorrowful and life changes that are radical.

At the same time, these steps are reinforced with encouraging promises: *the devil . . . will flee from you, God . . . will come near to you,* and *the Lord . . . will lift you up.* Such promises certainly direct us to a reliance on God rather than our good works. The assurance that God *will lift you up* is not explicitly defined. However, since *submit yourselves, then, to God* is the direct application from Proverbs 3:34, and since *humble yourselves before the Lord* restates that first imperative to summarize the paragraph, the promise of being lifted up probably refers back to the promise of grace in 4:6. From the context of the intervening imperatives, James would be telling us to expect that God will come near to forgive sin, to restore joy and to strengthen the repentant sinner to live in purity and righteousness. Seeing the requirement of radical life changes in 4:7-

---

4:11-12 Cf. Motyer's outline of these two verses, which, he says, tell us (a) how we should regard each other (as brothers), (b) how we should regard the law (as authoritative

10 expands our appreciation for that preceding promise in 4:6—*he gives us more grace*. Motyer comments, "What comfort there is in this verse! It tells us that God is tirelessly on our side. He never falters in respect of our needs, he always has *more grace* at hand for us. He is never less than sufficient, he always has more and yet more to give" (1985:150).

It would be accurate to say that James's entire letter is instructing us to live in reliance on God's grace. That sounded tame enough until James applied it to actual practice, such as ending hatred and fights. Now we see just how radical this proposition of grace-reliance really is. How do we manage not to curse people who treat us with such hostility and injustice that cursing them is exactly what we want to do? The answer is the course James has described: examination of one's own desires, choice to want God instead of the world, repentance for sin and reliance on God's grace.

Ralph Bell, an associate evangelist with the Billy Graham Evangelistic Association, is a godly man who tells of learning grace-reliance in a deeply personal way. Bell is a Canadian-born black man who lives and ministers in the United States. As a young man, he struggled with experiences of racial insults and discrimination. Being so treated by fellow Christians, who were disobeying James's instructions about impartiality, was especially hurtful. Bell shared his struggles with his mother, who counseled him to keep his eyes on Jesus, because Jesus would never disappoint him. As he sought to apply that advice, he began to find the grace to see others' racism as their problem. He further sought grace from God to purify his own life of hatred toward those who mistreated him. In James's terms, Ralph Bell humbled himself before the Lord, and he found himself being lifted up by the grace of God to be able to love his enemies. How does one love hostile and hurtful people? The answer is supernaturally, by relying on the grace that God gives to the humble.

Steps to Be Taken Toward Others (4:11-12) James could end this section at this point, having directed his readers with steps toward God. He is unrelenting, however, in making the explicit application to the problem with which he began—the problem of anger, impure speech

over us) and (c) how we should regard God (as the only Lawgiver and Judge) (1985:157-59).

and judging within the Christian community. He introduced this topic as early as 1:19. He focused on the aspects of judging and discriminating in 2:1-13. He returned to the issue of impure speech in 3:1 and specifically the problems of cursing and envy and fighting through chapter 3 and the beginning of chapter 4. Now he drives home his call to a life of faith in personal relationships. Here the coherence of James's letter is again evident, contrary to some commentators who see it as disconnected, self-contained pieces (e.g., Dibelius 1976:207-8; Laws 1980:186; and even Davids 1982:168-69).

First comes the pointed command *Do not slander one another.* The verb is *katalaleō* ("speak against"), which could include destructive verbal attacks, gossip behind another person's back and false accusations. Such offenses are not to be practiced among Christians.

Then James repeats this first verb in *anyone who speaks against his brother* but adds a second verb *or judges him* to make clear that the speaking against is a form of judging. Judging then becomes the real focus of these verses, and the remainder of the two verses is explanation of why judging is so wrong.

The fundamental notion of "judging" with the verb *krinō* is one of distinguishing or making a distinction. It is certainly right to distinguish between good and evil; James himself is not timid about condemning people's evil behavior. Yet he warns against judging. To see what he means, we need to draw together the line of thought James has pursued about judging all through the letter. We must begin with James's emphasis on faith, because that is still the unifying theme of the letter.

□ 1:1-18. Christians begin with a stance of faith. This faith could be summarized from 1:1-18 as confidence in God's mercy. James emphasized God's mercy with several examples: God is faithful to complete in us what we lack (1:3-4); God is generous to give to us without finding fault (1:5); God is kind to exalt us even in humble circumstances (1:9); God is reliable for us even when our own evil desires would entice us into temptation (1:13); God is, in fact, the gracious and consistent giver of every good gift (1:17-18).

□ 1:2-6. Faith in this mercy of God has radical implications for our lives. The first implication is that because of faith in God's mercy, Christians face trials with joy. They believe God instead of wavering with doubts *(diakrinō)*. If they act on the basis of doubts, they are distinguishing (or judging) a basis for life other than God's mercy.

□ 2:1-5. A second implication is that Christians are certainly not to practice partiality toward others, for then they would be discriminating *(diakrinō)* and making themselves judges *(kritēs)*. They would be treating people as if wealth instead of God's mercy were the factor determining people's value.

□ 2:8-13. The royal law commands us to be merciful. If we treat others with judgmental discrimination instead of mercy, we sin and will be judged *(krinō)* by that law. Our lives are based on God's mercy, by which we escape judgment and receive salvation; now in the law that we obey, our lives are again based on mercy. So both in being saved and in living the Christian life, "mercy triumphs over judgment!"

□ 3:1-2, 13-18. Everyone stumbles and so is vulnerable to judgment. But because of faith in God's mercy, a Christian will act in humility. A Christian will be *impartial (adiakritos,* "without judging") *and sincere (anhypokritos,* "without hypocrisy").

Drawing upon this background, in 4:11-12 James would now help us avoid the sin of judging. He instructs us in regard to three relationships that form the context for our lives. In each case, judging is inherently contradictory to the true nature of the relationship.

First mentioned is the relationship with each other. James chooses significant terms to identify the ones his readers would be judging: *brother* in 4:11 and then *neighbor* at the end of 4:12. Jesus used the term *brother* in his instruction against judging (Mt 7:1-5), and he used the term *neighbor* in the great commandment to love (Mt 22:39). In light of all that James has written so far about God's mercy toward us, these terms now come as reminders that our family bonds in God's mercy are violated when we who have received mercy turn to judge each other; and God's goodness to us is treated with contempt when we show judgment instead of mercy to our neighbors.

Second is the relationship with the law. James insists that we are to be doers under the law, which is contradicted when we try to be judges over the law. The "law" *(nomos)* could refer to the Old Testament command in Leviticus 19:16, which prohibits slander, and to Leviticus 19:18, "Love your neighbor as yourself," which James quoted in 2:8.

Given James's reverence for the teachings of Jesus as the royal law of the kingdom, it is likely that he also has in mind Jesus' specific command against judging in Matthew 7:1 and Jesus' own quoting of Leviticus 19:18. James's point is that if we accept God's mercy through Christ, we place ourselves under Christ's law, which commands mercy. If we then judge others instead of being merciful toward their faults, we are rejecting that law and so setting ourselves up as judges over the law. This contradicts our proper stance as recipients of grace—we are to be doers under the law.

The third relationship is with God. *One (heis)* as the subject of the sentence emphasizes that there is *only* one who is *Lawgiver and Judge.* When we judge each other, we are contradicting that fact. This is a revealing insight into our hearts. In judging people, what we really want is to take God's place. The United States government is arranged in judicial, legislative and executive branches, with a careful separation and balance of powers. In the realm of personal relationships, however, judging and lawgiving operate together; the one who judges another person is presuming to have authority to set the law or standard by which the other person is judged. Judging is an attempt to be in control as God is in control, which has been our rebellious desire ever since the serpent told Eve she could be "like God, knowing good and evil." Our sins of judging are attempts to set ourselves not only over the law but over the Lawgiver as well.

Now we can summarize. What James has been prescribing is a life of faith that has two facets: confidence in God's grace and passion for God's righteousness. The confidence and the passion are complementary responses to God's judgment and mercy. God's mercy triumphs over judgment on our behalf; therefore we may be confident in relying on grace. However, we who have genuinely grasped grace will become all the more eager to grasp righteousness, realizing that our lack of righteousness so nearly brought us to disaster in the fearful judgment of God. Once one has humbly sought grace for escape from judgment (4:10), it becomes unthinkable to set oneself up as judge over a neighbor (4:11). It is part of a single stance before God to submit to him for his grace (4:7) and to submit to him for his law; one cannot be both a judge over the law and a doer under the law (4:11). James is showing us a well-

integrated faith in Christ as both merciful Savior to be trusted and righteous Lord to be obeyed.

Applications for the Church Today Douglas Webster is very helpful
in telling us to see James as a "spiritual director" for the church. James's
counsel for the church goes beyond superficialities and guides the
church into holiness in its internal relationships. "True spiritual direction
not only challenges; it comforts" (Webster 1991:18), and this section of
the epistle is a fine example. James is faithful to confront sinful motives
and evil practices, and he is equally clear about the promise of God's
grace.

There should be no denying our need for James's instruction. It is all
too easy to find examples such as the troubled church I described at the
beginning of this section. Unspiritual wisdom, selfish fighting and un-
kind judging are all too common within our churches. Christians' experience of this is disheartening and disillusioning, undermining the health
and vision of our churches. James helps us recognize the source of all
this in our own sinfulness—not to leave us in deeper despair over it, but
that we may humble ourselves before the Lord and find grace for change.
Contemporary teaching from this passage must not be timid about confronting the specific sins; the harm being done to the church is too large
to avoid it. At the same time, teaching from this passage must not omit
the promise of the generous grace of God; our need for that grace is too
desperate.

We have found *judging* in James's text to refer to the act of setting
oneself up as a judge and lawgiver, as if one had the authority to determine what is right or wrong about another person's life. I observe it to
happen in the church today with particular frequency in three areas:
judging the motives behind others' words or actions in church business,
judging how others spend money and judging how others are rearing
their children. Judgmentalism needs to be confronted in specific areas
such as these, so that we can see how we are doing it. We make judgments about others when we have listened and understood too little
about them. James wrote earlier in the epistle, "Everyone should be
quick to listen, slow to speak and slow to become angry."

Whether it is studied in a small group, taught in a class or preached to a congregation, this word of God has been properly used if it leads the particular Christian community to repentance in personal relationships. This repentance will include several components:

1. Self-examination. James's word, properly applied, will move people to cut through self-justifying claims and accepted patterns to look beneath the surface. We will scrutinize our ways of relating. How are our relationships functioning? What are our underlying attitudes and motives toward each other?

2. Evaluation by God's standards. James's emphasis is on being doers of the law, and he identifies specifics of the law, including purity, peace, submissiveness, mercy, impartiality and sincerity. These will be taken seriously as the standards of holiness in application of this word. For example, in our church one of our relationship mottoes is "Talk *to* each other, not *about* each other."

3. Change. In repentance according to James's message, people will be growing. There should be an increasing measure of the specifics of the royal law in the way people treat each other.

4. Grace-reliance. It is woven throughout the passage that we need to learn to rely on God. God's grace gives wisdom from above; our fights are unnecessary and evil because they express our self-reliance instead of grace-reliance; God gives grace to the humble. The trait of humility before God and before each other is therefore emphasized repeatedly. Grace-reliance is the most far-reaching, life-changing, radical stance we need to learn.

□ Patience Until the Lord's Coming (4:13—5:11)

To what extent is your life directed by the knowledge that Christ is coming back? Much of our thinking and behavior is shaped by what we can see of present circumstances or past events. Yet Scripture speaks forcefully of Christ's return as a fact that should be directing how we live now. Christians are to be motivated by the certainty of this future event.

When I had been a Christian less than a year, I attended a conference for the InterVarsity chapters in our state. Among those in my cabin was a student from another campus who made a lasting impression on my life through one passing remark. During a discussion in the cabin about the events surrounding Christ's return, this student suddenly commented, "What a great day that will be!" He spoke briefly but with such fervor that I could not forget his words. I realized that the return of Christ was a fact of knowledge for me but had not become a moving force on my emotions, attitudes and behavior.

James writes now about a forward-looking stance of faith in which the realities of the future affect outlooks and behavior in the present. His flow of thought can be outlined in three sections evident in his three addresses in 4:13, 5:1 and 5:7. The first two begin with identical words, *age nyn* ("now listen" in NIV, or "come now" in the more literal NASB), and are negative in thrust. In the third section, James returns to his loving address, *brothers*, along with *then, oun,* showing that his thrust here will be his conclusion from what has preceded. The three sections are thus tied together and can be summarized as: "don't be arrogant; don't be materialistic; instead, be patient."

Don't Be Arrogant (4:13-17) The continuity from the preceding passage is the theme of humility. Humility is characteristic of the truly wise (3:13); it is the stance for receiving God's grace (4:6); it is commanded in the description of repentance (4:10); the opposite of humility is implied in the question immediately preceding this new passage: "But you—who are you to judge your neighbor?" It is natural for James now to confront directly the opposite of humility, which we would call arrogance.

Dibelius emphatically dismisses any literary connection between this passage and the preceding verses (1976:230). Davids also misses the continuity of theme and sees no direct connection to 4:1-12 (1982:171). He is perhaps overly distracted by the question of the identity of the *hoi legontes* ("you who say"). He and Laws perceive two distinct classes being addressed by James: merchants in 4:13-17 and wealthy landlords in 5:1-6. Laws concludes from the term *emporeusometha* ("carry on business") and from the rhetorical address "Come now!" that James is speaking about a distinct class of traveling traders who at this stage would not likely have been a part of the church in sufficient numbers to be singled out as a group of Christians (1980:190). If so, James would be addressing rhetorically people outside the church for the benefit of the Christians who are actually reading his letter. This is a possibility, since James refrains from calling them "brothers" and makes no distinctly Christian references about them. On the other hand, Davids believes James reserves the term *plousioi* for rhetorically addressing the "rich" who are not part of the church (as in 5:1). In this view, James's avoidance of the term *plousioi* in 4:13 means he is there addressing people within the Christian community.

Though Davids underestimates the continuity of the humility theme, this continuity actually supports his view of the identity of the entrepreneurs in 4:13-17. James has been addressing Christians about humility ever since 3:13 and has reached a climactic reference to arrogance at the end of 4:12. He would most naturally continue to address believers in 4:13, warning them about arrogance especially in their business endeavors. James will escalate this message in the next paragraph (5:1-6) through his rhetorical address to unbelieving rich oppressors. They will serve as examples of the arrogance described in 4:13-17, carried to the level of murderous greed. This is a more elaborate example of James's argument in 2:1-7, where he first warned Christians about their own sin of favoritism and then reminded them that they were acting like the unbelieving rich who were exploiting them and blaspheming the name of Christ.

Arrogance in Knowledge (4:13-14) James begins with the interjection *now listen (age nyn),* a short, blunt expression to get his readers' attention. He will call their attitude *boasting* by the end of the paragraph. Most of us do not think of ourselves as boasting people, because we do not go around making people listen to our bragging. As a good discipler, however, James makes us examine more subtle forms of boasting. Arrogance in knowledge occurs when we assume that we control time and events. By using the categories of 4:13, Douglas D. Webster observes how comprehensively we do this: "What else is there besides *time* ('today or tomorrow'), *purpose* ('we will go'), *place* ('to this or that city'), *goals* ('to carry on business') and *reward* ('make money')?" (1991:125).

James has touched what has become a major pathology in our society. It is alarmingly commonplace, even among Christians, to be overex-

Notes: 4:13 The imperative *age* has become a particle of exhortation and so is used in

tended in commitments, to be stressed because of time pressures and finally to become dissatisfied, compulsive people. Observing the sickness of contemporary family life, James Dobson has warned that if the devil can't make you sin, he will make you too busy, and that's just as bad. We are a driven people.

The attitude confronted in 4:13 is exposed as deception in 4:14: *Why, you don't even know what will happen tomorrow. What is your life? You are a mist that appears for a little while and then vanishes.* The verse begins as a relative clause continuing 4:13 as "who do not know . . ." The use of *hoitines* instead of *hoi* ("who") emphasizes a characteristic quality of the group being mentioned—to be rendered in this case as "who do not *even* know." *Poia* is the feminine of the interrogative pronoun *poios* ("of what kind?"), which brings a qualitative sense to the question: "What is your life like?" The question, however, is more likely the end of the longer sentence (as in the NASB). The NIV follows a textual variation to make it a separate question, but the variation seems best explained as an attempt to smooth and clarify the reading (Davids 1982:172). The preferred result is "who do not even know what your life will be like tomorrow."

The solution to our time-stress begins with humility, and humility comes from this knowledge: that we are like a vanishing mist unless the eternal God establishes us. James has employed an Old Testament image that captures an important biblical concept. In Hosea, for example, this image is used in judgment. The nation's weak love for God is condemned by its likeness to the morning mist and the early dew that disappears (Hos 6:4). Hosea combined the images of morning mist, disappearing dew, swirling chaff and escaping smoke to portray how easily the people who trust in idols will be blown away (Hos 13:3). In Psalm 1:4, the wicked are "like chaff that the wind blows away," in contrast to the righteous, who stand firmly planted. Isaiah described people who oppose God as being blown away like chaff before the wind (Is 17:13). The biblical concept is that human life is utterly dependent on God and completely incapable of standing before God's judgment.

---

this singular form even with the plural "you who say" or the plural "you rich people" in 5:1.

James would impress upon us this critical piece of knowledge: that God is the one who sustains our lives, that each day's twenty-four hours are not "ours" automatically, that God controls time and gives it as one of his good gifts, and that we would be already blown away in God's judgment were it not for his mercy. The biblical worldview is that "we receive another day neither by natural necessity, nor by mechanical law, nor by right, nor by courtesy of nature, but only by the covenanted mercies of God" (Motyer 1985:162).

This knowledge helps to dispel self-sufficiency, replacing it with the freedom to rely on God's faithful generosity. Again, far from preaching self-reliance and works-orientation, James is leading us into a life of grace-reliance.

Arrogance in Attitude (4:15-16) This life of reliance on God runs far deeper than the words we say, and care should be taken to apply James's words deeply and honestly. First, it would be a superficial spirituality to think that James's instruction is fulfilled merely by sprinkling our speech with "the Lord willing." At the same time, we should not judge those who do use this phrase; if it is done humbly as a way to keep oneself reminded of God's sovereignty, it can be a godly practice. Second, it would be a deformed spirituality to apply this by refusing to do any planning; 4:15 affirms the validity of planning to *do this or that.* Motyer writes, "James is not trying to banish planning from our lives, but only that sort of self-sufficient, self-important planning that keeps God for Sunday but looks on Monday to Saturday as mine" (1985:161). The spirituality James wants for us is a humble reliance on God which flows from knowing that one is in reality dependent on God for every moment. It is yet another example of how James would envision the manifestation of grace-reliance in our lives.

The sin of self-sufficiency is a serious matter. *You boast* is *kauchasthe,*

4:15 The phrase *if it is the Lord's will* is not even originated by James here. The concept and a similar phrase are found in pre-Christian Greek traditions. Dibelius lists a number of such references (1976:233-34).

4:16 The warning against overconfidence about the future is not original. Cf. possible background for James's thought in the Old Testament and Jesus' teaching (Prov 27:1; Lk 12:16-21). See Davids's comments on 4:14 (1982:172) for references to similar thought in extrabiblical sources.

The noun *alazoneiais* in the phrase *in your arrogance* is used only one other place in

a verb that can have a positive meaning, as in Romans 5:11 and 1 Corinthians 1:3, but clearly has a negative emphasis here. The NIV's *and brag* is actually not a second verb in the text but a prepositional phrase "in your arrogance" (cf. NASB). Moo (1985:157) points out that such a phrase in the New Testament, with the preposition *en* following this verb *kauchasthe,* always refers to the object of the boasting (for example, boasting in one's high position as in 1:9). This makes the arrogance not merely the manner of their boasting but rather the object of their boasting. The sin James is exposing is not merely a sin of omission (neglecting to recognize God's rule over their affairs); it is a sin of commission in that they even boast about their self-sufficiency. Such *boasting, kauchēsis,* is therefore especially evil; further, *all such boasting is evil.* It is a blasphemous denial of God's authority and grace to think that we instead of God control events.

Arrogance in Behavior (4:17) Suddenly James shifts his emphasis from whether we *know* God's will to whether we *do* God's will. Verse 17 seems at first not to fit the thrust of the paragraph. That, however, is a clue not that James is erratic in his thought but that we have not understood his meaning. The adverb *oun* ("then") provides grammatical evidence that James intends a connection in thought. He may have made a jump in his line of thought without articulating the intervening steps, but it is entirely consistent with the rest of the letter for James to tell his readers to carry out their inward attitude with outward actions. In fact, James capsulizes in this one verse much of what he has already taught in the letter. His double use of the verb *poieō (to do and doesn't do)* reminds his readers succinctly of his earlier emphasis on doing the word of God (1:22-25). The picture of one who *knows the good he ought to do and doesn't do it* recalls the earlier picture of one who finds the brother or sister in need but does not do the good that ought to be done

the New Testament: 1 John 2:16, there translated "boasting" (NIV) or "boastful pride" (NASB).

4:17 Commentators generally find that 4:17 reads like a proverb that James apparently assumes to be familiar to his readers. If so, he would also be assuming that they can connect the proverb to the context. Dibelius, however, finds all attempts at connecting 4:17 to the surrounding verses "futile" and is certain that "the verse does not tie in with either what precedes or what follows" except in having a "similar mood" (1976:230-31).

(2:15-16). The label of "sin" *(hamartia)* is applied with all the severe warning about sin given earlier (1:15).

James fully expects that a humble attitude will be manifest in humble actions, and an arrogant attitude will be manifest in arrogant actions. It is natural for him now to be saying in 4:17: "Do not merely say that you want to know God's will or that you recognize your dependence on his will; look carefully at what God has already said about his will, and do that."

Failure to do what one knows to be God's will is the same arrogance that James has been describing in knowledge and attitude, now carried out in behavior. Indifference toward God's will is commonplace sin today, and Motyer comments on this verse that "the whole idea of sinning by default has never been given more pointed expression" (1985:163). As we have previously found in this letter, here James carries the issues of faith into the realm of active obedience.

Don't Be Materialistic (5:1-6) The worldview of the preceding paragraph was that God rules over time and requires our obedience to his will in all use of it. The same worldview is extended now to encompass material wealth: God rules over wealth and requires our obedience to his will in all use of it. This is very much an Old Testament view as well. Leviticus 25, for example, asserts that the land and the people belong to God. This fact put the Israelites in the position of tenants rather than owners (Lev 25:23); they were obligated not to take advantage of each other and not to enslave each other (vv. 17, 42); they were to follow instead the admonition "Fear your God" (vv. 17, 43). James's paragraph flows from the same worldview and could be summarized with the same admonition.

Here a more definite case can be made that James is speaking rhetorically to unbelievers who are not receiving the letter. The evidence is fourfold. First, he refrains from his frequent addressing of "brothers," to

---

5:1 *Weep and wail* is actually one imperative verb, *weep* (translated "wail" in 4:9), followed by a participle to define the weeping as "wailing." It is the only New Testament occurrence of this verb "wailing," but Davids points out that its twenty-one uses in the Old Testament are all in the prophets, so that James's usage here "sweeps along with it the prophetic exhortations to cry out over divine judgment" (1982:175).

5:3 Cf. similar terminology in 3:6-8 about the tongue. Paul used the term *ios* while

which he will return in 5:7. Second, though he also refrained from any explicitly Christian address in 4:13-17, he goes beyond that in 5:1-6, employing his specific label *hoi plousioi* ("you rich people"). Third, James writes to the rich not with instruction or exhortation but with thorough condemnation, refusing to give the slightest hint that any redemption is expected. Finally, his approach is in keeping with many Old Testament passages condemning rich oppressors and affirming their needy, righteous victims (Ps 109:31; Ps 146; Is 5:22-24; Amos 2:6-7). James's passage similarly fits with Jesus' teaching about the poor and the "rich" *(plousioi)* in Luke 6:20-26. (For further discussion of this topic, see my appendix on the identity of the rich in James.)

Viewing the paragraph in this light, James would be intending two purposes for Christians as they read how he would address the rich. His Christian readers are suffering many trials, including economic hardship from persecution by the rich (2:6-7). These suffering Christians would be easily tempted to become discouraged, resentful, vengeful, jealous and covetous, and so to become just as thoroughly corrupted by materialism as are their rich oppressors. The first intended effect on the Christian readers, then, is encouragement from the fact that judgment will come to the rich, so the sufferers may leave that judgment to God and so persevere in righteousness without envying the rich. The second intended purpose is warning: judgment does come upon such sin, so they should be careful to avoid becoming materialistic themselves.

The Coming Misery of the Rich (5:1-3) The first half of the paragraph is a description of the awful misery that will come upon the rich. In the first place, they will lose their wealth. But that by itself is far too tame an exposition of James's words. The rich will find their hoarded wealth rotted, their fine clothes moth-eaten and their treasured gold and silver corroded (images that recall Jesus' words in Mt 6:20). James gives vivid and terrible images of the destruction of their wealth, indicating that the rich will experience horror and despair over their loss. They will

quoting the Old Testament in Romans 3:13, but James is the only New Testament writer to employ the term on his own—in 3:8 meaning "poison" and here in 5:3 meaning "corrosion" or rust. The fact that gold and silver do not actually rust does not indicate a mistake of ignorance on James's part. He is simply drawing on an image in Jewish literature in warning against hoarding material wealth since it rusts away.

weep and wail in misery. The verb *wail* is onomatopoeic—*ololyzō*—adding to the vividness of the imagery by sounding like the wailing it describes. It conveys the sounds of "weeping accompanied by recurring shouts of pain" (Kistemaker 1986:156), bringing to mind the experience of excruciating grief or anguish. The rich will lose everything they have devoted themselves to and everything they have relied upon. Theirs will be the despair of people who discover their dreams and treasures destroyed forever.

If the rich were only misguided in devoting themselves to their wealth, this first misery would be enough. But there is a second level to their misery: the destruction of the wealth will consume the rich people themselves. The imagery expresses forcefully that their sin has been a deliberate pursuit of evil. Literally, James says, the rust or corrosion on the gold and silver will be the active agent against the rich. The corrosive action will take two forms: first to testify against the rich (acting as evidence of their guilt) and then to eat their flesh like fire (acting as punishment for their sin).

There are, then, three miseries specified for the rich: despair from losing their wealth, guilt from the evidence against them and horrible pain from being devoured in the judgment upon them.

The Specific Sins of the Rich (5:3-6) Now we find out why these rich people are so condemned, as the second half of the paragraph is the indictment against them. The charges may be summarized as "greed and injustice." The greed of the rich has consisted of hoarding wealth and living in luxury and self-indulgence. The injustice has consisted of cheating workers of their wages and condemning and murdering innocent people. But these charges are not listed calmly, with the decorum of courtroom order; they seem to tumble off James's pen in outrage against gross immorality. Moral outrage such as this ought to come from one deserving James's reputation as "the Just."

These charges are made with reference to certain days—*the last days* and *the day of slaughter.* If these are both references to the time of God's judgment, they produce a twin irony. The rich have hoarded wealth—

5:3-6 Cf. similar portraits of the rich in Jesus' parables, such as Luke 12:16-21 and 16:19-31.

only to lose it in *the last days*. They have indulged themselves—only to become fat for their own *slaughter*. The first phrase most likely does refer to the future judgment (indicated by the future tense of the verbs in the middle of 5:3), and reflects the common apostolic viewpoint that the first coming of Jesus has already ushered in *the last days*, which will culminate in a future judgment. James, however, is not particularly amused with the irony of it all. He is moved far more by the offensiveness of the sin, that the rich have dared to hoard wealth even in the days when they should be most concerned to repent. In the context of *the last days*, when the rich should be most in fear of God, their greed amounts to a mocking of God, a hurling of arrogant insults into God's face.

The latter phrase, *the day of slaughter*, may also refer to God's judgment on the rich (as Davids contends, 1982:178-79). Certainly there is an Old Testament tradition for the image of God's judgment as a slaughter of his enemies (Is 34:5-8; Jer 12:3; 46:10). Yet there are problems with this view. The exact phrase does not occur in the Septuagint (as Davids acknowledges, 1982:178), and the connotations of the phrase are not clear (as Laws admits, 1980:203); it could be a description of the violent treatment of the poor by the rich (as Dibelius defends, 1976:239). The meaning advocated by Dibelius becomes the more likely one because of the immediate parallelism that emerges between 5:5 and 5:6, which could be paraphrased:

> You have lived on earth in luxury and self-indulgence,
> you have fattened yourselves
> —even in a day when you are slaughtering others!

> You have condemned,
> you have murdered the innocent one
> —who is not even opposing you!

The grammar lends support to the parallelism by each verse's series of aorist verbs to list the actions of the rich. These two series of verbs are

---

5:4 *Lord Almighty* ("Lord Sabaoth"). Cf. same phrase in Isaiah 5:9, where the context is also judgment upon abuses of wealth.

climaxed by the "slaughtering" and the "not opposing," which form a pair of complementary images about the same scene. Finally, the meaning fits with the entire paragraph's tone of moral outrage. Some have found the last sentence, "He is not opposing you" (or "not resisting you"), to be awkward and anticlimactic. The parallelism removes the dilemma by bringing out the fact that James is reaching the very peak of his moral outrage, as if shouting out the final, incredible and utterly offensive fact of what the rich are doing. They are victimizing people who are not even "opposing" them as enemies and who do not have the power to be "resisting" them. By this, James may also be encouraging his Christian readers to continue in nonresistance, reminding them that in doing so they are following Jesus' instruction in Matthew 5:39.

The two verbs translated *lived in luxury* and *self-indulgence* assess the lifestyle of the rich to be (by the first verb) disgustingly selfish and (by the second verb) extravagantly wasteful, "going beyond pleasure to vice" (Motyer 1985:167). The term *condemned (katedikasate)* in 5:6 is a judicial term, recalling James's earlier reference to injustices suffered by Christians through the courts in 2:6. The verb *murdered* could then refer to an indirect killing of the poor through control of a corrupt legal system by the rich. It may also refer to a direct killing of the poor by the rich.

A perspective from the standpoint of the very poor is provided by the Latin American Elsa Tamez, who views this verse from "the angle of oppression." She observes that the day laborers of James's day would have been so poor that they depended on daily wages for survival. "This salary was already low, but for day laborers it was very serious not to find work or not to be paid. For this reason James personifies the salary, seeing it as the very blood of the exploited workers crying out pitifully. The case was the same for the peasants. The peasants die because they pour out their strength in their work, but the fruit of their work does not come back to them. They cannot regain their strength because the rich withhold their salaries. Therefore James accuses the rich of condemning and killing the just (5:6)" (1990:20).

5:5 *Fattened yourselves* is literally "nourished your hearts." Cf. Jesus' warning in Luke 21:34.

5:6 Having taken *the day of slaughter* as God's future slaughter of the rich, Davids must account for the final present-tense sentence. Following Hort, he renders it as a question,

These terms give us a frightening glimpse of the injustice in which Christians lived, with all the power in the hands of the wealthy. Some have taken the singular *innocent man,* or "righteous man," to refer specifically to Christ. (Cf. Motyer 1985:168-69.) But it is difficult to imagine how James would have referred to the major offense of killing Christ without making it more explicit; instead, the term is probably a generic way of representing any of the innocent victims of the rich. However, for the application of this passage to our lives, Motyer is right to remind us of "the lone and wonderful figure of the Lord Jesus," whose model of nonresistance is ultimately "the most demanding example and the sweetest consolation in time of oppression" (1985:169). The present tense of the verb *antitassetai* ("opposing") simply reflects James's emphasis that the rich are continuing their ugly practice even in the present time. If the parallelism with 5:5 is correct, the slaughter of the poor should also be understood as a continuing offense.

Even with *slaughter* referring to the killing of the poor, the prospect of God's judgment is certainly James's message. These rich have arrogantly abused their positions of wealth to exercise evil power over others. This sin is answered by assurance that the cries of their victims are heard by the "Lord Sabaoth." The title *Sabaoth* is a transliteration of a Hebrew word for "army." The title is therefore often translated "Lord of Hosts," depicting God's position as mighty leader of a huge army, or "the Lord Almighty," as in the NIV. It is one of the most majestic images offered by the various Old Testament names of God. James is referring to God's awesome power and authority to judge sin. We are to fear this omnipotent God—fear him so much that we flee from the sins of the rich.

At the beginning of the discussion of 5:1-6, I identified two purposes (encouragement and warning) James would have for Christians who are reading how he would address their rich, non-Christian oppressors. His encouragement is for them to leave judgment to God while they persevere in righteousness. His warning is for them to beware of God's judg-

---

"Does he not resist you?" The implied answer is that the innocent victim does resist the rich, by calling for justice before God (1982:180). Moo also treats the sentence as a question (1985:167).

ment and flee from materialistic sin themselves. The implication for Christians with money today is that a huge responsibility goes with the possession of wealth. We dare not treat lightly the danger of sin. We dare not assume that because we are living respectable lives we are safe in our possession of wealth. James has warned us to take extreme care that we not tolerate in ourselves the sin of greed (in a self-indulgent lifestyle) or the sin of injustice (in how our use of wealth affects other people). The coming misery of the rich is too terrible to ignore.

A second area of application needs to be made today because of the spread of liberation theology. In light of James's teaching, how far shall Christians go in opposing the evils of wealth? The church needs to be instructed and led regarding four possible levels of action for the reformation of society: intercession, proclamation, resistance and revolution. First, the church should be stirred to intercessory prayer for its society. We have a biblical calling to pray for our society (Is 62:6-7), and prayer will be James's primary focus in the conclusion to his letter (5:13-18). Second, proclamation through clear prophetic warning is certainly proper, by the example of James's own letter. One of the ministries of the church today must be the prophetic sharing of truth. The world needs the church to address personal and societal abuses of wealth with James's twin messages of encouragement toward righteousness and warning against wickedness. Third, active resistance to injustice can be practiced through civil disobedience. Christians need to be given biblical instruction in the proper motives, methods and contexts for civil disobedience, so that this alternative can be practiced in righteousness. For the fourth possible level of action—armed revolution—James does not give any support. That will become clear as James develops the next stage of his message.

Instead, Be Patient (5:7-11) The particle *oun* ("then") makes definite the connection with the preceding paragraph; the picture of sin and judgment is the fresh motivation for telling the *brothers* now to *be pa-*

5:7-8 Whose coming does James have in mind with *parousia tou kyriou?* Davids's judgment is sound: "The majority of commentators note the strongly Christian tone throughout James, the doubtfulness of references to the parousia of God, and the common technical

tient. Be patient? What an incredible command to give after the preceding portrayal of offenses! "Be outraged" is more what we would expect. But James has not lost his moral perspective in the midst of his moral passion. He has already expressed his outrage, but his concern is still for purity among the Christians, and he discerns the danger of falling into sin here. James is practicing his own counsel from 1:9-15, recognizing the danger of temptation in the midst of trials inflicted by rich oppressors. He does not tell his readers to compete with or fight against the rich for their wealth, because it would be horrible to become drawn into the materialism of the rich and so to come under the same divine judgment.

James's other alternative might be to say, "Give up in despair, for the situation is hopeless; all the power is in the hands of the rich." This, too, would be falling into sin; it would be an affirmation of the values of the rich, saying that their materialistic power is the only goal to live for.

"Both giving in to the world and attacking the world are wrong," concludes Davids (1982:182). Instead, James says, *Be patient,* and he spends these next five verses explaining that patience.

The Nature of Christian Patience (5:7-8) I used to think of patience as a passive personality trait. I prayed for patience as if God might infuse me with this trait so that I would become unaffected by trying circumstances. It is certainly right to pray for patience; James is the one who urges prayer and reliance on grace so strongly. But if I want patience, I need to better understand what it is.

First, patience has a specific object in our own sanctification. James begins with the verb *makrothymeō,* which carries not only the idea of being patient but specifically the picture of waiting with patience. This implies some object of the waiting, but the object is not the parousia, the coming of the Lord. This becomes clearer in the analogy of the farmer who also "waits." James first uses the verb *ekdechomai* for the farmer's waiting, but he makes the continuity definite by adding a participle of *makrothymeō*—"being patient." The farmer is patient "over"

---

sense of parousia in the New Testament, and therefore argue that the event referred to here is the coming of Christ. . . . This seems to be the most reasonable position, for James is not a thinly Christianized Jewish document, but a thoroughly Christian one" (1982:182).

one thing and "until" another thing. The text says the farmer waits for the valuable fruit of the earth, being patient "over it" *(ep' autō)*, that is, over the fruit. He is patient "until" *(heōs)* it receives *the autumn and spring rains.* The description of the crop as *valuable* (or "precious" in NASB) would help the persecuted readers to identify with the farmer as not a wealthy landlord but a small farmer who depends on a good harvest for survival, even as the Christian readers are hanging on for survival. More important, it reminds the readers that there is something to be patient "over," something that is of more value than riches or ease. By this point in the letter, readers should be accustomed to James's conviction that the goal of becoming "mature and complete" is the goal of greatest value. James is telling the brothers to be patient over their trials to gain maturity and completeness until that process is crowned with the glorious coming of the Lord. The parallel is that farmers must be patient over their labor to gain the fruit of the soil until that fruit receives the coming of the rain. Do you want to learn patience? The first step is a choice of values. Set your heart on becoming "mature and complete" and having "the righteous life that God desires."

Second, patience has a specific hope in Christ's return. James tells the brothers to be patient "until" *(heōs)* the coming of the Lord. The future return of Christ is the event that motivates Christians to persevere in the endurance of suffering. In the life of the farmer, the autumn and spring rains have a similar role. If the farmer could not hope for the rains, all the plowing and planting and weeding would be futile. Rain (literally, the "early and late [rain]") is a standard Old Testament image of God's promised faithfulness (e.g., Jer 5:24 and Joel 2:23, as well as Deut 11:14, which would have been especially familiar as part of the regularly recited *Shema*). The effect is to leave no doubt about how appropriate it is to be patient. God has promised these rains; therefore the farmer can be patient in laboring. Even so, God has promised Christ's return; therefore believers can be patient in their hardships. Do you want to learn pa-

---

5:7 The subject of *labē* ("receives") is unclear grammatically, as reflected in the textual variants attempting to clarify the matter. It seems to give a more natural flow to understand the fruit or harvest, rather than the farmer, as the subject that receives the rain. Either way, it still remains that the farmer is patient *over* the harvest *until* the rain.

The reference to *the autumn and spring rains* may reflect merely the familiar Old Tes-

tience? Contemplate the hope of Christ's return.

Third, patience has a specific stance in deliberate behavior. In 5:8 James begins with the same verb *makrothymeō* in imperative form, exactly as at the beginning of 5:7. Then *kai hymeis* ("you too") adds emphasis to the force of the imperative and defines this verse as the application of the farmer analogy. The elaboration comes with a second imperative, "strengthen your hearts" (NIV "stand firm"). It communicates that the waiting is to be done not in weakness or defeat but in strength and action. This makes the patience "much more than passively waiting for the time to pass" (Kistemaker 1986:164). Finally, the hope is stated again; the Lord's "coming" *(parousia)* approaches or comes near. The perfect tense refers to a process viewed as having been completed and consummated. With the final verb *ēngiken* ("approaches" or "comes near") in the perfect tense, the coming of the Lord receives dramatic emphasis, as if James is saying with intensity, "It is so close and so certain—don't give up now!" Do you want to learn patience? Since you have set your heart on becoming mature and complete, and since you hope for Christ's return, now choose to stand firm. What that stance will mean in actual behavior is described in the next three verses.

I was talking with a woman who was facing circumstances of terrible hardship. She was telling me of a friend who had encouraged her significantly, and I was keenly interested to know what the friend had done to minister to her. "What helped me the most," she recalled, "was that he reminded me with assurance that these circumstances will come to an end. It looks so dark and unending now; I needed to be told that it would not last forever." In the same way James has encouraged his persecuted readers with the hope of Christ's return and so has helped them choose a stance of patience.

The Practice of Christian Patience (5:9-11) One view is that 5:9 is "quite isolated," with "scarcely any material connection with the admonition to patience" (Dibelius 1976:244, 242). Such a reading misses

---

tament phrase, or it may refer as well to the distinctive weather patterns of Palestine. If it is the latter, it could indicate the more limited dispersion of Christians before A.D. 70 as the setting for the epistle. In that setting, both the Old Testament phrase and the Palestinian weather would have familiar meaning for James and his Jewish-Christian readers.

the point that James is now turning from the nature of Christian patience to the very practical manifestation of it. What will it look like when we practice Christian patience? James gives one specific application and then reminds his readers of models to follow.

The one application of patience is that we will not *grumble against each other* (5:9). The imperative verb is *stenazō,* which means "sigh" or "groan." It refers to a proper groaning for something good in Mark 7:34, Romans 8:23 and 2 Corinthians 5:2. The only other New Testament usage is in Hebrews 13:17, where it has a sense more like the grumbling or complaining that James wants Christians to avoid. It is a grumbling specifically *against each other (kata* with genitive), thus referring to a complaining in which we blame each other. "Do not moan about one another," Davids translates it (1982:184). The warning *or you will be judged* is identical to Jesus' words in Mt 7:1 *(hina mē krithēte),* indicating that James regards this grumbling as a form of speaking against or judging one's brother, as in 4:11. No further explanation is given for the identity of *the Judge,* but *the Lord* in the immediately preceding verse is surely the most likely referent. *At the door* (translating the idiom "before the doors") would be an image for the nearness of the Lord's coming, as emphasized in 5:8.

It is valuable for us that James makes grumbling his singular point of application. We might want to sidestep this behavior while we try to practice patience in other ways. The trials being faced by those suffering Christians would have put their patience to the test and given plenty of opportunity for bickering and criticizing. The same happens in the church today, even when the Christians are more affluent and the trials more contemporary: "difficult marriages, frustrated dreams, demotions at work, commotions at home, insomnia, high blood pressure, allergies, credit-card bills and insecurity" (Webster 1991:149). Christians lose patience with each other under these pressures, and the church becomes infected with a readiness to criticize and blame. James would correct the problem with a renewed vision of the imminently returning Christ, particularly emphasizing that he comes as Judge.

5:9 For *at the door,* cf. Matthew 24:33 and Mark 13:29.
5:11 Some have seen in the *telos* of the Lord a reference to the Lord's purpose behind

The models given (5:10-11) are the prophets and Job. Here James's focus is on three elements that make up the portrait of patience at work in the believer's life: suffering, perseverance and blessing. James wants his readers to understand that these three develop in succession and that their outcome is as definite as the character of God. Suffering enters the believer's life; perseverance is the believer's response; blessing comes from the Lord, who is full of compassion and mercy. As in 2:20-26, James's choice of illustrations assumes a largely Jewish-Christian audience who would be familiar with Old Testament examples. A host of particulars might come to their minds from these models, but James chooses not to isolate specific instances as he did with Abraham and Rahab. Instead, he chooses to focus on the three elements: suffering, perseverance and blessing.

The suffering is *kakopatheia*, which can have a passive sense—misery that comes upon a person. It is also used in a more active sense to describe the deliberate endurance that a person practices in hardship. The latter meaning is James's emphasis here, since the prophets are an example of the pair of traits: literally, "an example . . . of suffering and patience," which would probably mean "patience in suffering." His term for patience is the nominal form of the verb with which he instructed his readers in 5:7 and 5:8 to *be patient*. It is clear that he is intending to give examples of those preceding imperatives. When he speaks of perseverance in the next sentences, he is using the verb *hypomenō* and the noun *hypomonē*, going back to the idea with which he began his letter in 1:3-4. He is using patience, *makrothymia*, and perseverance, *hypomonē*, as virtually synonymous.

God's work in the life of the persevering believer is to bless, conveyed by the verb *makarizō* ("consider blessed"). James's use of this verb in the first-person plural in 5:11, coupled with the reference to the prophets, indicates a common knowledge of Jesus' words recorded in Matthew 5:11-12. The source or reason for suffering is not identified. James's concern is not to answer that question, but to emphasize that God brings blessing. It was the same in chapter 1 of the letter. The origin

Job's sufferings. Here it more likely refers simply to the ultimate end of Job's story, that he was finally and abundantly blessed by God. Cf. Moo 1985:172.

of the trials was not specified, but it was important to be clear about this: God does not tempt us to do evil; he will use trials to bring good gifts to us. Now James emphasizes not merely that God will manage to bring some blessings but that God will ultimately accomplish his good purposes. The example of Job, who was ultimately blessed in abundance, reveals *to telos kyriou*—the end or goal of the Lord.

All of this demonstrates the character of the Lord, which is finally what James wants his readers to know with confidence. The description of God as compassionate and merciful would be as familiar to his readers as are the prophets and Job, from passages such as Exodus 34:6 and Psalms 103:8. Yet James places unique emphasis on this picture of God by introducing a term used nowhere else prior to or within the New Testament: *polysplanchnos* ("full of compassion"). This, ultimately, is the source of assurance by which we can be patient. What will it look like when we practice Christian patience? It will look like the prophets, who kept speaking, and like Job, who kept believing, in suffering and perseverance, with this specific assurance: God will bless.

This is the message of grace. God gives good gifts because he is full of compassion and mercy. Grace is the element in God's character which James wants his readers to know with absolute confidence. The Christian can be patient in suffering and consider trials pure joy because of the assurance that God will give wonderfully good gifts even through the hardships.

Fundamental for Christian practice is Christian belief. What is the truth about God? Is he this God of grace or not? We are called over and over in James's letter to believe this truth—believe it, believe it, believe it. And then act accordingly. Put belief into practice by being patient in the endurance of suffering.

□ The Encompassing Instructions (5:12-20)
I have heard Christians facing difficult trials say, "I need to know how great God is." A recent occurrence came while my wife's parents were visiting us for Christmas. Dad became ill, and I had to take him to the

---

Notes: **5:12** *Above all:* "It seems best to read the phrase *pro pantōn* as introducing rather

emergency room. We all spent a couple of anxious days while he was in the hospital. It is bad enough to be ill; it is worse when one is a thousand miles from home and the doctors are unable to diagnose the cause of the severe pain. On one of those anxious days, Mother was telling me about her quiet time that morning. She said she had thought about interrupting her current reading, which was in a section of Scripture about God's supremacy and authority, to look for some comforting passages about God's faithfulness and healing. She decided instead to stay in the section she'd been reading. She said, "This is what I need now. It doesn't answer all my questions, but I need to know how great God is."

I have experienced it myself. In the midst of still-unresolved trials, I need to submit my life consciously and deliberately to the greatness of God. That does not give me all the answers to the questions of why things are happening or what I should do, but it is what I need in order to deal with the fear and pain.

The original readers of James's letter are themselves in difficult circumstances. They are suffering under economic, legal and even violent persecution. Their trials are very much unresolved and current. In love for them, James has driven home the point of the greatness of God— that God is great in righteousness, unchangeableness and most of all faithfulness to give good gifts in compassion and mercy. Now, in the final section of the letter, James concludes his message with three particular things to do in light of the greatness of God: do not swear; instead, pray; and finally, keep bringing each other back to the truth. These are his three encompassing instructions.

Do Not Swear (5:12) There is agreement among commentators that the basic point of the instruction in 5:12 is to ensure the integrity of one's speech without having to rely on oaths. "Let your 'yes' be true and your 'no' be true" (Dibelius 1976:249). Additional issues surrounding the verse have to do with (1) the relationship of 5:12 with Matthew 5:33-37, (2) the relationship of 5:12 with the rest of James's text and (3) the

---

than concluding a section; the author moves on to a new line of thought with a transitional and emphatic 'most importantly' " (Laws 1980:220).

specific ways James would intend this verse to be applied. Some observations of the text to investigate the first two issues will clarify the meaning of 5:12 so that we can arrive at some reliable answers to the third and most important question of application.

This instruction is one of James's clearest references to the Sermon on the Mount (Mt 5:33-37), giving further confirmation of his deliberate remembrance of Jesus' teaching. James and Matthew recall Jesus' teaching with the same terms and order. In that teaching Jesus confronted the Pharisaic practice of using various formulas to create different levels of oaths, some of which were considered less binding than others. (Cf. Mt 23:16-22.) The Pharisees could thereby bind themselves to their promises in various degrees and so excuse themselves from keeping commitments they had made with lesser oaths. They could use their oaths to sound exceedingly pious and to justify themselves as deeply religious, while being in fact hypocritical. (See Stott's discussion of Mt 5:33-37, 1978:99-102.) Jesus commanded his followers therefore not to swear but to invest their simple words of yes or no with complete integrity. James follows that passage; we might conclude that he is simply prescribing honesty in speech.

But in two ways James departs from what Matthew records. First, James lends a priority to this particular point of behavior by his introductory *above all.* Second, James concludes with a warning of judgment (literally, "that you may not fall under judgment," translated "or you will be condemned" in NIV). This is not to imply that James and Matthew disagree about what Jesus said. James is making a reference to what Jesus said and then adding the particular emphases he wants to make. The introductory words *above all* indicate that James has in mind a meaning larger than honesty in everyday speech. After all he has said about large issues of purity and patience and perseverance, why would he settle upon oaths as the sin to avoid *above all?* His concluding mention of judgment draws upon the context in 5:1-6 and 5:9, but it also adds further weightiness to this matter of oaths. Why would James make it such a priority?

To answer this we must address the second issue, concerning the context for 5:12 in the epistle. Dibelius blinds himself to this avenue of investigation by insisting that 5:12 "has no relationship with what precedes or follows" (1976:248). It is certainly proper to investigate the context for a possible connection. If the surrounding text provides a reasonable context to explain a verse, and if there is no textual evidence for regarding the verse as a later addition, then there is no basis for rejecting the observed context as the *intended* context for the verse. We can investigate the matter by asking simple inductive questions. First, does the context tell us anything about why these Christians would be swearing with oaths? Then, does this contextual reason for swearing connect to any fundamental issue in James's letter?

First we consider the preceding context. Throughout the letter and especially in the preceding passage, James has been concerned to encourage his readers' patience and perseverance in the midst of trials. It is clear that he anticipates in their suffering the temptation to compromise their moral standards and so become polluted by the world. He has just been telling them about the need for patience in the face of suffering. In the immediately subsequent context, we will find James prescribing prayer as the proper recourse for Christians in trouble. This context does in fact provide a readily understandable and very possible reason for these Christians to be swearing with oaths. They would be tempted to strike bargains with God, swearing to do one thing or another if only God would deliver them from their persecutors. Religious people have tried this kind of bargaining all through the centuries. Animists who live in fear of their gods are driven to make such promises. The unconverted young Martin Luther made his famous promise to become a monk when a bolt of lightning terrified him in 1505. James has been saying, "Be patient in your suffering. Remember the Lord is coming. Remember the example of the prophets. Remember the perseverance of Job. Remember the Lord's full compassion and mercy." Now he says, "Above all, don't fall into swearing, as if you could manipulate God by your oaths. Instead, speak honestly and directly, and rely on God in prayer."

Does this contextual reason for swearing connect to any issue so fundamental in the letter that James would make this a matter of encompassing importance? It connects to the underlying issue of the entire letter: the meaning and practice of faith. From the very beginning, James has said that his readers' faith is being tested in the trials (1:3). In the midst of trials, Christians are to ask God in faith (1:6). It is because they hold faith in Christ that they are not to show favoritism (2:1). It is faith that constitutes true riches (2:5). James has gone to great lengths to emphasize that genuine faith will manifest itself in deeds (2:14-26). His whole letter is a plea for his readers to be not merely religious people, but people of faith.

Now it is the lack of faith that must appall James in the act of swearing. It is unbelief that would move his readers to try to save themselves by a manipulative use of oaths. It is through lack of faith that we disbelieve God's "compassion and mercy" and so want to strike a bargain. Striking a bargain with God cuts at the very heart of the gospel; it is an attempt to rely on the worth of one's own offering instead of relying on God's grace in the offering of Christ on the cross. Bargaining is a reliance on works; James is insisting that we rely on grace. He is again teaching the opposite of what some have portrayed as an anti-Pauline works-righteousness. James says *above all* and *you will be condemned* because he is addressing not just a simple matter of dishonesty but a fundamental lack of faith and denial of grace. *Above all* makes sense if it introduces not just 5:12 but this entire final section of the letter, in which faith is the real focal point.

Now we can see the proper application of 5:12. We are getting sidetracked if we focus on whether Christians should take oaths in courts of law. We are being too superficial if we see this verse merely as an injunction against "frivolous and indiscriminate oaths and the thoughtless mention of the divine name" because such speech would violate God's law and hinder one's witness to unbelievers (Tasker 1983:125). Those are important matters, but James is here (as usual) cutting to an essential difference between genuine and false religion. He is saying: Do not allow suffering to pressure you into unbelief. Do not try to impress each other or to manipulate God as if your works were what counted instead of God's grace. If you are trusting in God's grace, you have no need to impress God or people, and you can be at peace with saying honest words. Integrity should characterize Christians, and integrity will flow from wholehearted reliance on grace. Unbelief manifests itself in bargaining, manipulating and trying to impress. The opposite manifes-

---

5:13 "The misfortune expressed in *kakopathei* is not illness, but physical circumstances or personal situations that cause the person distress. In other words, the inner experience

tation, flowing from faith, will be prayer.

Instead, Pray (5:13-18) These next verses, then, are a continuation of 5:12 and give the alternative to swearing, which is praying. Most commentators miss this connection between 5:12 and 5:13, which should be noted because it is based on the letter's underlying theme of faith. See, for example, the interpretations attempted by Moo (1985:175), Motyer (1985:187), Laws (1980:224) and Davids (1982:181). Tasker seems to perceive the connection (1983:126). Martin suggests that the praying is perhaps James's proposed alternative to fighting (1988:205). This is certainly true in the verse's larger context, but in the more immediate context praying is the alternative to swearing. In James's view, oaths and prayers are simply the verbal expressions of underlying stances of unbelief and faith, respectively. Because James is a man of faith, he has a passion for prayer. For his concluding instructions to suffering Christians, he dwells on this matter of prayer with three emphases· when to pray, how to pray and why pray.

When to Pray (5:13-14) James's first emphasis is on the diversity of circumstances for prayer. Dibelius regards these sentences as declaratives followed by imperatives: "Someone among you is suffering; let him pray" (1976:241, 252). Davids argues well that James intends interrogatives followed by imperatives, as in the NIV. The result Davids describes as "the lively discourse of oral style" (1982:191). It reflects James's desire to engage his readers personally, because he wants so much for them to put prayer into practice.

With a poetic pattern to his sentence construction, James shows that he intends one point with his three questions: Pray in all circumstances.

A. Question: *Kakopathei tis en hymin.*
Answer: *proseuchesthō.*
B. Question: *euthymei tis.*
Answer: *psalletō.*
A. Question: *asthenei tis en hymin.*
Answer: *proskalesasthō . . . kai proseuxasthōsan.*

of having to endure misfortune is indicated more than a specific form of misfortune" (Davids 1982:191).

James's vocabulary also indicates his intention. With general verbs and indefinite pronouns, he keeps the focus broad and inclusive. Prayer is the encompassing instruction, because it is the right course of action for the full range of life-situations and for *any one* in these situations.

1. Pray in times of trouble. The kind of trouble is not specified; it is a general verb, *kakopatheō*. "Is anyone among you suffering?" (NASB). Like James's original readers, we might allow the fact of trouble to suggest that God is uncaring or unknowing or unable to help, and so we would pray less. The biblical instruction is the opposite: pray more. Trouble is the very time to pray.

2. Pray in times of happiness. No single cause for happiness is specified; it is a general verb, *euthymeō*. "Is anyone cheerful" (NASB) or encouraged? Like James's original readers, we might allow times of happiness to make us complacent, and so we would pray less. The biblical instruction is again the opposite: pray more. Happiness is the very time to *sing songs of praise.*

3. Pray in times of sickness. No particular disease is identified; it is a general verb, *astheneō*, meaning to be weak or sick. Like James's original readers, we easily feel defeated in times of sickness. Weakness makes us feel hopeless, as if there were nothing to do. The biblical outlook is the opposite: there is something very significant to do, namely, to pray. Weakness is the very time for prayer. O. Hallesby, the great teacher on prayer, wrote, "Your helplessness is your best prayer."

In other words, pray in all kinds of circumstances. "The habit of prayer should be, and indeed is, one of the most obvious features which differentiates a Christian from other people" (Tasker 1983:126).

How to Pray (5:14-16) James proceeds to instruct his readers in how to pray. His purpose is still to motivate them to pray, but now he encourages prayer by his vision of how he expects prayer to operate in

---

5:14 The reference to elders is no ground for assigning a later date for the writing of the letter or assuming a later addition to the text at this point. There is no sound reason for thinking the exiled recipients of James's letter would not have had elders at this early stage in church history. These Christians may have been persecuted, but that does not mean they were simply frightened and disorganized. They were having the assemblies to which James referred in 2:2. The office of elder was already familiar from Jewish synagogue tradition (Acts 4:5, 8, 23). When Paul embarked on his missionary journeys, he appointed elders in each new church as a normal, accepted practice (Acts 14:23; Tit 1:5). Some have

the church. The meaning of the verses can be seen by isolating four practices which are pictured here for an effective prayer life.

1. We should call upon *the elders of the church* for prayer. The fact that the sick person calls is an expression of faith, which is one condition for effective prayer (1:6-7). The fact that the elders are the ones called is an expression of submission and unity in the church, which are additional conditions for powerful praying. There is no indication of specialized spiritual gifts here (as in Paul's letters). James envisions a spiritual power available to the church and exercised through the elders. This is not at all to diminish the importance of personal prayer by each Christian. It is to affirm the value of agreement by the church, for Jesus promised that agreement among Christians would unleash power for answered prayer (Mt 18:19-20; Jn 15:7-17).

2. We are to pray *in the name of the Lord.* If the first practice expressed submission to each other in the church, this second practice expresses submission to the Lord himself. In this sense, it is not just a formula with which to pray but a state in which to be praying: pray in union with Christ. Similarly, when James instructs his readers to *anoint . . . with oil,* it is not the oil that heals. See Mark 6:13 for a use of anointing with oil within the time of Jesus' public ministry; yet most of the stories of healing by Jesus and his disciples have no mention of oil, and James's emphasis here is certainly on the power of the Lord rather than any power in the oil. The promises of Jesus (Jn 14:13-14; 15:16; 16:23-24) give basis for expecting great power as we practice the principle of praying in his name. These promises apparently led the early church from its very beginning to practice a deliberate calling upon the name of the Lord in the context of baptizing, healing and casting out demons. Examples may be found in Luke 10:17 and Acts 2:38, 3:6, 9:34 and 10:48. The phrase *in the name of the Lord* means that the power comes from

argued that James describes an institutionalizing of the earlier exercise of spiritual gifts—that is, elders are here replacing the charismatic healers of an earlier stage. However, if James's letter precedes Paul's as I have argued, the charismatic healers functioned within a church structure already governed by elders.

Concerning the praying and anointing in 5:14, Dibelius concludes that "the whole procedure is an exorcism" designed to "remove the demon of the disease" (1976:252). Laws is certainly correct to dismiss this as "an unwarranted elaboration" (1980:228).

God and that the one praying acts in union with Christ to call upon the power of God.

3. We are to offer prayer *in faith*. This phrase is James's explicit return to his underlying theme as he concludes his letter, and all he has said about faith is the background for his meaning here. In 1:6 he told the person needing wisdom to ask "in faith" *(en pistei)*, not doubting. He has spent this letter exhorting his readers about the goodness and purity of God, showing their selfish fighting to be a lack of faith, both unnecessary and evil. Now he refers to the prayer "of faith" *(tēs pisteōs)* and would again expect his readers to repudiate unbelief as they pray. (See, in the section on 1:5-8, an earlier discussion concerning modern distortions of praying without doubting.)

4. The fourth principle for effective praying is to pray united as repentant sinners; we should *confess . . . sins to each other and pray for each other*. James introduces the mention of sin at the end of 5:15 in the context of praying for a sick person: *If he has sinned, he will be forgiven*. It is a conditional clause *(kan,* "and if"); the connection between sin and illness is a possibility, not a necessity in every case. The implication is that the physical illness and the guilt may be interwoven, and the cure promised in 5:16 seems to encompass both physical and spiritual healing. We are to pray as repentant sinners asking for a comprehensive healing of our lives.

We are reading James's concluding remarks here; he would expect us to recall what he has been saying in the course of the letter. He is writing to people struggling in hardship. Martin is right to comment that in urging them to pray, James is "allowing for a positive response to hardship" instead of "advocating a stoic or impassive response to adversity" (1988:205). But it is more than that. These verses, coming as the conclusion to all James has addressed in his readers' lives, describe a healing of their relationships with God and with each other.

Their relationships *need* healing. As a first result of their hardships, their relationship with God has been suffering. They are falling into temptation to doubt God (1:6), to blame God (1:13) and to bargain with God (5:12). James is directing them back to God in faith with a reliance on him in prayer.

A second result of their adversities is that their relationships with each other have been suffering. James has had to warn them against the evils of playing favorites with each other (2:1), verbally attacking each other (3:9), fighting with each other (4:1), slandering each other (4:11) and judging each other (4:12). Now this present passage helps us realize what a dramatic transformation of relationships James envisions. He points out the oneness we have with each other because of our common need for forgiveness. If we consciously stand together before God as sinners needing grace and wanting righteousness, that stance has compelling application to our relationships. Instead of judging each other, we will be driven to confess to each other. Instead of desiring to place guilt on each other, we will become eager to forgive each other. Instead of moving to criticize, we will move to intercede for each other. A spirit of reconciliation will pervade the church. This, too, James learned from Jesus (Mt 5:23-24; 6:12-15; 7:1-5).

To catch the importance of this for the church, we need to notice that James is writing about spiritual freedom given to the church, not spiritual gifts given to certain ones in the church. The freedom happens because "the Lord is full of compassion and mercy," and in that mercy James exults. Picture this exultation happening in modern churches, and you have something of James's vision: elders leading worship with a spiritual authority in the name of Jesus; Christians praising God joyfully, confessing their sins openly and praying for each other lovingly; the church together experiencing spiritual cleansing and physical healing. This is the exciting power of prayer.

Why Pray (5:15-18) I remember a sign that read, "A funny thing happens when you don't pray," followed by a large, nearly empty space carrying just one word in small print: "(nothing)." James is certainly convinced that prayer brings results. Therefore his final way to encourage his readers to pray is to describe the effectiveness of prayer.

1. The results. The conviction that prayer will bring results was implicit in 5:13-14. It becomes explicit in 5:15-16 with James's assurance of four results. The prayer *will make the sick person well . . . the Lord will raise him up . . . he will be forgiven . . . so that you may be healed.* The first result, *make well,* is the NIV's translation of the verb *sōsei* "will save." It is a proper translation for this context, where "will save" is in the sense of healing rather than spiritual salvation. See Mark 5:23. Similarly, the verb *egerei, will raise up,* would refer to physical restoration rather than spiritual resurrection in this context. When James declares that the penitent sinner *will be forgiven,* what he has described as the context is prayer of intercession, not absolution, with emphasis on God as the one answering prayer. It is a final reminder that God is the giver of every good gift. The concept of being *healed* can have a spiritual sense with the verb *iaomai,* as in 1 Peter 2:24, which refers to Isaiah 53. Here in 5:16 it seems to refer to physical healing, although James recognizes in 5:15 a possible combination of illness and sin. The vision he is sharing with his readers is for both physical and spiritual healing of their lives.

2. The principle: The prayer of a righteous man is powerful and effective. In Greek this is a compact, five-word sentence waiting to be unpacked by the student or expositor to reveal the vigorous expectation that God dynamically answers prayer. James begins with the substantive *poly* ("much") as the matter he wants his readers to see first and foremost: how very much can be accomplished through prayer.

After the main verb *ischyei* ("has power" or "is able"), James introduces two terms with apparent deliberateness. For *prayer* as the subject of the sentence, he shifts from the general term *euchē* to the more specific term *deēsis* ("supplication" or "entreaty"), denoting the sort of prayer his readers would be doing because of their trials and persecutions. Then the person praying is designated as *dikaiou* ("righteous"), even though righteousness has not been mentioned thus far in the passage. To pray as repentant sinners is what James commanded at the beginning of 5:16. This is the stance Jesus taught his followers to take. But it is not a position of despair; Jesus also awakened in his followers the hope of becoming righteous. Within Matthew 5:3-10 he capsulized that progression from being spiritually poor to hungering for righteousness and finally becoming so righteous that one would be persecuted for it. James now affirms that hope to be *righteous* and applies it as encouragement for praying.

The term *righteous* in 5:16 is more than an automatic statement that "holds good for every believing petitioner," as Dibelius characterizes it

---

5:16 The participle *energoumenē* is translated by Dibelius as a direct adjective, "the energetic prayer" (1976:241), implying that the person is to pray with earnestness and force. Laws is similar with her rendering "the active prayer" (1980:234). Ropes translates it "when

(1976:256). It is a call for every believer to reach toward righteousness. All along, James has been urging his readers to resist the temptation to compromise righteousness in their trials. Now, with the designation of the one praying as *righteous* and with the shift in terms from general "prayer" to specific "entreaty," the implication is as follows: In your trials, you don't need the power gained by money or favoritism or selfishness or fighting or swearing; use the power of prayer, for which you need righteousness. Commit yourself to doing what is right without compromise; then you may rely on God in prayer for all your needs.

As has become clear within the letter, James is not denying salvation by grace through faith; he is merely convinced that genuine faith will express itself in righteousness, and the prayer of genuine faith is the prayer that is effective. After all, what causes me to try to protect myself by unrighteous means in trials? It is my unbelief. On the other hand, confident belief in God's grace will make me strong for acting righteously in the midst of trials. It is a message similar to that of 1 Peter 4:19 and 5:6-7.

The last word in the sentence is *energoumenē* ("effective"). This is actually a middle-voice participle of the verb *energeō*, which means "to work" or "to be effective" with such an energized sense indeed that the NIV renders it as a predicate adjective (in contrast to the direct adjective in the more literal NASB). This participle describes the subject, *prayer,* and enhances the idea of the verb *ischyei,* "has power." The result is a highly charged affirmation of prayer as both "powerful and effective."

3. The example: Elijah. This power of prayer is further emphasized by an Old Testament figure known for his miracle-producing prayers. The bulk of 5:17-18 is devoted to the basic facts surrounding one of Elijah's prayers: the long drought and the renewed rain recorded in 1 Kings 17—18. Those chapters do not record what James supplies, that Elijah *prayed earnestly that it would not rain.* The story in 1 Kings begins directly with Elijah's declaration to King Ahab that it would not rain again except at Elijah's word. The chapters include the miracles done by Elijah when continuous food was provided for the widow at Zarephath during the

---

it is exercised" (1916:309). Adamson is right to reject this emphasis on the fervor with which one prays and instead to join the participle to the main verb: "is very powerful in its operation" (1976:196, 199). Kistemaker is similar: "powerful in its effect" (1986:180).

drought, and when Elijah prayed earnestly for the widow's dead son and he was restored to life. The climax was the confrontation between Elijah and the prophets of Baal on Mount Carmel, in which Elijah prayed earnestly again and God answered dramatically with fire upon the water-drenched altar and then with rain upon the drought-stricken land.

James has chosen as his illustration an episode that is not only prominent and familiar from Old Testament history but also clearly supportive of the point he wishes to make. The miracles in 1 Kings 17—18 were undeniably beyond Elijah's human power. They were divine answers to prayer. With his concern for his readers to have faith instead of doubt, James may also be remembering that when Jesus' power to do miracles was hindered by people's unbelief in Nazareth (Mk 6:4-6), Jesus himself drew attention to Elijah's powerful praying over the rain (Lk 4:25).

But the primary intended effect of this illustration is revealed in the brief introductory sentence in 5:17. Having emphasized righteousness as a condition for effective praying, James is not wanting Christians to postpone praying while they try to attain some level of perfection or super-spirituality. His foremost emphasis about Elijah is that he *was a man just like us.* James is saying: Strive earnestly for the goal of righteousness, but get down immediately to the business of praying.

The NIV conveys the sense that Elijah *prayed earnestly,* from *proseuchē proseuxato* which is an aorist indicative verb coupled with a dative noun—literally, "he prayed in prayer" or "he prayed with prayer." Such a construction suggests intensity or frequency. Laws renders it "he prayed and prayed" (1980:235). It is important to define the intensifying effect intended by James. His desire in the passage is not to erect a standard of fervency for his readers to attain; he seems more intent on pushing them into the active prayer life that is so readily available. Adamson describes it as emphasis that praying is precisely what Elijah did (1976:201). Motyer comments that "the meaning is not his fervency, nor even his frequency of prayer, but that 'he just prayed'—that, and nothing more!" (1985:206-7). James's message in these two verses includes both

---

5:17 James's term *homoiopathēs* ("just like" or "with the same nature as") is used only one other place in the New Testament, by Luke in Acts 14:15.

the great expectations and the common availability of prayer. The mighty power of prayer is for us!

Keep Bringing Each Other Back to the Truth (5:19-20) The emphasis on prayer brings James to his closing message: As you hold onto the truth and trust God in prayer during your trials, keep helping others to do the same. In making this the conclusion of his message, James is explaining his own letter. He began the letter saying he was "a servant of God." Now he adds the complementary calling: he is a servant of sinners. He has written forthrightly, insistently and passionately about what is sinful and what is righteous. In fact, someone has called James's letter "the Ouch! book" because it is so pointed. James makes no apology for that. But why such a passion for righteousness? Three concepts that appear in these closing verses reveal James's heart.

Truth Is Available James has written about a God who is personal and good; he gives good gifts and gives them generously (1:5, 17). James has also written about a God who is absolute; his word is true and his judgments are supreme (1:18; 4:12). In this context, it is possible for human beings to know absolute truth. It is also possible to "wander from the truth" and to be brought back to the truth. James understands this wandering especially in moral terms; his passion is for righteousness, not merely correct doctrine. "Truth is a way to go, a way of life" in both Old Testament and New Testament thinking (Davids 1982:199).

This concept forcefully thrusts the church today into confrontation with the world. Surveys indicate that two-thirds of American adults believe that there is no such thing as absolute truth (this percentage is 74 percent among people 18-25 years old) and that it does not matter which god or higher power is addressed when one prays. Even though serious Christians would not count themselves among those percentages, the assumptions of relativism tug at them daily and influence them subtly, because relativism is such an accepted part of our cultural worldview.

This cultural context makes it all the more urgent that the church be absolutely clear about this: Absolute truth is available and knowable.

5:20 *Cover over a multitude of sins:* Cf. a similar phrase in Proverbs 10:12, quoted in 1 Peter 4:8. This is evidence again of a familiarity of thinking between Peter and James.

There are absolute moral standards. God's will for our lives is holiness. Salvation is to be worked into our character and daily life in the form of righteousness.

Death Threatens Us James's conviction is that sin represents a life-threatening danger, not just a harmless blemish on our otherwise good character. Sin is not to be tolerated complacently; it destroys us. James may have in mind physical death from the illness associated with sin in 5:15. (Consider Paul's teaching in 1 Cor 11:30.) But when he speaks of saving the sinner's *psychēn*, "soul," from death, he "appears to go beyond physical death and recognize death as an eschatological entity" (Davids 1982:200). The reference to covering a multitude of sins refers to gaining forgiveness and is a benefit parallel to the saving from death.

If we make this verse merely an occasion to argue whether Christians can lose their salvation, we will miss the real impact James wants to make on his readers. He is again, with passion and forcefulness, warning his readers that genuine faith includes repentance for sin and a life of obedience to Christ as Lord. What James is saying in 5:20 is simply consistent with his view throughout the letter. See the discussion of 1:15, where he first brought up the notion of death. His point is not that true believers may lose their salvation by sinning, but that sin full-grown ultimately destroys the sinner, and that genuine faith compels us to flee from sin and to help each other do the same. To the very end, James insists on the lordship of Christ as an essential part of the gospel.

Again the church is put into confrontation with the world. In America today, 83 percent believe that people are basically good. That view of human nature will make James's letter seem offensively harsh and ridiculously outdated. Yet when we believe the danger present in sin, we will begin to share James's passion for righteousness.

We Are Called to Turn Sinners from Error If truth is available, and if death does so threaten us, then love demands that we call each other to repentance. If I turn a fellow sinner from sin, I save that person from death and cover over that sinner's multitude of sins. Some commentators have tried to assign one or both of these benefits to the Christian who helps the sinner—for example, saying that Christians cover over their own sins when they turn a sinner from error. (See Adamson 1976:203; Dibelius 1976:258-259; Laws 1980:239.) Davids is right to reject this as unlikely logic for James to be using (1982:201). James is more probably thinking of the saving from death and the covering of sins as two parallel benefits coming to the sinner. Repentance is a necessary step of faith and is the only route by which one can be saved from death and freed from guilt.

The verb translated in 5:19 as "bring back" is *epistrephō;* it is the same verb in 5:20 as "turns." It can mean "convert," but there is no distinction made here between evangelizing a non-Christian and discipling one who believes. In either context, James wants his readers to see the urgency of bringing people to repentance. This is why he has written so severely to people whom he loves so dearly as "brothers." He has persistently called them to turn from sin. He concludes his letter saying, "I have called you to repentance; now you do this for others. Hold each other to righteousness just as firmly as I have held you."

This is what Douglas Webster calls "the work of spiritual direction" (1991:13). It is a ministry of cutting through the deceptive complexities of a relativistic culture and setting before others a clear path of obedience. It is a ministry that simplifies and clarifies life by defining godly commitments and directing people toward maturity (Webster 1991:15-19). It is a ministry of mutual discipling in the church, and it is based on one of the most crucial principles for effective church discipline: that the whole church is called to exercise discipline, not just pastors or elders. "For while God has given different gifts, the most basic training he gives is meant to come from fellow Christians in everyday encounters. *Church discipline* is the training *of* the church *by* the church. Trained professionals have their place, but they cannot and never were meant to be a substitute for the whole body" (White and Blue 1985:18).

These are the realities of life with which James concludes his letter: There is truth to be followed. There is death to be avoided. There is ministry to give to each other. James has called us to serve both God and sinners.

Appendix on the Task of Biblical Interpretation: How Can We Identify the Rich in the Epistle of James?

There is a fundamental difference between any word and that which is signified by the word. The complexity of the difference is multiplied when whole sentences are involved, and then multiplied many times over with paragraphs, letters, essays or entire books. There is additional difference, and therefore an automatic communication gap, between the writers themselves and even their most immediate readers. The gap is widened still more when there are years or centuries between writers and readers.

Both phenomenology and deconstruction have so founded their modern theories of interpretation on this rupture between word and meaning, between writer and reader, that meaning in a given message has become viewed as indeterminate. This results in a contemporary skepticism regarding the possibility of knowing the true meaning of any text; and it makes the task of biblical hermeneutics all the more urgent for Christians today. If our discussions of interpretive problems in the biblical text are, in the end, nothing more than assertions of personal opinion ("Well, I think the passage means this . . ."), then we are conceding the crucial arguments of interpretive skepticism. We may as well agree: truth is relative; communication is subjective; the establishment of meaning is hopelessly lost in the gap between the biblical writer and the modern reader.

It is not that we have to be able to resolve every interpretive difficulty with an absolutely clear solution. Some aspects of certain biblical texts may remain obscure. Yet we need to be prepared to demonstrate by careful procedure whether we have hermeneutical principles and tools by which we can bridge the gap and arrive at sound conclusions about the original, intended meaning of a biblical text. Do our hermeneutical tools yield results?

The Problem My intention in this appendix is to put these tools to a modest test by focusing on one interpretive problem in the biblical text—a problem sufficiently confined and specific that we may look for definite results. The problem to be addressed is the meaning of one word (*plousios*, "rich") in one verse (Jas 1:10). Were the rich in this verse believers in Christ included in the address "brother" in 1:9—that is, people within the Christian community and part of the actual, intended audience for the letter? Or were they outside the Christian family, non-Christians being addressed only rhetorically in James's letter?

The importance of this question is seen in two respects. First, if hermeneutics properly includes both exegesis and application of the text, the latter portion of the task is seriously affected by whether the message in James is directed to rich Christians about themselves or to poor Christians about rich non-Christians. Second, this issue is not minor or tangential in James. The relational dynamic between rich and poor and the role of material wealth or need in Christians' lives are significant and repeated themes in the letter. Our understanding of several passages in James will be affected, including (1) passages that make explicit reference to *plousios* (1:9-11; 2:5-7; 5:1-6) and (2) passages that discuss wealthy people without making explicit mention of *plousios* (2:1-4; 4:13-17).

Our hermeneutical goal now is to identify as accurately as we can what was signified by James's use of the signifier *plousios*, to understand the discourse meaning of the term *plousios* in the letter and at least to point to some directions to be taken for contemporary applications.

Analysis of Past Approaches The more common approach among biblical commentators has been to argue primarily from straightforward grammatical structure that James 1:10 speaks to rich Christians. The verb *kauchaomai* ("take pride in") at the beginning of 1:9 is understood as the verb for 1:10 as well; likewise, *ho adelphos* ("the brother") in 1:9 is understood as the subject to be supplied for 1:10. The contrast then would be between the brother who is *ho tapeinos* ("in humble circumstances") and the brother who is *ho plousios* ("rich"). Examples of this approach can be found in Joseph B. Mayor 1897, J. H. Ropes 1916 and James B. Adamson 1976.

An alternative approach has been to argue primarily from the content of the message that James 1:10 must be speaking about rich non-Christians. The exultation of the poor brother is seen as too dissimilar to that of the rich person to be parallel. The absence of any hope or commendation given to the *plousios* here or elsewhere in the letter seems to indicate a non-Christian identity for the rich. Not just their riches but they themselves "will pass away like a wild flower." Examples of this approach can be found in the work of the German Martin Dibelius (1964), the British Sophie Laws (1980) and the American Peter H. Davids (1982).

The difference between these two approaches leads to significant differences in understanding and application. Taking Mayor as a spokesman for the first view, James 1:10 is rendered "Let the rich brother glory in his humiliation as a Christian." The meaning of the verse then has to do with "the intrinsic effect of Christianity in changing our view of life." And the application of 1:10 is for the proud rich to learn "self-abasement," even as the application of 1:9 was for the despised poor to learn self-respect (Mayor 1897:43). Working from this understanding, preaching that captures the intent of James 1:10 should be directed to Christians who have wealth, should urge them to take pride in their abasement and should instruct them in practices of self-abasement.

On the other hand, taking Davids as representative of the second view, it is argued that the text about the rich never says "humiliation *as a Christian.*" What the letter does do is uniformly condemn "the rich" in all three passages that refer explicitly to *plousios* (1:9-11; 2:5-7; 5:1-6).

They are seen as persecutors and blasphemers. "Some wealthy individuals" were coming into the church as inquirers or new converts; these are the ones James would have in mind in 2:2 and 4:13. But James avoids calling them "the rich" and reserves the term *plousios* for pejorative use. "These rich are not Christians, but rather the enemies of the church" (Davids 1982:46). Application of the text must be made with understanding that James is writing with "great sympathy for the poor and that the term is virtually identical in his mind with 'Christian' " (Davids 1982:45). Proceeding with this view, preaching that is faithful to the biblical writer's intention in 1:10 should be directed to Christians who are poor, assuring them of the ultimate futility of material riches as a goal in life and encouraging them to be faithful to Christ even in their poverty.

How can this hermeneutical problem be addressed? We will examine in turn the text's linguistic and lexical context, historical context, literary context and canonical context.

Linguistic and Lexical Context Though the hermeneutical value of etymology has been exaggerated in many biblical studies, we can still begin with the linguistic and lexical data as the starting point for contextualizing James's term *plousios.* Friedrich Hauck and Wilhelm Kasch describe the basic sense of the term as "fullness of goods" (Hauck and Kasch 1968:319). Arndt and Gingrich list two senses of *plousios:* a literal sense ("rich man") and a figurative sense ("rich in something") (1957:679). Both of these senses can be carried in the related words *plouteō* ("be rich, become rich"), *ploutizō* ("make rich") and *ploutos* ("wealth, riches"). The adverb *plousiōs* ("richly, abundantly") completes the list of related terms of similar lexical form. Other terms of different lexical form include

  agathos good thing, possession, treasure
  euporeō, euporeomai have plenty, be well off
  euporia means, prosperity
  mamōnas wealth, property
  timiotēs abundance of costly things
  chrēma property, wealth, money
All of these terms, both similar and dissimilar to *plousios,* should be included as relevant terms in a search for passages about wealth in the

canonical context. For now, no definitely Christian or non-Christian meaning appears for *plousios*.

Historical Context Determining the historical context for the writing of the biblical text is important because it reveals some of the "Presupposition Pool" (T. Venneman's phrase used in Cotterell and Turner 1989:90) shared between the writer and the original intended readers. A thorough presentation of the evidence and arguments is not possible in the framework of this study, but a summary of the major points will indicate the basis for my conclusions.

First, the scant references to James's epistle by early church fathers is best explained by an early dating of the letter, before the church became more predominantly Gentile and before the Pauline writings overshadowed James's letter in church usage. Second, the very minimal introduction of James's identity in the letter suggests James the Just, brother of Jesus, as the author. Only one James was well known enough after the death of James the brother of John to have written this letter to the scattered Christians without needing further identification. Third, although the letter puts particular emphasis on the law ("the royal law" and "the law that gives freedom"), there is no reference to controversies over Gentiles, circumcision or ceremonial law. None of this was yet an issue prior to the events of Acts 15, which indicates that this letter was likely written prior to that time.

Fourth, the approach to faith and deeds in James has been seen by some as a response to Pauline writings. This assumed context has made James's teaching confusing and troubling to many. However, it can be shown that James is using his terms *deeds* and *righteous* in 2:14-26 with a purpose different from Paul's. James is writing about how one is shown to be righteous; Paul writes about how one is declared righteous. James's teaching on this matter becomes far less confusing and more consistent even with the rest of his own letter when it is seen to be not anti-Pauline but pre-Pauline in origin. The conclusion we reach is that the epistle of James was written by James the Just, brother of Jesus, between A.D. 40 and 50, during the early diaspora described in Acts 8:1-4 rather than the later diaspora of A.D. 70.

This conclusion provides us with a narrative setting in Acts 8 by which to discern some of James's purposes in writing. His audience would be primarily people of Jewish upbringing with a fairly recently acquired Christian faith who were experiencing a severe persecution at the hands of their erstwhile leaders in Judaism. They were mourning deeply because of the death of a loved and respected leader, Stephen (Acts 7). Almost all the Christians (except for the apostles such as James) had been driven from their homes in Jerusalem and scattered to other places. Almost all of them had likely lost homes or possessions or normal means of income; they had been separated from relatives and friends. There were abundant circumstances to cause them confusion, fear, loneliness, anger, sorrow, poverty, hardship—in fact, "trials of many kinds" as James acknowledges in 1:2. James's probable purpose in this context is confirmed in the letter: to encourage suffering Christians in the face of hardship and to strengthen them for faithful Christian living.

It would fit this historical setting that James would be writing primarily to poor Christians and that one of his goals would be to instruct and encourage them in the face of hardship at the hands of rich unbelievers. In speaking of "the rich," James would likely have in mind the unbelievers who were using their wealth as power to oppress the very vulnerable Christians.

Literary Context The literary context comprises evidence from within the epistle of James itself. It is worth enumerating the various aspects of this context.

1. Genre We are dealing with writing that is certainly more didactic than narrative, but we can qualify this classification in two respects. First, the instruction makes frequent reference to the readers' historical circumstances ("scattered among the nations . . . you face trials of many kinds . . . fights and quarrels among you"), showing the writer to be consciously addressing particular events and situations. The historical narrative behind the writing of the letter will therefore be relevant. Second, the instruction displays a definite rhetorical flavor. Second-person address is prevalent throughout the letter. That James would employ the second person rhetorically toward people not actually receiving the letter is most clearly confirmed in 5:1-6. Both Mayor and Adamson, while wanting to allow for some possible address of professing Christians even in this vehement passage, do admit that 5:1-6 seems to be referring primarily to unbelievers (Mayor 1897:148; Adamson 1976:183-84). Adamson even compares it quite appropriately to Churchill's wartime speeches, which were formally directed at the enemy but intended to encourage his own people.

2. Syntax Understanding *adelphos* in 1:9 to be the referent for both *tapeinos* in 1:9 and *plousios* in 1:10 does seem to be a natural way to read these verses. The important caution in using this argument of "natural" reading is that it may simply be making the ancient text fit with what seems natural to our modern ears. The difference between the ancient text and our modern thinking is precisely the gap we are trying to cross. The fact is that the grammar in 1:9-10 does not require this reading of *adelphos* as a common referent. Another very possible way to read the passage would be to see *ho adelphos ho tapeinos* standing together as a unit and *ho plousios* as the contrasting subject, with *adelphos* not repeated because the rich here are not "brothers," and with *kauchastho* the verb for both subjects.

3. Style of Writing The writer of the epistle typically employs contrasts in successive clauses, sentences or groups of sentences. Examples are found within 1:19, 2:5 and 4:7-8. This stylistic device is used at times to make emphatic contrast between the "rich" and "brothers," as in 2:5-6 and 5:1, 7.

There is a frequent use of diverse similes and metaphors, as in the hunting and fishing imagery of 1:14 followed immediately by the childbearing imagery in 1:15. This manner of description is definitely applied to the rich in 1:10-11 (with the wild flower image) and in 5:1-6 (with the images of destruction) for vivid emphasis. This use of imagery is part of the pattern of strong, intense language throughout the letter. Douglas Moo captures the tone of James's letter as "profound moral earnestness" (Moo 1985:9). In the case of 5:1-6, Adamson describes James's writing as "sarcastic," "dramatic" and "forceful" (Adamson 1976:183).

4. Associated Terms and Messages for the Rich Whenever James speaks of the rich as *plousios* there is a consistently negative message without any hope offered. In 1:10-11, the rich will pass away like a wild flower. In 2:6-7, the rich are seen as persecuting Christians and slandering the name of Christ. In 5:1-6, the rich are guilty of greed, injustice, self-indulgence and murder. They are promised only misery. The only other use of *plousios*, in 2:5, is not a contradiction to this rule, since *plousios* is used here in its figurative sense: those who are poor in material wealth are said to be "rich in faith." The fact that James's other descriptions of people with wealth (in 2:2 and 4:13) do not employ the term *plousios* does leave the term with a uniformly negative connotation in this letter. This, of course, is the heart of the case made by Davids and others in viewing "the rich" in 1:10 as non-Christians. Their argument is quite plausible and consistent with the entirety of James's message.

5. The Author's Use of Narrative The narratives authors employ can reveal intended meaning that may be unclear from their didactic statements alone. James's narratives about the rich and the poor become additional evidence of his meaning.

□ 1:2. The prevalent situation of James's readers is the suffering of diverse trials. Though this does not mention poverty explicitly, the "humble circumstances" in 1:9 seem to be brought up as a prime example of the trials.

□ 1:27. The example chosen to illustrate pure religion is action on behalf of needy people.

□ 2:2-4. Rich people may attend a Christian meeting, but they are not to be shown favoritism above the poor.

□ 2:6-7. The rich typically exploit Christians and blaspheme the name of Christ.

□ 2:15. The example of proper deeds accompanying genuine faith is to help a "brother or sister" who is poor.

□ 4:13-17. Those who have any money are warned to know their complete dependence on the Lord.

□ 5:1-6. The rich are seen as people who arrogantly abuse the power that their wealth brings.

The picture derived from this narrative material in the letter is that James wrote with a particularly intense concern for the poor, and that this was probably because his Christian readers were predominantly poor or at least suffering some significant economic hardship. There would have been exceptions—some rich people would be turning to Christ, and these would have been the referents of 2:2 (Davids 1982:108). However, in general *adelphos* and *tapeinos* became almost synonymous.

6. Conclusions from Literary Context Adamson dismisses the view that the rich of 1:10 are non-Christians as having "little to commend it" (1976:61). He lists the weaknesses of that view as being that it is unnatural not to supply the term *brother* to complete *rich* in this context, that it requires an excessively ironical sense for 1:10 and that it makes the verse only loosely connected to the context of trials begun in 1:2. These arguments now appear rather surprising since, on the contrary, so far the view that the rich are unbelievers seems to be very possible from the syntax, quite appropriate to James's intense, imaginative, rhetorical style of writing and thoroughly in keeping with the historical context of Christians suffering trials.

Gathering together the connotations with which James uses the term, we can say that the discourse meaning of *plousios* is one who has material wealth and typically displays arrogance in abusing its power.

Canonical Context We can look for confirmation or contradiction of this conclusion from other biblical writings that have a demonstrated background or affinity to James.

First, a survey of Old Testament references to the rich and wealth shows that riches are judged favorably in the Law as a blessing from God. The Writings have the largest volume of Old Testament references, especially concentrated in the Wisdom literature, where riches are generally valued and approved. It is in the Prophets that we find a significant amount of criticism of the rich as a class of people.

Perhaps the most important prophetic reference is Jeremiah 9:23-24, because of its use of both *kauchasthō* and *plousios* in the Septuagint. James certainly knew the Jeremiah passage and could have applied it as Paul did in 1 Corinthians 1:31—"Let him who boasts boast in the Lord." Instead, James's emphasis is on the destruction of the rich. He seems to expect the rich to continue in their materialism only to find themselves brought low in the end, as in the common prophetical denunciations of the rich. It is a description of the rich as unbelievers.

Second, it can be shown that James's letter is saturated with a knowledge of Jesus' teachings, especially his sermons in Matthew 5—7 and Luke 6 (well documented by Mayor, Davids and Kistemaker). This gives us reason to examine the references to rich people and wealth in the teachings of Jesus to get a very important picture of what was informing James's thinking.

1. Matthew 6:19-24. Treasures on earth are not of lasting value. "You cannot serve both God and Money."

2. Matthew 13:22. Wealth has a harmful influence on people in the parable of the sower.

3. Matthew 19:23-24. It is very hard for the rich to enter the kingdom.

4. Matthew 27:57. Joseph of Arimathea is a rich man who is a friend to Jesus.

5. Mark 12:41. The rich are compared unfavorably to the poor widow who could give only a little.

6. Luke 1:53. Mary thanks God for caring for the poor and sending the rich away empty.

7. Luke 6:20, 24. "Blessed are you who are poor. . . . But woe to you who are rich."

8. Luke 12:16-21. The rich man in the parable is declared a fool.

9. Luke 14:12-14. Jesus tells his host to invite not his rich neighbors but the poor.

10. Luke 16:1-15. Jesus warns against love of money, and the Pharisees are characterized as ones "who loved money."

11. Luke 16:19-31. In the story of the rich man and Lazarus, the rich man is in torment in hell, while the poor man Lazarus is blessed to be at Abraham's side.

In these references (and their Synoptic parallels, which are not listed) there is a consistently negative picture of wealth and of the rich. The one exception is the loyalty of Joseph of Arimathea. The demonstrated saturation of James's mind with the teachings of Jesus makes still more likely the conclusion that James is thinking of the rich primarily as non-Christians.

Conclusions from All the Contexts The various contexts for trying to understand James's intent give us abundant reason to conclude that he was speaking in 1:10 with rich non-Christians in mind. Therefore he was speaking rhetorically, formally addressing non-Christians in 1:10 as well as later in 5:1-6, but saying this really for the benefit of his Christian readers, who were suffering at the hands of rich persecutors. He wrote

1:9-11 to encourage these Christians to rejoice nevertheless in their real exaltation in Christ.

Areas for Contemporary Application When the observation and interpretation of a text are carefully done, the proper areas of application become more readily apparent. In this case, the obvious common thread between the original readers of James's letter and today's readers is the spiritual significance of material wealth. Poor individuals today know full well that the wealth of the rich is power. Poorer nations know the same reality in regard to rich nations. On both the individual and international level, then, James's earnest encouragement for "the brother in humble circumstances" has very contemporary applications.

Jacques Ellul is one cultural analyst who gives expression to modern thinking about the dehumanizing function of money. He observes that in both socialism and capitalism money has the function of measuring value, and that it therefore leads people to pursue the goal of *having* something instead of *being* something (Ellul 1984:22). He writes about Jesus' statement in Luke 16:13,

> What Jesus is revealing is that money is a power. This term should be understood not in its vague meaning, "force," but in the specific sense in which it is used in the New Testament. Power is something that acts by itself, is capable of moving other things, is autonomous (or claims to be), is a law unto itself, and presents itself as an active agent. This is its first characteristic. Its second is that power has a spiritual value. It is not only of the material world, although this is where it acts. It has spiritual meaning and direction. Power is never neutral. It is oriented; it also orients people. Finally, power is more or less personal. (Ellul 1984:75-76)

This contemporary wrestling with the spiritual power of wealth suggests ready areas for current application of James's teaching.

From what we have found in James's meaning, we can define some errors to avoid in making these applications. Careful hermeneutical work shows that it would be going beyond James's teaching to make a doctrinal classification of rich people as automatically evil or to reject all that wealthy people do. This would be the error of systematizing and absolutizing what is rhetorical language. On the other hand, we are not to ignore or reduce the powerful force of James's meaning. He brings a vehement condemnation of the unjust use of materialistic power.

Three specific areas of application do suit the intention of James 1:9-11.

1. Our beliefs about wealth. The verses are a warning that material wealth is spiritually dangerous. We must believe that in our minds if we are going to act with our wills to avoid becoming like the rich in this passage.

2. Our attitudes about wealth. The verses are encouragement for Christians in hardship not to envy the rich, and certainly not to think their wealth is worth pursuing, but instead to take pride in exaltation in Christ, which is of real value.

3. Our actions related to wealth. The verses instruct Christians in the theological context for actions such as those prescribed elsewhere in the letter. We are especially to care for the needy (1:27; 2:15-17); we are not to show favoritism to the rich (2:1-4); we are not to hoard wealth or treat others unjustly or live in self-indulgence (5:1-6).

Bibliography

Adamson, James B.
1976   *The Epistle of James.* New International Commentary on the
               New Testament. Grand Rapids, Mich.: Eerdmans.
Barclay, William
1976   *The Letters of James and Peter.* The Daily Study Bible, rev.
               ed. Philadelphia: Westminster.
Barker, Glenn W.,
William L. Lane and
J. Ramsey Michaels
1969   *The New Testament Speaks.* New York: Harper & Row.

Bauer, Walter,
William F. Arndt
and F. Wilbur
Gingrich
1957   *A Greek-English Lexicon of the New Testament.* 4th ed.
               Chicago: University of Chicago Press.
Blanchard, John
1986   *Truth for Life: A Devotional Commentary on the Epistle of
               James.* Hertfordshire, U.K.: Evangelical Press.
Burns, John A.
1986   "James, the Wisdom of Jesus." *Criswell Theological Review*
               1:113-36.
Cotterell, Peter,
and Max Turner
1989   *Linguistics and Biblical Interpretation.* Downers Grove, Ill.:
               InterVarsity Press.
Davids, Peter H.
1982   *The Epistle of James.* New International Greek Testament
               Commentary. Grand Rapids, Mich.: Eerdmans.

Dibelius, Martin
1976   *A Commentary on the Epistle of James.* Revised by Heinrich
              Greeven, translated by Michael A. Williams. Philadelphia:
              Fortress.
Dyrness, W.
1981   "Mercy Triumphs Over Justice: James 2:13 and the Theology
              of Faith and Works." *Themelios* 6 (no. 3): 11-16.
Ellul, Jacques
1984   *Money and Power.* Downers Grove, Ill.: InterVarsity Press.

Eusebius
1890   *Church History.* Nicene and Post-Nicene Fathers 1. New
              York: Christian Literature.
Evans, M. J.
1983   "The Law in James." *Vox Evangelica* 13:29-40.

Foster, Richard J.
1981   *Freedom of Simplicity.* New York: Harper & Row.

Greidanus, Sidney
1970   *Sola Scriptura.* Toronto: Wedge Publishing Foundation.

Grudem, Wayne A.
1988   *The First Epistle of Peter.* Tyndale New Testament
              Commentaries. Grand Rapids, Mich.: Eerdmans.
Guthrie, Donald
1990   *New Testament Introduction.* 4th ed. (rev.). Downers
              Grove, Ill.: InterVarsity Press.
Hanks, Thomas D.
1983   *God So Loved the Third World.* Maryknoll, N.Y.: Orbis Books.

Hauck, Friedrich,
and Wilhelm Kasch
1968   "πλοῦτος κτλ." In *Theological Dictionary of the New
              Testament.* 10 vols. Edited by G. Kittel and G. Friedrich.
              Grand Rapids, Mich.: Eerdmans. 6:318-32.
Hiebert, D.
Edmond
1979   *The Epistle of James.* Chicago: Moody Press.

Hort, F. J. A.
1909   *The Epistle of St. James.* London: Macmillan.

Howard, Tracy L.
1986   "Suffering in James 1:2-12." *Criswell Theological Review*
            1:71-84.

Johnson, L. T.
1982   "The Use of Leviticus 19 in the Letter of James." *Journal of
            Biblical Literature* 101:391-401.

Kistemaker,
Simon J.
1986   *New Testament Commentary: Exposition of the Epistle of
            James and the Epistles of John*. Grand Rapids, Mich.: Baker
            Book House.

Knox, W. L.
1945   "The Epistle of St. James." *Journal of Theological Studies*
            46:10-17.

Laws, Sophie
1980   *A Commentary on the Epistle of James*. London: Black.

Lea, T.
1986   "James: Outline and Introduction." *Southwestern Journal of
            Theology* 29:5-11.

Lenski, R. C. H.
1966   *The Interpretation of the Epistle to the Hebrews and the Epis-
            tle of James*. Minneapolis: Augsburg.

MacArthur,
John F., Jr.
1990   "Faith According to the Apostle James." *Journal of the
            Evangelical Theological Society* 33:13-34.

Martin, Ralph P.
1988   *James*. Word Biblical Commentary. Waco, Tex.: Word Books.

Mayor, J. B.
1897   *The Epistle of St. James*. London: Macmillan.

McGavran,
Donald A.
1980   *Understanding Church Growth*. Grand Rapids, Mich.:
            Eerdmans.

Mitton, C. Leslie
1966   *The Epistle of James*. Grand Rapids, Mich.: Eerdmans.

Moo, Douglas J.
1985   *The Letter of James*. Tyndale New Testament Commentaries.
            Grand Rapids, Mich.: Eerdmans.

Motyer, Alec
1985   *The Message of James.* The Bible Speaks Today. Downers
                Grove, Ill.: InterVarsity Press.
Peterson,
Eugene H.
1980   *A Long Obedience in the Same Direction.* Downers Grove,
                Ill.: InterVarsity Press.
Plummer, Alfred
1900   *The General Epistles of St. James and St. Jude.* The
                Expositor's Bible. New York: Funk & Wagnalls.
Radmacher, Earl D.
1990   "First Response to 'Faith According to the Apostle James' by
                John F. MacArthur Jr." *Journal of the Evangelical Theological
                Society* 33:35-41.
Rakestraw,
Robert V.
1986   "James 2:14-26: Does James Contradict the Pauline
                Soteriology?" *Criswell Theological Review* 1:31-50.
Reese, J. M.
1982   "The Exegete as Sage: Hearing the Message of James."
                Biblical Theology Bulletin 12 (no. 3): 82-85.
Ropes, J. H.
1916   *The Epistle of St. James.* International Critical Commentary.
                New York: Scribner's.
Ross, Alexander
1954   *The Epistles of James and John.* New International Commen-
                tary on the New Testament. Grand Rapids, Mich.: Eerdmans.
Saucy, Robert L.
1990   "Second Response to 'Faith According to the Apostle James'
                by John F. MacArthur Jr." *Journal of the Evangelical
                Theological Society* 33:43-47.
Sider, Ronald J.
1977   *Rich Christians in an Age of Hunger: A Biblical Study.*
                Downers Grove. Ill.: InterVarsity Press.
Simmons, B. E.
1986   "The Epistle of James: An Introduction." *Theological
                Educator* 34:3-16.
Sloan, Robert B.
1986   "The Christology of James." *Criswell Theological Review* 1:3-
                30.
Songer, H. S.
1972   "James." In *The Broadman Bible Commentary,* vol. 12.
                Nashville: Broadman.
1986   "Introduction to James." *Review and Expositor* 83:357-68.

Stibbs, Alan M., and
Andrew F. Walls
1959 *The First Epistle General of Peter.* Tyndale New Testament
Commentaries. Grand Rapids, Mich.: Eerdmans.

Stott, John R. W.
1975 *Christian Mission in the Modern World.* Downers Grove, Ill.:
InterVarsity Press.
1978 *Christian Counter-Culture: The Message of the Sermon on
the Mount.* Downers Grove, Ill.: InterVarsity Press.

Tamez, Elsa
1990 *The Scandalous Message of James: Faith Without Works Is
Dead.* New York: Crossroad.

Tasker, R. V. G.
1983 *The General Epistle of James.* Tyndale New Testament
Commentaries. Grand Rapids, Mich.: Eerdmans.

Ward, Roy Bowen
1969 "Partiality in the Assembly: James 2:2-4." *Harvard
Theological Review* 62:87-97.

Webster,
Douglas D.
1991 *Finding Spiritual Direction.* Downers Grove, Ill.: InterVarsity
Press.

Wells, C. Richard
1986 "The Theology of Prayer in James." *Criswell Theological
Review* 1:85-112.

Wenham, John W.
1974 *The Goodness of God.* Downers Grove, Ill.: InterVarsity
Press.

White, John, and
Ken Blue
1985 *Healing the Wounded.* Downers Grove, Ill.: InterVarsity
Press.

Williams, R. R.
1965 *The Letters of John and James.* Cambridge Bible
Commentary on the New English Bible. Cambridge, U.K.:
Cambridge University Press.

Yancey, Philip
1977 *Where Is God When It Hurts?* Grand Rapids, Mich.:
Zondervan.